BUILDING COST CONTROL
TECHNIQUES AND ECONOMICS

or 8/93

Building Cost Control Techniques and Economics

PETER E. BATHURST, F.R.I.C.S.
and
DAVID A. BUTLER, F.R.I.C.S.

SECOND EDITION

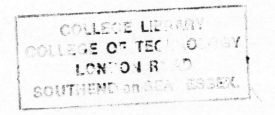

HEINEMANN : LONDON

William Heinemann Ltd
10 Upper Grosvenor Street, London W1X 9PA

LONDON MELBOURNE TORONTO
JOHANNESBURG AUCKLAND

Printed in Great Britain by
Redwood Burn Limited, Trowbridge, Wiltshire
and bound by Pegasus Bookbinding, Melksham, Wiltshire.

Contents

Introduction to First Edition

Our principal guide in deciding the contents of this book has been the examination syllabus in building economics and cost planning set by the Royal Institution of Chartered Surveyors and the Institute of Quantity Surveyors. The basis of the book has been the lecture notes we have used in discussing these subjects with surveyors and architects over a number of years. We have also included additional matter prepared for conferences and multi-professional seminars at the Architectural Association, York Institute of Advanced Architectural Studies, the College of Estate Management at Reading University, and at courses for Government Quantity Surveyors at The Polytechnic of Central London.

An examination syllabus reflects the work of a profession at a particular period but this work is continuously changing in character with the varying demands of its clients, the requirements of colleagues in other professions, and changes in the building industry. We have, therefore, avoided placing emphasis on exercises in estimating that relate to present costs or to the current problems of metrication or commodity coding. We have directed our attention instead to describing basic skills of analysis and calculation which may be applied to a wide range of circumstances and lead to a general mathematical understanding of the problems.

The work of the quantity surveyor traditionally covers the measurement and preparation of the contract documents, the preparation of the final account, and estimating and furnishing cost advice to the architect and client. These tasks have been undertaken at different times, and in different countries, by architects, engineers, builders, and also specialist planning or management consultants. The present concentration by quantity surveyors on cost-control services and the provision of cost advice to the client, during both the design and construction stages, can, therefore, be seen more in terms of reallocating tasks rather than creating completely new services, but, whoever is responsible for preparing the advice on cost and communicating it to the client and however these responsibilities change in the future, it is clear that clients no longer believe that the cost of building is solely related to market conditions and simply determined by the pressures of competition. Almost all now expect that the buildings they commission should be designed to meet a precise brief in terms of performance, space, and cost. Sometimes the client will be able to set these standards himself and require the professions to work to them, at others the client will need advice on the formulation of his brief and also the probable cost; but, however the brief is written, once the advice has been given the building owner will expect the building and the contract sum to conform to the standards laid down. Whatever changes in technology lie in the future and whatever organizations and professional skills are developed, this expectation of cost control is likely to be an unvarying factor in the service provided.

The fact that changes are inevitable, though unpredictable, makes it difficult to produce a textbook illustrated with practical exercises that will remain up to date for more than a few years. This is the main reason why we have concentrated on the description of general skills rather than costed examples, and why we have also described the work and the methods of quantity surveyors carrying out research studies and of those in Government service responsible for establishing cost indices and expenditure limits. However, the main difficulty in writing convincingly on the subject of building economics is the divisions in the industry between the designers and the constructors. In speculative house- and factory-building a direct relationship exists between the architect as designer and the builder who has initiated the brief, financed the work, and is responsible for carrying out the construction. In these circumstances there is the possibility of feedback of cost information from the builder to the designer, though this information is private and will not normally be passed to anyone else.

In building contracts it is extremely difficult to trace the cost effect of decisions to employ particular forms of design. For example, a designed detail affecting a suspended ceiling may produce a difficulty apparent to the operatives on the site, but they are likely to be employed by a sub-contractor rather than the main contractor, and unless the problem is of sufficient importance to be reported back to their management, it may be solved without comment on the site. Even if the information was passed to the sub-contractor, there is no guarantee that it would reach the main contractor or the architect and quantity surveyor. The action taken by the sub-contractor would also depend on whether he thought that the responsibility for the difficulty came from his own misunderstanding of the detail when pricing, or whether in fact, although working to the detail had caused extra costs, these were covered by some contingency sum deliberately added

1

to his tender, or had merely arisen by the application of average prices to gross measured areas. If working to the detail had turned out to be exceptionally advantageous, there would be no reason for the sub-contractor to disclose this fact to the main contractor or to the designer, and if such working resulted in extra profits, it would be difficult for the contractor to be certain that these had not resulted from factors affecting the output of his work people or from an over-pessimistic tender. It would be impossible for him to relate his increased profits to the particular design detail without an exceptionally efficient system of cost records, and a system that was in continuous operation.

This hypothetical example illustrates the difficulty of relating extra costs or cost savings directly to design decisions and also the difficulty of arranging a line of communication along which cost information could flow. It is possible to relate tender prices to actual building prices by using operational bills, or, to some extent, elemental bills, but this appears to be more useful in controlled research situations and for the reasons described above is unlikely to be helpful in general competitive contracts. The quantity surveyor is forced to accept that cost information based on actual expenditure on design details does not exist, and, even if it did, there is no contractual or practical reason why it should be passed on to the professions. Advice on building economics is, therefore, based on the prices offered by the industry in their tenders. Without doubt this is second-best information, not only reducing the effectiveness of the contribution that the professions and also the management of contractual firms could make in increasing building efficiency but also disguising true cost relationships because short-term economic pressures are affecting the prices. This is a further reason why we have not emphasized detailed pricing or labour constants and work measurements in this book. We feel that the quantity surveyor must familarize himself with the general level of prices that he may expect in the bills of quantities currently submitted in competition, and, by making use of such services as the Building Cost Information Service of the Royal Institution of Chartered Surveyors and other published cost indices, the probable cost to be expected for typical buildings. The detailed advice that he can give on building economics must be worked out from 'first principles' for each situation, and he must ally his skills of measurement and estimating with an understanding of the management objectives and the methods used by contractors in constructional operations.

We have placed considerable emphasis on statistics, mathematical analysis, and cost in use studies, since we regard these as being extensions to the quantity surveyors' skills of measurement. By extending his knowledge to the relations between capital expenditure and the income that may be expected, the cost of borrowing, or the cost of maintenance and renewal, he is taking into account factors that are fundamental to the financial basis of every building, private or public.

In conclusion, the quantity surveyor's position among his professional colleagues is based on his detailed work in measurement and contract documentation, and his understanding of contract law. New entrants to our profession are now required to have a much deeper understanding of the work of the other professional partners in the building team and to have reached higher standards in economics, management, and data-processing. The training syllabuses of the institutions are concentrating on breadth of knowledge rather than emphasizing single skills. We hope that this book by its inclusion of descriptions of the work of quantity surveyors peripheral to the more traditional tasks will help in widening the general field of experience. For quantity surveyors trained to an earlier syllabus we hope that this book will link their practical day-to-day work with new opportunities for professional service in the future.

To this end the book has an informal structure of six sections. The first (Chapters 1–3) gives the essential background to the industry and the professions connected with building, their clients, and the legal control of development. The second section (Chapters 4–9) studies the methods by which designs may be evaluated, including preliminary estimating, cost yardsticks and analysis, cost geometry, statistics, and cost in use theory. The third section (Chapters 10–12) covers the design and cost consequences of architectural decisions, including the effect of plan shape, planning efficiency, and the choice of specification for buildings and service installations. Section four (Chapters 13–15) describes various methods of arriving at a total cost limit for the building, either by the use of financial formulae or by statutory cost limits, and the calculation and use of cost indices. Section five (Chapters 16 and 17) deals with the theory and practice of cost planning, and the final section (Chapters 18 and 19) describes the application of cost in use theory and statistical exercises to cost planning and design control. The general pattern follows the description of techniques and their application in current practice and possible future developments. The appendixes contain a detailed example of cost analysis in the form adopted by the Royal Institution of Chartered Surveyors Building Cost Information Service, together with notes on graphical methods of calculation, further cost studies, and examples of discount tables.

We would like to express our great appreciation of the help and encouragement given by many colleagues and students in the preparation of this book. Particularly we are grateful to the Royal Institution of Chartered Surveyors Building Cost Information Service for their permission to reproduce their 'Standard Form of Cost Analysis' as an appendix, and to Elizabeth Browne, Marilyn Clifford, and Anne Elliott for their patience and efforts in typing the manuscript. We also express our thanks to Mr. Frank Thomas for having compiled the index.

2

Introduction to Second Edition

The objectives of this book have not altered from those we intended for the earlier edition, but variations have been introduced to both the presentation and contents to meet some of the changing needs of the professions and industry. The most obvious need for revision resulted from the pressures of inflation: it came as a very considerable shock to calculate the extent to which the many numerical examples needed to be updated, not least because of the differential between the increases in fuel costs and those for construction. In addition rates of interest, which were tending to fall as the First Edition was prepared, are standing higher than at any time in the past. The effect of these two issues is to place even greater importance on the evaluation of total expenditure throughout the life of buildings taking into account both construction and running costs. However, the response to this issue is tempered by the fact that the calculations are considerably more sensitive to error and misinterpretation when interest rates are high.

Another major change we have reflected is the move from a demand economy to one based on cash considerations. The period in which we compiled the First Edition was towards the end of the post-war reconstruction. It was also an era where the development of city centres and new industrial complexes was accelerating, financed by the realization that the potential of many industrial and commercial estates was seriously undervalued. The success of these developments and indeed many of the post-war programmes are now called into question, and it is clear that decisions taken to ensure high volume construction produced problems, which indicate a lack of technical foresight and can often only be solved by immediate replacement or major reconstruction. In addition to problems of building construction the social implications of many developments are being challenged. The favoured solution to these problems appears to rely on a greater degree of public consultation at local level, an increasing pressure to justify all construction works by evaluation studies and a release from the more mechanical aspects of expenditure limits and planning controls. For this reason we have placed rather more emphasis on general economic issues as they affect the industry and professional consultants, and this has resulted in a change to the contents of some chapters described in the introduction to the first edition.

The authors would like to thank numerous individuals who have commented on the earlier publication and who provided ideas which have been incorporated in the new sections of this edition, and as before we would like to thank all who have helped with the preparation of this manuscript.

1

The Building Industry

Relation to the National Economy

The building industry, with a total value of building work in 1978 amounting to £16,147 million, accounts for more than 50 per cent of the gross fixed investment and for over 10 per cent of the gross domestic product of the nation. It also employs approximately 10 per cent of the total male working population of the nation.

Activities on such a massive scale make the building industry a focal point of the national interest. Major changes in the industry become matters of national economic importance and changes in the state of the national economy become in turn matters of major concern to the industry. Government measures to control the economy usually affect the industry, either directly, by the control of output, by licensing or by reducing the programme of public expenditure, or indirectly, by restriction on borrowing. Either way the amount of work available to the industry is reduced, employment falls off, and the financial structure of the industry is affected; in addition, consequential reduction in the consumption of building materials affect the business of merchants and manufacturers to a degree which often goes beyond the short-term nature of the controls.

Annual Output

The Department of the Environment *Housing and Construction Statistics*, the source of the information set out in Table 1.1, in addition to providing the figure for total output in 1978 of £16,147 million, also provides information enabling a closer examination of the building industry to be made.

Building Operations

The essential difference between building and all other manufacturing industries is that the product is assembled on the site where it is to be used. Apart from general work such as excavation and concreting, the labour force is mainly engaged on the assembly of large or small scale pre-manufactured components, but this labour force must move from site to site and operate under any conditions imposed by the environment or weather. This produces difficulties of management, organization, and even output that are not experienced by industries working from a fixed base and in controlled conditions. Development in the various forms of industrialized building changes the

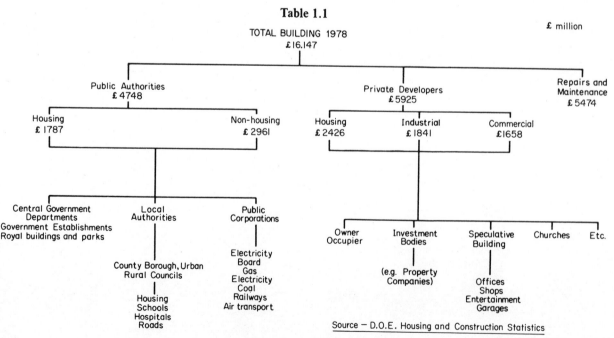

Table 1.1

£ million

Source – D.O.E. Housing and Construction Statistics

proportion of work carried out on the site to that in factories, but except in the manufacture of the fully prefabricated timber building, the amount of site labour has not fallen to any marked degree and there is no such thing as building in factories.

The persons engaged in carrying out building operations include the building employers and operatives, together with the members of the allied professions – architects, engineers and quantity surveyors.

Table 1.2
Construction firms – October 1978
Number of Firms sized according to Number of Operatives Employed

Number of Operatives Employed	0–1	2–7	8–59	60–299	300–1,199	1,200+	Total
Number of Firms	28,551	42,007	18,667	1,902	339	54	91,520
Value of Work Done in 3rd Quarter 1978–£million	56·4	319·6	936·7	720·3	698·7	540·4	3,272·1

Table 1.3
Trade of Firms

	Number of Firms	
	April 1965	Oct. 1978
TRADE OF FIRM		
General Builders	36,578	36,407
B. & C.E. Contractors	3,095	2,380
Civil Engineers	1,260	1,886
Sub-total	40,933	40,673
Plumbers	8,744	7,463
Joiners and Carpenters	5,727	5,855
Painters	15,136	12,350
Roofers	1,556	2,441
Plasterers	3,231	2,775
Glaziers	291	933
Heating and Ventilating Engineers	970	3,952
Electrical Contractors	4,568	6,958
Constructural Engineers	425	683
Plant Hirers	707	2,556
Other Specialist Firms	1,408	4,881
TOTAL	83,696	91,520

Table 1.4
Operatives Employed

	Number in Thousands	
	April 1965	Oct. 1978
OPERATIVES EMPLOYED		
TYPE OF WORK		
Housing	325·9	198·0
Non-Housing	496·4	327·0
Total New Work	822·3	525·0
Repairs and Maintenance	315·7	232·0
TOTAL ALL WORK	1,138·0	757·0

Building Trade Employers

Building trade employers can be considered as falling into two groups: the contractor and the public authority.

THE CONTRACTOR

In October 1978 contractors comprised 91,520 separate firms. As Table 1.2 shows, these ranged from the large firm, capable of dealing with any type of work of any size, either in this country or overseas, to the small jobbing builder engaged primarily on repairs and maintenance or small, speculative housing-development work.

It can be seen in Table 1.2 that rather less than ½ per cent of the firms employ over 300 operatives. This ½ per cent is engaged in approximately 40 per cent of the total value of building work. In contrast, the one-man concerns, while accounting for over a quarter of the total number of firms, are engaged for less than 2 per cent of the total value of building work.

Classification of firms according to the number of operatives employed can, however, be misleading. It is a feature of the industry that employment is largely 'casual' in the sense that employees are usually engaged for a particular contract. This can cause a firm to move from one classification to another temporarily between contracts.

Many firms engaged on contracts both large and small actually employ very few operatives themselves, but act primarily as co-ordinators, the bulk of the work being carried out by firms of specialist sub-contractors.

CHANGES IN THE BUILDING INDUSTRY

The preceding paragraphs illustrate the position at one point in time, but the industry is continually changing and reacting to the demands placed upon it. At the time of publication it appears that the period 1967—8 represented a maximum for both employment and output. Since that time the value of output at constant prices has dropped by about 10 per cent. There are also significant changes in the number of operatives employed. In 1965, the peak year, the average number over the year, including direct labour and all administrative and clerical staff, was 1,128,000, in 1978 the figure had dropped to 750,000. This particular development merits further analysis.

Table 1.5 shows that the reduction is greatest in new construction work and appears to be out of proportion to any reduction in output over the period. It is also surprising that there should be such a marked reduction in the numbers involved in maintenance, which might be thought immune from short-term social and political pressures on the industry. In fact these figures probably represent not a reduction in numbers involved in the industry but changes in the methods of employment.

It has always been a feature of the industry that the experienced craftsman could, if he so wished, move into the field of management either as a foreman or clerk of works, or, alternatively, set up in business on his own account. Traditionally, if he followed the second choice he became an employer of labour with a direct financial responsibility and relationship to his clients. One development has been the 'labour only' contractor, the craftsman who sets himself up in business but does not enter into a contract with clients or accept responsibility for the materials he uses. Relieving the main contractor of his normal responsibilities as an employer makes it possible to reduce overhead costs, but it is debatable whether this advantage, if such it is, is not completely outweighed by the consequential complication of site organization and management.

Another change has been the number of large well-established firms who have amalgamated with others or gone out of business. The changes in the industry, therefore, comprise a concentration into large-scale contracting organizations coupled with an increase in the numbers of self-employed labour-only firms.

THE PUBLIC AUTHORITY

In 1978 the public authorities engaged their own direct labour for £1,400 million of building work. Work carried out

Table 1.5

Number of Operatives (in thousands) employed by Contractors

Quarterly Average	Housing	Non-Housing	Maintenance	Total
July 1965	315	489	317	1,121
July 1967	311	462	293	1,066
July 1969	264	439	276	979
July 1971	205	394	234	833
Oct. 1978	198	327	232	757

by direct labour consisted mainly of repairs and maintenance to existing buildings. This policy has proved sensible, since this type of work does not attract the building firm that is not organized to do it at an economic price. In only a few instances do the local authorities use their direct labour force on major new projects.

The size of the direct labour forces of the Department of the Environment and the Greater London Council would rival the largest of the contracting concerns.

The 'casual' nature of employment that is a feature of the contracting side of the industry is absent from public authority employment, where more stable conditions apply, although this attraction is offset, particularly for the younger building worker, by the comparatively high wage rates paid by the contractors.

The Professions

The professional consultants, though appointed either directly or indirectly by the building owner, have a responsibility to both the owner and the contractor. These responsibilities are set out in codes of professional practice and in the form of contract.

THE ARCHITECT

The Architects' Registration Act of 1938 provides that no person may carry on business under the description of 'architect' unless registered with the Architects' Registration Council established under the Act.

The architect may be engaged in private practice and appointed by the building owner for a specific work, or he may be employed on a salaried basis by a public authority or industrial undertaking. Essentially, the architect is the leader of the building team. From completion of the briefing by the building owner until the signing of the final certificate of payment to the contractor, the architect is in command, occupying a position at the centre of the complex operations necessary for the fulfilment of the building owner's brief.

The architect is responsible for obtaining the necessary approvals from appropriate authorities, designing the work, specifying the materials to be used and the methods of construction to be employed, inviting tenders and advising on selection of contractor, supervising the works in progress, and certifying payments to the contractor. In his design and specification of materials and methods of construction, the architect has a responsibility to the building owner to consider his interests not only through the effectiveness of the design but also by ensuring both economic initial capital cost and subsequent maintenance costs.

THE ENGINEER

If the architect requires advice on the design of foundations, structures, or mechanical or electrical services, he may recommend the appointment of consultant engineers. Unlike the architect, the engineer is not required by law to be registered or necessarily to be qualified, although a court of law would hold that a person acting as an engineer should perform to the levels of competence expected of an engineer. The engineer may act as a consultant to the architect or, where the building is of an engineering character, he may assume total responsibility and act in a capacity similar to that of an architect.

The engineer will work within the brief prepared by the client and developed by the architect, and within the limits of economic costs that may be agreed.

THE QUANTITY SURVEYOR

As a member of the building industry the quantity surveyor is unique to this country and to certain of the Commonwealth countries. Quantity surveying developed after the emergence of the general building firms in the latter half of the nineteenth century, which made it necessary to select a single organization to carry out a project. In 1922 the first edition of the *Standard Method of Measurement for Building Works* was published, leading to uniformity in measuring building work. This cleared the way for the evolution of the modern bill of quantities, which, in addition to providing the industry with a standardized basis for tendering, also enabled one to obtain comprehensive cost data.

The quantity surveyor's main function is to advise on all matters related to cost that involve measuring the work, preparing documents to enable prices to be obtained from contractors, assessing the value of work done as it proceeds so that interim payments can be made, and preparing accounts to enable the final payments to be made.

Recent developments in the building industry have turned the quantity surveyor into a building cost accountant. As such he may inform the architect of the likely effect on cost of various design solutions, material specifications and methods of construction, and prepare estimates of cost from preliminary designs or schedules of accommodation. Costing may now also influence design, and the quantity surveyor, armed with information made available by analysis of costs of previous building projects, is often brought in at the early brief stage. Indeed a client may well consult the quantity surveyor first if he needs advice on the feasibility of a project before deciding whether or not to buy a particular site or embark on a speculation.

2
Clients of the Industry

It can be seen from Chapter 1 that the two clients — public authority and private developer — utilize the output of the industry in almost equal proportions.

Public Authorities

Public authorities are governed generally by Acts of Parliament. Central government control over their capital building expenditure is exercised on their long-term capital programme and on their annual capital budget. The government of the day sets a policy for the distribution of the total national resources, and decides in broad outline the amount to be expended on the building sector of the economy and the amount to be allocated to each of the main services. Following this, the Treasury, the Department of Education and Science, the Department of the Environment, the Home Office, the Department of Health and Social Security, etc. distribute the money and take steps to ensure that 'value for money' is obtained on individual schemes.

Table 1.1 shows public-authority expenditure divided between housing and non-housing. The non-housing work is made up of expenditure on schools, hospitals, government offices, libraries, fire stations, police stations, roads, etc. The expenditure on repairs and maintenance includes work carried out by direct labour, although no detailed breakdown is available. The public sector can also be divided into three groups according to the way it is administered.

1. Central government departments, e.g. the Department of the Environment, which is responsible for all government and Royal establishments;
2. Local authorities, e.g. county, borough, urban and rural councils who are responsible for housing, schools, roads, etc; and
3. Public corporations, e.g. gas, electricity, coal, railways and air transport boards, etc., each responsible for buildings required for their own particular field of operation.

Private Developers

The sector of the private developer ranges from the large organization controlled by a board of directors to the owner-occupier providing the 'one off' type of building for his own use.

Central government control of building in this sector is exercised through legislation requiring the developer to obtain planning permission and, in many instances, licence to build. Financial control is generally exercised through the project balance sheet, which sets expenditure on building operations against the anticipated returns, usually in the form of rents.

Financial Classification

In general, all projects can be classified financially under one of three headings:

1. Commercial — where the project is expected to yield a revenue for profit, e.g. projects involving shops, offices, etc., which the client will let to produce a rent.
2. Quasi-commercial — where the project is expected to yield a revenue but not for the purpose of profit, e.g. local authority housing.
3. Non-commercial — where the project is not expected to yield a revenue, e.g. schools, hospitals, churches, etc.

Clients in each of these three financial classes will be influenced when working out their project budgets by different considerations.

COMMERCIAL

The first considerations will be the need for the project to yield a profit. On one side of the balance sheet will be the expected income and on the other will be the likely capital outlay on the building, on the site, on the maintenance, and running costs during the life of the building, and on the servicing of any mortgages or loans.

The commercial client would normally make his appreciation of the finances of a project before buying the site. When a site worthy of consideration becomes available, he should approach the local planning authority to find out to what

extent the site may be developed. From this information his financial advisers can prepare a budget of income and expenditure. Included in this budget must be an item for the cost of building. The architect and quantity surveyor must, therefore, be prepared to advise upon the feasibility of providing the required accommodation on the site, and to indicate the order of expenditure likely to be needed to ensure an acceptable development.

Quite clearly, when the question of the building cost has played an important part in the decision to embark on a project, it is absolutely essential that the budgeted building cost is not exceeded. Equally it is also essential that within the budgeted building cost the building must be designed to provide at least the floor area upon which the rent calculations were based.

QUASI-COMMERCIAL

This class covers almost exclusively local-authority housing, a most complex field of building. It is sensitive to political and social issues but nevertheless subject to the same overriding consideration, associated with the commercial project, that income must be balanced against expenditure.

On the income side of the balance sheet will be the rents received from the tenants, monies received from central government subsidies, and the local authority's own contribution from the general rate fund. This last item is the amount required to balance any deficit in the year's accounts between revenue and expenditure, a variable figure governed by the particular authority's rent policy.

The expenditure side will be made up of loan charges on

any capital sum borrowed to finance the project, and outlay on maintenance and running costs.

Local-authority rent policies often strike a balance between the 'economic rent' for a property and the ability of tenants to pay. The economic rent is the level of rent that would show no deficit on the housing account.

Even with differential rent schemes, few authorities can look to their rents to cover all their housing costs and, therefore, some contribution from the general rate fund is often necessary; but the amount of this contribution must be kept as low as possible to reduce the burden on the authorities' ratepayers and also to avoid curbing the authorities' activities in other fields.

For buildings in these first two financial classes it will be apparent that the budgeted building cost must not be exceeded, since any substantial excess expenditure would invalidate the financial basis of the whole project.

This would be no less true of buildings in the third – the non-commercial – class, though budgeting for projects in this class cannot normally be based on money income.

NON-COMMERCIAL

In the absence of an income from the property the amount to be spent can only be determined by the needs to be satisfied by the building. For example, in schools we can use the number of student places required as a basis of assessment, or in hospitals the number of beds. Having chosen the basis, a reasonable cost per unit can be assessed by reference to past experience. The non-commercial client can then be sure that the amount allowed is realistic, and can reasonably expect that it should not be exceeded.

3

Financial Control of Development

One of the basic rules of management is that no project is likely to be successful unless the objectives are properly defined and the necessary allocations made for the labour and materials. This rule is no less true when applied to the economy of a country. It is imperative for the Government to decide which objectives are to be met within its programmes — choosing between a number of conflicting and overlapping social needs and laying down the proportion of the nation's resources that is to be devoted to each.

In a simple 'desert island' economy it is possible for the 'Government' to decide which site should be cleared for the village school. They could choose the workmen by name and direct which local building materials should be used. In a situation like this the various buildings would be built as they were needed, and as the workmen and materials were available. There would be no need to consider expenditure. In a complex industrial society the situation is very different. Those responsible for meeting the social needs of housing, schools, hospitals, whether at the local or central government levels, cannot be involved with all the operational decisions needed in the siting or the construction of the buildings. There will be a series of decisions at different levels, starting with agreement on the need to provide a building in a certain area, that the building should be on a particular site, and continuing through to the ordering of materials and hiring the labour. This chain involves, at different levels of responsibility, politicians, administrators, architects, surveyors, and contractors. Apart from a common motivation to meet the requirements, the only factor common to all their decision making is the expenditure of money. In short, finance acts as the framework in which all the decisions are made. The decisions made by the Treasury on finance in a complex economy are as effective in general terms, as the direct operational decisions made on the 'desert island'.

This situation can be illustrated by reference to the post-war expansion of school building. There was a need for new schools, arising from a number of factors, such as replacement of war-damaged and obsolete buildings, the movement of populations from city centres to new suburbs, the creation of new towns, a general increase in the numbers of school-children following the post-war rise in the birth-rate, new educational concepts, and changes in school-leaving age.

The first approach to this problem was to allow local authorities to develop their plans for new schools as quickly as possible alongside the provision of new houses, factories, and the repair of war damage. However, in the decade spanning 1945—55, there was a period when many contracts started were not completed because the labour and material resources were not available. For schools this problem was solved and its recurrence prevented by the decision to programme, within close limits, the amount to be spent both in total and for individual schemes. This is an illustration of the underlying purposes of cost control to direct and define the objectives of the political, administrative, professional, and contractual team within the constraints of the country's economy and not just to limit standards of area or specification.

In addition to financial control the Government may make a direct impact on building developments by such methods as restricting the amount of office buildings, or developing design disciplines such as the 'nucleus' hospital.

Individual projects are usually controlled by a system of expenditure limits. These systems lay down the maximum cost that can be allowed for the particular function to be satisfied, coupled with minimum requirements expressed in terms of areas or design provision. Once a system of control has been established for a particular class of building, it is possible to forecast what financial programme will be necessary to meet the estimated levels of demand. This allows the Government to balance demands and priorities between departments and to allocate building programmes with a reasonable degree of confidence.

The development of expenditure limits and their application are described in a later chapter. At this point it is useful to discuss how expenditure on individual contracts is integrated into the capital programmes determined by Government. To this end it is necessary to examine some of the 'terms of art' used in this area of financial control.

The first consideration is whether the nature and application of the capital programmes is in terms of 'starts' or 'expenditure'. A capital programme of 'starts' is simply a sum of money that is to be distributed, for example, between a number of individual contracts let by Local Authorities or Universities. The aggregate value of the contracts let in a particular year are related to the published programme for that year although the actual expenditure on these contracts will fall to be paid in later financial

years. Control by 'expenditure' requires that the total expenditure on all contracts in progress for a particular category of building type amount to the designated capital sum for that year.

For officers controlling capital expenditure and for their client bodies and professional advisors there is no doubt that control by starts is easier to manage. This follows from the fact that as schemes are developed through the design stages towards the point where contracts are to be placed accurate estimates of the eventual contract sums can be produced. Therefore the aggregate total can be predicted and appropriate action initiated if it appears that the programmes may be under or over fulfilled. The control of buildings within a programme of expenditure is more complicated since although the expenditure on future contracts can be estimated the number of schemes that can be started will depend on what is happening to all the other contracts that are already in progress. It will be appreciated that the final cost of a project will be affected by variations and through the fluctuations clause in the contract. This extra expenditure must be met within the overall programme but the actual incidence and timing is difficult to pre-determine.

It should be apparent that although the decision that a particular contract should be allowed to start is based on the effect that will have on the total expenditure, the actual control lies in placing the contract. In most situations once contracts have started the client is not in a position to affect the rate of expenditure.

In practical terms, if capital programmes are held more or less constant there will be little difference in the effect of either method since the total expenditure certified in each year will tend to equate to the value of contracts let in that year. Similarly if any particular facility is to be expanded the controlling agency can arrange to increase programmes at the appropriate time to meet either the aggregate value of the new contracts or the value of the certificates which will fall to be paid. In circumstances where capital spending must be reduced programmes controlled by expenditure can only be adjusted by cancelling existing contracts or by preventing new contracts being let. The second of these methods will have only a limited effect since schemes may be scheduled to start late in the financial year and therefore the potential savings may be small. In addition the spending in the first few months of any contract is low. Exactly similar considerations apply where programmes are controlled by starts: real reductions in public expenditure can only be achieved by reducing the quantity of building work being carried out. Therefore, it is clear that even where control is apparently concerned simply with the number of building contracts that can be let, the ultimate effect on the computation of public liability must relate to the flow of expenditure that results.

There are two other aspects of financial control that merit examination, first the distinction between capital and revenue expenditure and secondly the difference between control by cash limits or by the normal methods of financial accounting.

In ordinary commercial practice capital expenditure implies investment in buildings, plant and machinery that assist in the creation of revenue and exist as a saleable asset adding to the value of the shares. In the field of public investment this distinction has less meaning since all funding is in the end supported by the public purse. Nevertheless all government departments in their budgets indicate revenue or recurrent expenditure separately from capital spending. The primary reason for this is that the year-by-year spending is designed to support policies that have been approved by Parliament and established by statute. Capital expenditure may imply making additional commitments and this must be considered against all other priorities in public investment. In normal circumstances revenue expenditure will be continued from one year to the next but capital spending is usually considered against short-term economic yardsticks. For most government departments maintenance of buildings is financed from the year-to-year revenue allocations. New buildings, major repairs and plant replacement are funded from capital. It is usual for there to be some facility for interchange between the two budgets and there is constant debate about how far the distinction should be maintained. For example, if new buildings were financed from revenue, which is normally spent in accordance with decisions made at local level, it could release central government departments from the need to be involved in much controversy. It is already the case in the fields of housing and school building that local authorities borrow from the Public Works Loan Board and make repayments from their rate income. However for other public works, particularly hospitals, where no income is received from the public, it is impossible to accumulate sufficient funds out of the revenue supported by government subvention to finance large-scale redevelopment.

To summarize, for expenditure supported by share capital there are real reasons to distinguish between capital and other forms of spending. In the public sector the asset value of the stock or estate is rarely taken into account and although both revenue and capital are funded by taxation nevertheless there are political and procedural reasons for maintaining the two categories.

The second point, relating to the current emphasis on monetary control by cash limits, is also based on theories of control found in commercial practice. The basic objective is quite simple: in the private sector unless expenditure is closely related to income the business will fail. However, if a commercial enterprise does not produce a constant flow of income to match continuing expenditure it can resort to borrowing. This practice is adopted by many companies and as long as the eventual income can cover costs and loan charges, and from the point of view of the banks if the

11

capital assets are adequate in relation to the size of the loan, no particular problem results. Nevertheless it will be appreciated that large-scale borrowing must increase costs and there is the argument that it is an undesirable factor in the economic affairs of the country. For example in a period of high inflation repayments of loans are made in coin that has been devalued. The banks must protect their investment by charging high rates of interest, this produces a ripple effect on many other aspects of the economy including the rate of return on Government stocks and mortgages. There is, therefore, overt pressure to reduce borrowing; and if interest rates are high company accountants will as far as possible plan the cash flow of expenditure and receipts to keep borrowing to a minimum. This philosophy has been extended to the vocabulary of public expenditure. At the Treasury level, the situation is precisely the same as for private industry, over spending, not directly supported by revenue, must be met by borrowing. Therefore there is every reason to reduce expenditure to match income. For individual departments the perspective is different. For example in the National Health Service the income is determined by the Department of Health and Social Security, borrowing is not permitted, and there is little other income. The basic argument for cash limits is therefore not directly applicable. Nevertheless, the operational managers have the responsibility to draw up expenditure profiles predicted on a monthly basis for the year and to control their spending within these ceilings and this procedure achieves the objective of controlling the rate of government expenditure.

In practice it is not easy to monitor overall financial control from the month to month cash statements because these simply indicate the value of cheques drawn against the cash profile. The difficulty being that the total expenditure is often affected by arbitrary factors in the timing of payments such as the implementation of a wage award or an unexpected bank holiday giving rise to overtime payments — thus the figures can be misleading. Treasurers therefore continue to draw up financial statements of income and expenditure taking account of debtors and creditors as well as actual cash transactions. These allow the actual cost of services to be analysed year by year.

This very simplified account of the economic background to the constraints applied to development, underlines the need for procedures to estimate the pattern of expenditure arising from building contracts. The basic principles behind these procedures relate to the conditions of contract i.e. payments are made by monthly certificates, a retention is deducted, at practical completion half this retention is released the remainder being paid after the period of final measurement. The situation is complicated by the fact that the month-by-month expenditure is not constant; at the start only a few trades are involved and certificates will be low. As the building work develops more trades and sub-contractors will be involved and monthly certificates will increase, but as work is completed the average value will fall away.

This pattern is shown by the graphs illustrated in Appendix D but in addition the cost and timing of contracts will be affected by the inevitable variations and contractual delays. A further consideration is the impact of inflation on contracts with construction times exceeding twelve months. This will affect certificates to an increasing degree as the contract nears completion and usually represents a significant proportion of the final settlement. Therefore any professional involved in predicting expenditure needs to analyse the statistical probabilities of change in the contract as well as the likely incidence of inflation on the certificates.

Table 3.1 gives an extract from such an analysis for hospital buildings over a period of years. It will be realized that since this survey is based on contracts of a particular

Table 3.1

Contract Value (1975–76)	Indicated Contract Period Average (months)	Actual Contract Period Average (months)	Expenditure at Indicated Completion Date Average (per cent)	Expenditure at Practical Completion Date Average (per cent)	Commencement to final Account Average (months)
Up to £100,000	12	15	80	90	39
100–200,000	15	18	80	90	45
200–300,000	18	21	85	95	40
300–400,000	18	21	90	95	48
1–10,000,000	48	60	90	100	90

type placed by one agency in a single locality it should not be expected to apply universally.

The table shows that for the largest schemes the time overruns are quite significant and on average the total cost of the contracts was above the original tendered figure. This point is underlined by the fact that the full sum has been paid before the retention is released and the final account settled.

The methods described in Appendix D combined with studies of the type illustrated can be used to determine the total spending that may be expected to fall within the financial years covered by the contract period. Thus, where it is necessary to keep within a programme controlled by cash limits the aggregate spending on contracts in progress and those proposed can be calculated. If the programme limit is likely to be exceeded the placing of new contracts must be delayed.

This chapter has been mainly concerned with public works programmes but the principles of prediction and monitoring are applicable to all contracts. The need to assess the timing of payments under building contracts is particularly important in the private sector where development projects are financed from the cash flow of income from earlier enterprises.

4

Preliminary Estimates and Cost Yardsticks

Approximate Quantities

The method of preliminary estimating most commonly used is that of approximate quantities.

The procedure followed is similar to that employed to obtain building tenders, except that, instead of producing detailed bills of quantities for the contractors to price, the surveyor takes off composite items of quantities that are then priced at all-in rates.

The extent to which items of work are brought together will depend on individual preferences, the degree of accuracy required, and the stage the drawings have reached in the planning process. No particular rules of measurement and pricing exist, and many composite items result from research into pricing carried out by the estimator.

Let us take an example from concrete work. Research may have shown that for a particular building the cost of concrete in beams is roughly the same as the cost of formwork, which in turn is about the same as the cost of 1 per cent reinforcement. In other words the cost ratio between concrete, formwork, and 1 per cent reinforcement is 1:1:1, inclusive of all labour and sundry items. If this cost ratio can be established, then the beams can be measured as a total cubic content, the composite item being 'Concrete in beams of average section including formwork and reinforcing with 1 per cent reinforcement'.

This item can then be priced at three times the concrete rate.

Engineers will usually be able to indicate the percentage of reinforcement in particular beams and columns accurately enough for the estimate being prepared.

Similar items in composite form could read:

'150 mm concrete bed spread and levelled on and including 150 mm bed of hardcore and building paper, and including all necessary excavation and reinforcing with and including fabric reinforcement'.
'Brick cavity wall faced externally in facings £100 per thousand and plastered internally, including decorating with emulsion paint'.
'Stoneware drainpipe laid in trench on and including 150 mm concrete bed haunched up at sides, including excavation in normal soil average 1·50 m deep'.
(N.B. the rate will allow for a reasonable number of bends and junctions, etc.)

In this way the work involved in a building may be taken off for estimating purposes in considerably fewer items than would result from the application of the rules set out in the *Standard Method of Measurement of Building Works,* and those items required for the tender Bills of Quantities.

The amount of information required for this method of estimating means that planning must have reached an advanced stage.

At earlier stages estimates must be based on information that can only be related to the general characteristics of the building, i.e. the number of occupants, the floor area or the volume. In the past the cost of buildings on tender has been analyzed against three yardsticks, and the resulting single price-rate figures used for approximate estimating.

Cost Yardsticks

UNIT METHOD

The building cost is expressed in terms of the accommodation it provides, for example:

Schools   – cost per student place
Hospitals – cost per bed
Theatres – cost per seat
Hostels   – cost per residential place
Car Parks – cost per car space

This method, because of the size of the unit used and the difficulty of adjusting the figure to meet particular situations, is unreliable for most estimating purposes; so it is restricted to the very early stages of a project, before any drawing is begun. It may be noted that these units can be used to establish the project budget cost or cost limit, as with Department of Health and Social Security hospital projects and Department of Education and Science school projects.

CUBIC METHOD

The volume of the building is calculated according to a set of rules illustrated in Figure 4.1. The cube is made up by taking plan dimensions from the outside faces of brick walls, and vertical dimensions from the top of foundations to halfway up a pitched roof or 0·61 m above a flat roof. Any projections such as tank rooms or chimneys are added as a net extra.

As a yardstick for use in Cost Planning this method is unreliable, since two buildings having identical areas of accommodation but differently designed and constructed could have very different volumes.

The cubic method has, nevertheless, some value in that it may enable a notional figure to be given when there is insufficient time to allow a more accurate estimate of cost to be prepared. The Building Cost Information Service of the Royal Institution of Chartered Surveyors in the 'Standard Form of Cost Analysis' uses the internal cube (*see* Appendix A).

STOREY ENCLOSURE METHOD

An adaptation of the single price rate methods, which gained publicity in the 1950s and which attempted to make the cubic method more realistic is the Storey Enclosure method, illustrated in Figure 4.2. Factors are introduced to account for storey heights, basements and areas of enclosing walls. The unit obtained is known as the Storey Enclosure Unit and the rules of measurement are as follows:

1. Measure the area of the lowest floor and multiply any part above ground level by two, and any part below

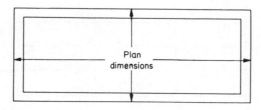

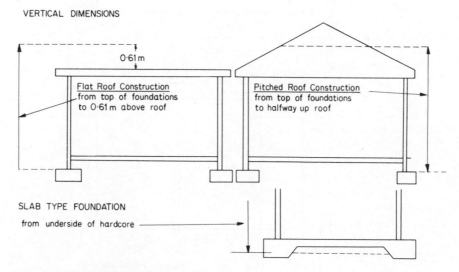

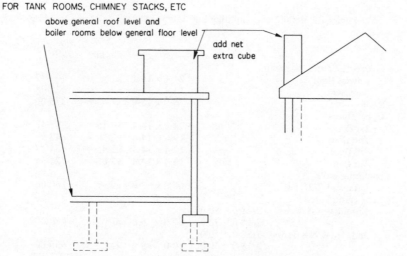

Figure 4.1 Method of computing the cubic content of a building.

ground level by three (these areas being measured within the external walls).

2. Measure the area of the roof (measured flat to the extremities of the eaves).
3. Measure the area of the upper floors and multiply by two, and also adjust each upper floor area by multiplying by a progressive factor of 0·15 (i.e. first floor by 2·15; second floor by 2·30 and so on).
4. Measure the area of the external enclosing walls, the area of any enclosing wall below ground level to be multiplied by two.

Insufficient use prevents any judgement being passed on the effectiveness of this method. As a yardstick for cost-planning purposes it has similar disadvantages to those of the cubic method.

SQUARE METRE METHOD

This method, now more commonly met with, is illustrated in Figure 4.3. It is more easily calculated than the other methods, and it offers a more satisfactory means of obtaining a reasonably reliable estimate, provided the plan shape

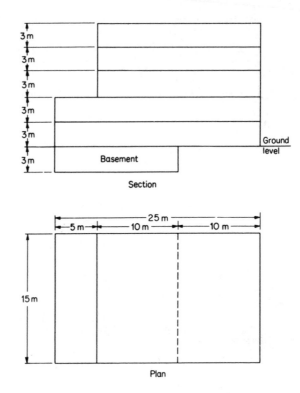

Figure 4.2 Method of computing the storey enclosure units of a building.

		Area	Factor	*Storey Enclosure Units*
Lowest floor and basement				
Lowest floor		24·4 x 14·4	x2 =	702·72
Basement		14·4 x 14·4	x3 =	622·08
Roof		25·0 x 15·0	x1 =	375·00
Upper floors				
1st floor		24·4 x 14·4	x2·15 =	755·42
2nd floor		19·4 x 14·4	x2·30 =	642·53
3rd floor		19·4 x 14·4	x2·45 =	684·43
4th floor		19·4 x 14·4	x2·60 =	726·34
Enclosing walls				
Basement 2/2/15·0		60·0 x 3·0	x2	360·00
Above ground level				
Ground & 1st floors	2/25·0 = 50·0			
	2/15·0 = 30·0	80·0 x 6·0	x1	480·00
2nd, 3rd & 4th floors	2/20·0 = 40·0			
	2/15·0 = 30·0	70·0 x 9·0	x1	630·00
Total Storey Enclosure Units				5978·52

and storey height of the building are taken into account when deciding on the rate to be applied. The area is calculated by measuring between the internal faces of the external walls on each floor. Despite the fact that the measurements taken do not take into account the vertical dimensions of the rooms, the method has proved in practice to be the most convenient basis for estimating. This argument is pursued in more detail in Chapter 5.

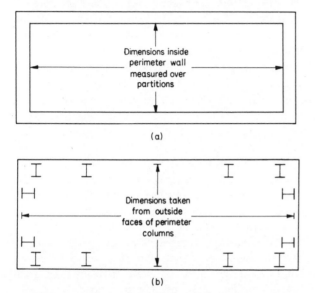

Figure 4.3 Method of computing the superficial floor area of a building.

The area is calculated by measuring between the internal faces of the external walls on each floor with *no* adjustments for internal walls and partitions.

In cases where columns to frames are situated inside the external walls these columns are ignored and the dimensions taken from the internal face of the perimeter walls.

Where there is no external wall at floor level (as in the case of freight sheds) the dimensions are taken from the external face of columns as illustrated in (*b*).

TENDER ESTIMATING

The methods of approximate estimating previously described in this chapter may often be used in sequence on an individual scheme – firstly a unit cost estimate used for investigating the feasibility of the project, followed by an estimate based on floor area at the sketch planning stages, and approximate quantities for cost checking. The next estimate of cost produced by the contractor for use in his tender is of vital importance, since it forms the financial basis for the contract and, as a by-product, provides all the cost information used by surveyors. Nevertheless, despite the fact that the tender is based on an accurate measurement of the items of work to be carried out, presented in the

standardized form required by the method of measurement, the calculation of the rates is another form of approximate estimating.

It is, therefore, necessary at this point to examine the methods of building up a tender estimate and find out how reliable its figures might be.

The price for an item such as 'one-brick wall in facing bricks PC £140 per thousand' is built up in the following way:

Number	£
Bricks 130 @ £140 per thousand	18·20
Mortar (say)	1·00
Labour 2½ hours craftsmen (inclusive rate of craftsmen & labourers). £4·50 x 2½ hours =	11·25
	30·45
Profit and overheads 10 per cent	3·05
	£33·50

In this dummy calculation only the costs of bricks and mortar can be considered reasonably accurate. In fact many contractors in preparing their tender will calculate the total value of materials first, and work out all other figures in relation to this known figure. In effect they are reducing the scope of the competition to the variations in labour, plant and overheads.

Even when the basic materials can be computed accurately, the allowances for waste and fixing accessories (in this example mortar) are matters for judgement. Clearly the value of mortar is not large in relation to any individual item of brickwork, but the cost of producing mortar, in terms of machinery, labour, materials, petrol, oil, repairs, cleaning, etc. is not inconsiderable and would merit a separate and detailed valuation. Such a calculation would only indicate an average price for the total production; it would be purely a matter of chance whether a particular cubic metre of mortar had cost the average figure, and, therefore, whether the 'correct' cost was attached to the particular square metre of brickwork.

This comment is also true for labour costs. The cost of laying bricks will vary with where the work is being done in the building, which will affect the time taken to transport the materials; with the complexity of working from scaffolding or around openings; and even with the time of the day, the day in the week, or the week in the year. Furthermore, the calculation of the labour cost is usually related to the composition of a particular gang size, in this instance three craftsmen and two labourers. This might be a

'standard' gang, considered by the management to be the most efficient, but on site when the work is carried out the actual gang could be quite different.

Finally, in the calculation, nothing has been allowed for unloading materials, insurance or plant, and scaffolding. Some contractors' estimates would include a proportion of those costs with each rate, and others would include them in the 'preliminaries'. An alternative might be to price the scaffolding in the 'preliminaries' and the insurances in the summary. There would also be differences in the treatment of the allowances for future cost increases in fixed price contracts.

These remarks simply underline the fact that the rate inserted against an item in the bill is an assumption of the cost of an average situation. In addition, the cost of an item is only complete when considered in the context of all parts of the bills of quantities. There is an obvious temptation to feel that if there were more efficient measurement of site costs, then the usefulness and accuracy of tenders might be improved. But it is arguable whether tender rates can be or should be considered as an accurate statement of the price which the contractor must pay for the work he sells to the client.

The tender rates in the bills of quantities represent only one part of the method of arriving at a lump sum price, and part of the procedure for determining the cost of variations. The rates are part of a competitive offer, and, even if the results of work study could suggest more accurate constants for labour and materials, there is no contractual reason why this information must be used in pricing individual items in the bills. Sometimes it is suggested that a price for a particular item is 'wrong', the contractors' estimator having failed because he has been misled by the descriptions, or has not grasped the possibilities of prefabrication or standardization. This shows a lack of understanding of the commercial nature of the contractor's bid. If the contractor had to represent the actual expenditure week by week throughout the contract, it would bear little direct relationship to the execution on site of the parcels of work measured in the bills. It might, indeed, suggest that the proper basis of payment would be a direct charge for materials plus a management and labour service fee for each week the contract was operating, a method perhaps close to a prime cost plus fixed fee contract. However, for most purposes it is necessary to sign contracts on the basis of lump sum tenders. Prime cost methods usually have the disadvantage that the client cannot know his total commitment at the start of the contract.

The paradox in this situation is that more accurate pricing implies that descriptions should be more closely related to the operations made necessary by the particular design, yet the strength of the bill as a tendering instrument lies in standardization. Similarly the quantity surveyor, although he will bend his efforts to producing accurate data on quantities and specifications, will be aware that he is working in a commercial situation where the 'right' price is the highest compatible with success in the competition.

The situation is little different for negotiated tenders, since even here the surveyor is often doing little more than transferring prices from one bill to another, or in effect pricing the bills in competition against the general level of prices received in his office. Even in situations outside normal competition, where there can be collaboration between contractors and surveyors it is perhaps unusual to find that individual rates are calculated any more accurately in relation to the operations to be performed.

The concept of the 'right' price and the 'right' estimate is the philosopher's stone of quantity surveying. Many research studies are initiated with the intention of stripping away the obscuring veils of the influences of site conditions, design and specifications to reveal the 'true' cost. These studies are really attempts to find a magic number which, by some manipulation, will always give the 'right' answer. The fact that these studies rarely produce any useful general results is perhaps an indication that they are striving after an impossible ideal. The lesson that should be drawn is perhaps that the purposes of research should be to reveal the differences between buildings rather than to search for ephemeral similarities.

5

Cost Analysis

The object of cost analysis is to provide a method of comparing the costs of alternative designs. The development of such a method was an essential preliminary to the study of building economics. Any comparison between alternative purchases must take into account a wide range of factors: the purchase price and the terms of payment, the quantity offered, the quality, the speed of delivery, the after-sales service and the cost of repairs and running costs. For a building the purchase price, terms of payment and speed of delivery are established by the conditions, rates and quantities in the contract bill. This purchase price is the sum paid by the client and does not represent the actual cost to the contractor, so it is necessary to accept the reservation that any economic conclusions drawn from such a figure will depend on the contractor's view of profit margins and the competitive situation at that time.

The first essential of any form of comparison is a standard yardstick for measurement. The contract price from the bill of quantities is a 'unique' figure, and, without some method of measuring the 'quantity' of building, it is of no use for comparative studies. It is necessary to measure or describe the complete building and not simply the items within the building; in fact, to establish a yardstick that can be applied not only to certain classes of buildings but to all buildings. For housing, the following range of methods of measurement might be possible:

1. Description of user requirements — a five-person house
2. Description of provision — a three-bedroom house
3. Description of size — a house with rooms totalling x m^2
4. Description of size — a house with a total area y m^2
5. Description of size — a house with a cubic volume z m^3

In addition there might be other measurements, such as the total area of the enclosing surfaces or even the weight of the components.

Examples 1 and 2 could be descriptions that would be useful in classifying buildings and for comparing total costs, but be less useful for detailed investigation because the size of the building within the classification would vary as well as the methods of construction, specifications and level of prices. Method 3 is more useful, since it is a measurement that relates to the actual value of the building to the occupiers, but for detailed investigation it suffers from the disadvantage that comparison would be complicated by the relation between the room areas and the circulation spaces resulting from different planning solutions. Methods 4 and 5 allow costs to be related to size. Cost comparisons are then possible within the building type, and with buildings designed for different uses.

The representation of the total cost as an amount per unit of area or volume produces a figure of limited use that gives no indication of the effect which decisions on design, specification and prices may have had on its composition. In fact, a system of detailed analysis is required. The following examples show the genesis of a method of elemental cost analyses using both superficial area and cubic volume as the unit of measurement.

Each example in Figure 5.1 represents a similar building constructed of four elements — wall foundation, walls, roof and floor. The same specification and costs have been assumed for unit quantities in each example.

Table 5.1 illustrates firstly, that the total cost will increase as the building size increases, as the storey height increases, and where the building outline is rectangular rather than square. The build-up of the total cost figure reveals the reason for these changes. Although Examples 1 and 3 have the same floor area, the amount of external walling is greater in Example 3 because of increased storey height.

Table 5.1 also shows the total costs and cost of the individual elements for each example, divided by the respective floor areas and volumes. Each set of figures is a cost analysis on the basis of area or volume, and these can be compared to determine which method is most likely to offer the most useful information.

On the basis of area the comparison of Examples 1 and 2 shows that the total cost per m^2 is higher for the rectangular building. The costs per m^2 are constant for both the roof and floor elements, but in Example 2 the cost of external walls and foundation show an increase. The ratio of the elemental costs of the walls is the same as the ratio of the wall areas; similarly the ratio of the elemental costs of the wall foundation is the same as the ratio of the wall lengths. For this reason it would be possible to cost Example

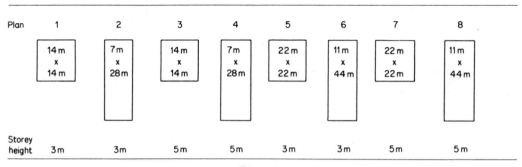

Figure 5.1

2 from the elemental costs of Example 1, together with the measurements of the wall lengths and wall areas.

i.e., cost of walls for Example 2 =

$$\text{cost of walls for Example 1} \times \frac{\text{Area of walls Example 2}}{\text{Area of walls Example 1}}$$

$$£8,400 = £6,720 \times \frac{210}{168}$$

Since the two have the same floor area it is also true that:

$$£42 \cdot 86 = £34 \cdot 29 \times \frac{210}{168}$$

A similar adjustment could be made for the increase in storey height in Example 3 or the effect of increased storey height and the rectangular plan in Example 4.

The comparison of Examples 1 and 2 shows in simple terms how building costs may be affected by the plan shape. This effect can also be illustrated by comparing Examples 1 and 8. In Example 1 the ratio of wall area to floor area is 168/196 = 0·86, the cost per m² of walls £34·29, in Example 8 the ratio is 550/484 = 1·14. The cost of the external wall per unit of floor area in Example 8 is, therefore £34·29 × (1·14/0·86) = £45·45. On the basis of volume similar comparisons can be made, but from Examples 3 and 1 and 4 and 2, it can be seen that the total cost per m³ falls as the storey height is increased. The cost per m³ of the individual elements other than the walls shows a reduction, but the cost of the wall element remains the same. Since the buildings with increased storey height are more expensive in total cost, it seems perverse that they should appear

Table 5.1

Example		1	2	3	4	5	6	7	8
Floor area	m²	196	196	196	196	484	484	484	484
Volume *	m³	588	588	980	980	1,452	1,452	2,420	2,420
Wall foundation length	m	56	70	56	70	88	110	88	110
Wall area	m²	168	210	280	350	264	330	440	550
Roof area	m²	196	196	196	196	484	484	484	484
		£	£	£	£	£	£	£	£
Wall foundation costs	£35 m	1,960	2,450	1,960	2,450	3,080	3,850	3,080	3,850
Wall costs	£40 m²	6,720	8,400	11,200	14,000	10,560	13,200	17,600	22,000
Roof costs	£45 m²	8,820	8,820	8,820	8,820	21,780	21,780	21,780	21,780
Floor costs	£25 m²	4,900	4,900	4,900	4,900	12,100	12,100	12,100	12,100
TOTAL		22,400	24,570	26,880	30,170	47,520	50,930	54,560	59,730

	cpm²	cpm³	cpm²	cpm³	cpm²	cpm³	cpm²	cpm³	cpm²	cpm³	cpm²	cpm³	cpm²	cpm³	cpm²	cp
Wall foundation	10·00	3·33	12·50	4·17	10·00	2·00	12·50	2·50	6·36	2·12	7·95	2·65	6·36	1·27	7·95	
Walls	34·29	11·43	42·86	14·29	57·14	11·43	71·43	14·29	21·82	7·27	27·27	9·09	36·36	7·27	45·45	
Roof	45·00	15·00	45·00	15·00	45·00	9·00	45·00	9·00	45·00	15·00	45·00	15·00	45·00	9·00	45·00	
Floor	25·00	8·33	25·00	8·33	25·00	5·00	25·00	5·00	25·00	8·33	25·00	8·33	25·00	5·00	25·00	
TOTAL	114·29	38·09	125·36	41·79	137·14	27·43	153·93	30·79	98·18	32·73	105·22	35·08	112·72	22·55	123·40	24

* These figures refer to the actual enclosed volumes within the building, and are not measured in accordance with the rules for cubing in approximate estimating.

cheaper when the costs are analysed on the basis of volume. Also, if the elemental costs of Example 1 were known on this basis, with a storey height of 3 m, and it was required to estimate the cost of a building with a height of 5 m, the procedure would be to adjust the rate per m³ for all elements other than the one that had changed in total cost.

The contrast between using area or volume as the method of measurement, is therefore, the difference between a system that allows for the ready adjustment of the figures and one in which these adjustments are much more complicated and difficult.

The figures in Table 5.1 are in effect based on simple approximate estimates for the various elements. The relations between the costs and the method of comparing the values would hold true if the figures had been produced from the tender sum by the addition of the costs of those items associated with the 'Foundation' or the 'External Walls'.

The other factors to be considered in comparing design solutions are quality and running costs. The example above shows how quality can be indicated. The walls were given an all-in rate of £40·00 per m², which in itself indicates a certain possible range of specifications, and if the figures were compiled with brief notes, comparisons with the same element in other buildings would be possible. However, it is more difficult to indicate the quality of workmanship and quite impossible to consider matters of appearance. The question of running costs and maintenance are considered in later chapters.

Elemental Cost Analysis

The object of cost analysis is to obtain a representative set of figures related to the major elements of a building, to allow examination and comparison. The source of these costs is the priced contract bill of quantities. The amount of data contained in the measured quantities, the descriptions, rates, and prices is overwhelming. It is, therefore, necessary to devise a method of classification and grouping of data before it can be understood.

Any method of analysis can provide cost information of interest, but the example described earlier in the chapter showed that a useful analysis is possible if the basic yardstick of area is used and costs are grouped in the simple constructional parts of the building. The analysis is prepared by bringing relevant items in the bills together and calculating total costs. For convenience the groups are chosen so that as much of the work as possible can be based on the written document. For a particular building the division into constructional sections will be a matter of convenience, but there are obvious advantages if a standard list of elements can be used for all analyses, since it enables easy comparisons between different buildings. The choice of elements in such a standard list is arbitrary. For example, a simple classification such as 'Roofs' would have a universal application, but other classifications such as 'Pitched Roofs', 'Flat Roofs', 'Glazed Roofs', 'Load-bearing Roofs' or 'Inflatable Roofs' could be chosen. However, although more sub-divisions might appear to give more accuracy of definition, they also make the analysis of the tender more difficult. For example, a canvas roof suspended on cables could clearly be classified under 'Roofs', but if multiple classifications were used, unless they happen to include this particular case, it would be necessary to make an *ad hoc* addition to the list. Clearly, the more items that are included on an *ad hoc* basis, the more difficult it becomes to make comparisons between buildings and the less useful becomes the analysis.

The list of elements developed by the Building Cost Information Service of the Royal Institution of Chartered Surveyors has been adopted for general use (*see* Appendix A). The choice of elements and their definitions represents a compromise, to make it as useful as possible both for traditional buildings and other designs in industrialized forms. For some buildings certain elements will not be used, and in others two or more elements will have to be amalgamated. For example, the cost information on the external cladding for a building using patent glazing would have to be analysed under a combined element of external walls, windows, and external doors. The methods of analysing the cost information and the measurement of quantity factors and unit elemental rates are fully described in the notes attached to the list of elements.

6

Cost Geometry

The examples described in Table 5.1 showed that the total costs of the buildings with a square plan were lower than those with a rectangular form. These examples were based on approximate estimates for the cost of the various elements, but the results would be the same if they had been based on costs established by the analysis of a building tender. In these simple examples the change in the total cost was directly related to the change in the quantity of the external walls and wall foundations. Similarly the change in the cost per m² was directly related to the change in the quantity factors, i.e. the change in the quantity of the element related to the area of the building.

It is suggested that the phrase 'Cost Geometry' should be used to describe the study of the effect on cost by (1) the relative proportion of the quantities of the various elements within a particular building, and (2) the changes in quantity factors between dissimilar buildings. In this chapter the study of the first of these aspects is extended to show how the mathematics of these relationships can be used to suggest the optimum solution to the building brief. The second part of the study is developed in Chapters 10 and 11, and it also forms the basis of procedures of cost planning described in Chapter 17.

The final part of this chapter discusses how the study of cost geometry could be integrated with the use of computers.

Cost Equations

The calculation of the total cost in Examples 1 and 2 from Table 5.1 can be written as follows:

Cost = Wall length x Foundation Cost + Wall Area x Wall Cost + Roof Area x Roof Cost + Floor Area x Floor Cost, i.e.

$$\text{Cost}_1 = 4.14.35 + 4.14.3.40 + 14.14.45 + 14.14.25 \qquad \text{(Eq. 6.1)}$$

$$\text{Cost}_2 = 2(7 + 28).35 + 2(7 + 28).3.40 + 7.28.45 + 7.28.25 \qquad \text{(Eq. 6.2)}$$

Since the area of these two examples is identical, the cost of the last two elements in these equations will be the same. The change in total cost is related to the dimensions 4.14 and 2(7 + 28). In verbal terms it could be said that

these dimensions are indicators of the 'shape' of the building and that the equations could be written:

Total cost = Cost of elements affected by shape x 'shape' + constant

This equation is similar to the familar general form for a linear function:

$$y = ax + b$$

where a and b are constants and the change in y is dependent on the change in x. In the equation above the change in 'cost' would be dependent on the change in 'shape'.

Differentiation

An equation in the general form $y = ax + b$ can be plotted to give the graph shown in Figure 6.1.

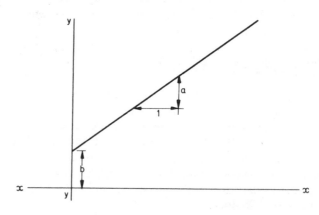

Figure 6.1

It is clear from an inspection of this figure that a unit change in the value of x will produce a change in the value of y equal to the constant a. The gradient of the graph, which is a measure of the relationship between the changes in x to the changes in y, is therefore $a/1$. It will be noted that the value of the constant b does not affect the gradient but serves to fix the position of the graph in relation to the origin of the axes.

The gradient may also be obtained by using the techniques of differentiation by rule. In an equation where $y = $ (function) x, then dy/dx, the gradient, is given by multiplying

the coefficient of the terms containing x by the power of x and reducing the power of x by one.

i.e. where $y = ax + b$
$$dy/dx = 1 . a . x^{(1-1)}$$
$$= 1 . a . x^0$$

But since any number raised to the power zero is equal to unity then:

$$dy/dx = a$$

The constant b is ignored since it contains no terms in x, and, as could be seen from the graph, its presence does not affect the gradient.

The same procedure for finding the gradient can be applied to equations that are in a quadratic form. For example the general equation $y = ax^2 + b$ produces the curve shown in Figure 6.2.

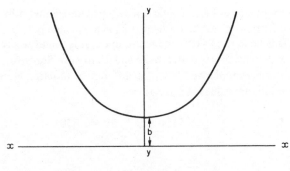

Figure 6.2

The gradient of this curve is variable, depending on the point at which it is measured. By differentiation the gradient is

$$y = ax^2 + b$$
$$dy/dx = 2ax$$

Examination of Figure 6.2 shows that where $x = 0$, the variable y will be equal to the value $0 + b$. For this equation this is also the minimum value of y. The minimum value of the curve is at the point where the gradient is zero. It follows that if the value of the differential function is found for a curve and put equal to zero, the solution of the resulting equation will show where the minimum value is to be found.

For the equation above $dy/dx = 2ax$. At the minimum dy/dx will equal 0.

$$dy/dx = 0 = 2ax$$
$$0 = x$$

This serves to confirm the observation from Figure 6.2 that the minimum value of y is where $x = 0$.

Differentiation of Cost Equations

EXAMPLE 1

The cost equation for Example 2 in Table 5.1 set out at Eq.6.2 can be written in algebraic terms, substituting the letters x and y for the dimensions on plan where $x . y = A$, the area of the building. The letters W, F, and R represent the costs per unit area of the walls, floors and the roof respectively, and Q the cost per linear unit of the wall foundations. The storey height is indicated by the letter H.

$$\text{Cost} = 2(x + y) Q + 2 (x + y) H . W + x . y . F + x . y . R$$

But $x . y = A$ and $y = A . x^{-1}$

$$\text{Cost} = 2 . x (Q + H . W) + 2 . A (Q + H . W) x^{-1} + A(F + R)$$
(Eq. 6.3)

This equation will take the form of a curve because the variable x is included as a reciprocal. The differentiation of a function with a negative power is performed in the same way as before, but the sign of the function will change and the value of the power will increase in a negative direction.

The differential of Eq.6.3 with respect to the x dimension is

$$d \text{ Cost}/dx = 2 (Q + H . W) - 2 . A (Q + H . W)x^{-2}$$

This curve will have a minimum value when this differential is equal to zero, i.e.

$$0 = 2(Q + H . W) - 2 . A (Q + H . W)x^{-2}$$
$$x = \sqrt{A}$$
$$\text{and } y = \frac{A}{\sqrt{A}} = \sqrt{A}$$

This result is confirmation of the fact that the minimum cost of walling or wall foundations in a rectangular building will be found where the x and y dimensions are the same, i.e. the special case where the rectangle is a square.

Table 6.1 shows the cost of the wall element alone, extracted from Eq.6.3, for a range of values for the x dimension and using the area and costs used in Table 5.1. Figure 6.3 shows the first two parts of the equation plotted separately. The first part, which is directly related to x, gives a straight line; the second part, which is related to

Table 6.1

x	$2 . H . W . x$ $= 2 . 3 . 40 . x$	$2 . A . H . W . x^{-1}$ $= 2 . 196 . 3 . 40 . x^{-1}$	Total
6	1,440	7,840	9,280
10	2,400	4,705	7,105
14	3,360	3,360	6,720
18	4,320	2,615	6,935
22	5,280	2,135	7,415

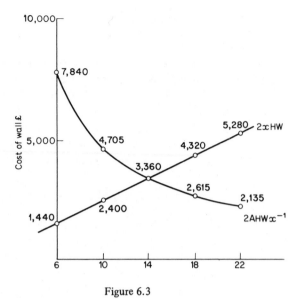

Figure 6.3

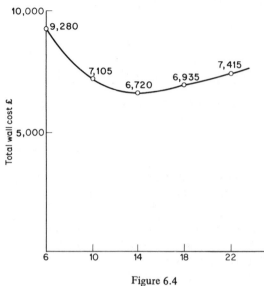

Figure 6.4

$1/x$ or x^{-1}, gives a curve with a value that falls as x is increased. Figure 6.4 shows the combined effect of the two sets of calculations, producing a curve with a minimum value of cost found where $x = 14$.

EXAMPLE 2

Figure 6.5 illustrates a simple building with a single partition bisecting the accommodation. If the cost of the partition is represented as P per unit of area, the total cost of the external walls and the partitions will be given by the following equation where total area = $2A$:

$$\text{Cost} = 2 \cdot x \cdot H \cdot W + 4 \cdot A \cdot H \cdot W \cdot x^{-1} + 2 \cdot A \cdot H \cdot P \cdot x^{-1}$$

The differential $d\,\text{Cost}/dx$

$$= 2 \cdot H \cdot W - 4 \cdot A \cdot H \cdot W \cdot x^{-2} - 2 \cdot A \cdot H \cdot P \cdot x^{-2}$$

The cost will be a minimum when $d\,\text{Cost}/dx = 0$

$$0 = 2 \cdot H \cdot W - 4 \cdot A \cdot H \cdot W \cdot x^{-2} - 2 \cdot A \cdot H \cdot P \cdot x^{-2}$$

$$x = \sqrt{\frac{A(2 \cdot H \cdot W + H \cdot P)}{H \cdot W}}$$

Substituting the same numerical values for the walls and

the room area as before, a rate of £30 per square metre for the partitions gives the total costs shown in Table 6.2.

This table shows that the minimum cost is found where the x dimension lies between 20 and 28 metres. Substituting in the equation derived from the differential function gives the minimum values as follows:

$$x = \sqrt{\frac{196\,(2 \cdot 3 \cdot 40 + 3 \cdot 30)}{3 \cdot 40}}$$

$$= 23 \cdot 2$$

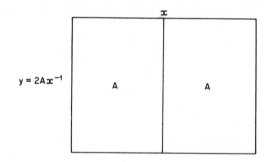

Figure 6.5

Table 6.2

x	$2 \cdot x \cdot 3 \cdot 40$	$4 \cdot 196 \cdot 3 \cdot 40 \cdot x^{-1}$	$2 \cdot 196 \cdot 3 \cdot 30 \cdot x^{-1}$	*Total*
16	3,840	5,880	2,205	11,925
20	4,800	4,700	1,765	11,265
24	5,760	3,920	1,470	11,150
28	6,720	3,360	1,260	11,340
32	7,680	2,940	1,105	11,725
36	8,640	2,615	980	12,235

EXAMPLE 3

A building made up of a number of cells (Figure 6.6) can be analysed in a similar way, although the cost equation is correspondingly more complicated:

If W = cost of walling per metre run
  P = cost of partitioning per metre run
  F = cost of foundations and lower floor per square metre
  U = cost of upper floor per square metre
  R = cost of roofs per square metre
  S = cost of stairs

In this example the storey height has not been included as a parameter of the equation, and the costs of walls and partitions are expressed in linear terms.

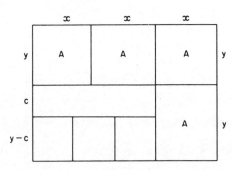

Figure 6.6

Total cost to provide eight rooms each with area A on two storeys is:

$$2 . 2 . 3x . W + 2 . 2 . 2y . W + 2 . 3x . P + 2 . 3y . P$$
$$+ 2 . 2x . P + 2 . 2(y-c) . P + 3x . 2y . F + 3x . 2y . U$$
$$+ 3x . 2y . R + S$$

If c, the width of the corridor, is 1 metre, and substituting $xy = A$ and $y = Ax^{-1}$ then:

$$\text{Cost} = 12 . x . W + 8 . A . W . x^{-1} + 10 . x . P$$
$$+ 6 . A . P . x^{-1} + 4 . A . P . x^{-1} - 4 . P$$
$$+ 6 . A(F + U + R) + S$$

$$\frac{d\,\text{Cost}}{dx} = 12 . W - 8 . A . W . x^{-2} + 10 . P - 6 . A . P . x^{-2}$$
$$- 4 . A . P . x^{-2}$$

Cost is a minimum when $\dfrac{d\,\text{Cost}}{dx} = 0$

$$0 = 12 . W - \frac{8 . A . W}{x^2} + 10 . P - \frac{10 . A . P}{x^2}$$

$$x = \sqrt{\frac{A (4 . W + 5 . P)}{(6 . W + 5 . P)}}$$

Suppose W = £100·00 per m run
  P = £ 75·00 per m run
  F = £ 50·00 per m^2
  U = £ 40·00 per m^2
  R = £ 60·00 per m^2
  S = £500

Area of room to be 20m^2

$$x = \sqrt{\frac{20 (4 . 100 + 5 . 75)}{(6 . 100 + 5 . 75)}}$$

$$= \sqrt{15.89}$$
$$\simeq 4$$

Substituting the same cost figures and $y = 20/x$ in the initial equation gives:

$$\text{Total Cost} - 2 . 2 . 3 . 100 . x + 2 . 2 . 2 . \frac{20}{x} . 100 + 2 . 3 . 75 . x$$
$$+ 2 . 3 . \frac{20}{x} . 75 + 2 . 2 . 75 . x$$
$$+ 2 . 2 \left(\frac{20}{x} - 1\right) . 75 + 3 . 2 . 20 . 50$$
$$+ 3 . 2 . 20 . 40 + 3 . 2 . 20 . 60 + 500$$

$$\text{Cost} = 1{,}950x + \frac{31{,}000}{x} + 18{,}200$$

Table 6.3 shows total cost for varying room widths:

Table 6.3

x (m)	3	3·5	4	4·5	5
Total (£)	34,380	33,880	33,750	33,860	34,150

This table confirms the calculation. It also shows in this instance that the variation of total cost around the optimum figure is not large.

As in the earlier examples, the horizontal elements of floors, foundation and roofs are eliminated in the development of the equations. To some extent this is unrealistic, since these costs will bear some relation to the spans and lengths controlled by the x dimensions and in addition the perimeter conditions will have an effect on the cost. This suggests that if cost analysis figures are used for these studies, they should be in two parts — the horizontal element and a perimeter or junction element. It would also seem essential that the horizontal element should contain a factor related to span lengths which would have a mathematical relationship to the room width.

EXAMPLE 4

The example above is based on a particular arrangement

of the accommodation. The equation could only be built up after the decision had been made to have four usable rooms on each of two floors. It is, of course, impossible to produce an example of this type without assuming plan shapes and some relations between rooms and the areas of corridors, stores and lavatories. However, it is possible to base a cost equation on a more general proposition, which can be modified to meet some particular brief.

For residential hostels it has been found that rooms on either side of a central corridor will normally provide the most economic solution, and that the area of the lavatories, stores and stairs usually amount to about one-third of the area of the residential rooms.

These generalizations led to the plan shape and disposition of accommodation shown in Figure 6.7.

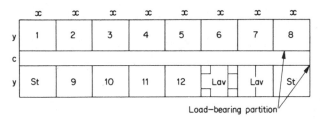

Figure 6.7

Total number of occupants in building $= O$

Number of residents per floor when N is the number of floors $= \dfrac{O}{N}$

Length of building $= \dfrac{2}{3} \cdot \dfrac{O}{N} \cdot x$

Number of partitions between residents $= \dfrac{2}{3} \cdot \dfrac{O}{N} - 1$

Number of partitions between residents and stairs, lavatories, etc. (an arbitrary assessment) $= (\text{say}) \dfrac{O}{N}$

Width of building $= (2y + c)$

A = Room area
H = Storey height
W = Cost of walls
G = Cost of windows (assumed 25% of floor area of rooms)
P = Cost of partitions
L = Cost of load-bearing partitions
F = Cost of foundation slab
U = Cost of upper floors
R = Cost of roofs
S = Cost of stairs per floor rise
B = Cost of land (assumed area required is equivalent to six times the ground floor area of the building)
D = Cost of lifts per floor rise

The total cost of the building and the differential in respect of the number of floors would be as follows:

Cost of windows

$$= 2 \cdot \frac{2}{3} \cdot \frac{O}{N} \cdot \frac{A \cdot 25}{100} \cdot N \cdot G = \frac{O \cdot A \cdot G}{3}$$

$\dfrac{d\,\text{Cost}}{dN}$ = Nil because after simplification N is cancelled.

Cost of walls

$$= 2 \cdot \frac{2}{3} \cdot \frac{O}{N} \cdot x \cdot H \cdot N \cdot W + 2(2y + c) \cdot H \cdot N \cdot W - \frac{O \cdot A \cdot W}{3}$$

$$\frac{d\,\text{Cost}}{dN} = 4 \cdot y \cdot H \cdot W + 2 \cdot c \cdot H \cdot W$$

Cost of foundations

$$= \frac{2}{3} \cdot \frac{O}{N} \cdot x(2y + c) \cdot F$$

$$\frac{d\,\text{Cost}}{dN} = -\frac{4}{3} \cdot O \cdot x \cdot y \cdot F \cdot N^{-2} - \frac{2}{3} \cdot O \cdot x \cdot c \cdot F \cdot N^{-2}$$

Cost of roofs (*similar to foundations*)

$$\frac{d\,\text{Cost}}{dN} = -\frac{4}{3} \cdot O \cdot x \cdot y \cdot R \cdot N^{-2} - \frac{2}{3} \cdot O \cdot x \cdot c \cdot R \cdot N^{-2}$$

Cost of upper floors

$$= \frac{2}{3} \cdot \frac{O}{N} \cdot x(2y + c) \cdot (N - 1) \cdot U$$

$$\frac{d\,\text{Cost}}{dN} = \frac{4}{3} \cdot O \cdot x \cdot y \cdot U \cdot N^{-2} + \frac{2}{3} \cdot O \cdot x \cdot c \cdot U \cdot N^{-2}$$

Cost of partitions

$$= \left(\frac{2}{3} \cdot \frac{O}{N} - 1 + \frac{O}{N} \right) \cdot N \cdot y \cdot H \cdot P$$

$$\frac{d\,\text{Cost}}{dN} = -y \cdot H \cdot P$$

Cost of load-bearing partitions

$$= 2 \cdot \frac{2}{3} \cdot \frac{O}{N} \cdot x \cdot H \cdot N \cdot L$$

$\dfrac{d\,\text{Cost}}{dN}$ = Nil because after simplification N is cancelled

Cost of stairs

$$= 2 \cdot S(N - 1)$$

$$\frac{d\,\text{Cost}}{dN} = 2 \cdot S$$

Cost of land

$$= 6 \cdot \frac{2}{3} \cdot \frac{O}{N} \cdot x(2y + c) \cdot B$$

$$\frac{d\,\text{Cost}}{dN} = -8 \cdot O \cdot x \cdot y \cdot B \cdot N^{-2} - 4 \cdot O \cdot x \cdot c \cdot B \cdot N^{-2}$$

The total differential, substituting A for xy and A/x for $y =$

$$4 \cdot \frac{A}{x} \cdot H \cdot W + 2 \cdot c \cdot H \cdot W - \frac{4}{3} \cdot O \cdot A \cdot F \cdot N^{-2}$$

$$- \frac{2}{3} \cdot O \cdot x \cdot c \cdot F \cdot N^{-2} - \frac{4}{3} \cdot O \cdot A \cdot R \cdot N^{-2}$$

$$- \frac{2}{3} \cdot O \cdot x \cdot c \cdot R \cdot N^{-2} + \frac{4}{3} \cdot O \cdot A \cdot U \cdot N^{-2}$$

$$+ \frac{2}{3} \cdot O \cdot x \cdot c \cdot U \cdot N^{-2} - \frac{A}{x} \cdot P \cdot H$$

$$+ 2 \cdot S - 8 \cdot O \cdot A \cdot B \cdot N^{-2} - 4 \cdot O \cdot x \cdot c \cdot B \cdot N^{-2}$$

If the cost is to be a minimum $\dfrac{d\,\text{Cost}}{dN} = 0$

it follows:

$$N = \sqrt{\frac{\frac{2}{3} \cdot O(F + R - U + 6 \cdot B)(2 \cdot A + x \cdot c)}{\frac{A}{x} \cdot H(4 \cdot W - P) + 2 \cdot c \cdot H \cdot W + 2 \cdot S}}$$

If the following values are substituted in this equation: $A = 12$, $x = 3$, $c = 1$ and $H = 3$, $O = 100$ occupants, land cost £125,000 per hectare, or £12·50 per m², and the elemental costs those used in the earlier exercises, then $N = 7$. If land costs had been ignored, the optimum number of storeys would have been approximately five.

STUDY OF COST IN RELATION TO ROOM SIZE AND SHAPE

The preceeding section discussed a method of finding optimum values for one parameter in geometrical equations when all others are held constant. To discover the most economic arrangements of accommodation where dimensions and room areas can vary requires a more detailed analysis.

An exercise carried out to check the design of a students' residential building provides an example of one possible

methodology. The building had sixteen rooms 3,050 mm by 3,660 mm on three floors planned as shown in Figure 6.8.

The method used was to calculate the cost of a strip 305 mm wide parallel to the corridor on both the front and rear faces and to add the cost of these strips, or subtract them from the basic cost of the building, thus giving the extra costs or savings introduced by increasing or reducing the length of the rooms at right angles to the corridor. The items of measured work occurring in the horizontal elements of foundations, floors and roof are priced at the rates in the contract bills, the strip on the front face 40, 132 mm long cost £1,560 and the strips on the rear face passing through the projections cost £540. The vertical elements of walls and partitions contained within the strips cost £1,116. The effect of making these adjustments is shown in the upper part of Table 6.4. The total cost of strips at right angles to the corridor passing through each study bedroom was also calculated and added or subtracted to the basic cost to produce the variation resulting from adjusting the width of the rooms. The horizontal and vertical elements cost £3,984 and £2,856 respectively and the results of making these adjustments are shown in the lower part of Table 6.4. A variation in this method was next used to calculate the cost of a block with rooms 2,743 mm by 3,963 mm. The reduction of 305 mm in the width of each room reduces the total lengths of the strips parallel to the corridor by 4,865 mm with an appropriate reduction in cost of horizontal elements, the cost of the vertical elements remaining constant. In the original building the average length of the strips at right-angles to the corridor was 8,128 mm. When the room length is increased to 3,963 mm the average length of the strips increased by 406 mm with a corresponding increase in the cost of the horizontal elements. The procedure was then repeated to calculate costs for rooms with widths varying at 305 mm increments but with a constant depth of 3,963 mm and for depths varying above and below 3,963 mm but with a constant width of 2,743 mm. The next application of the process calculated the cost of a basic building with rooms 2,440 mm by 4,267 mm and so on, to produce the results summarized in Table 6.5. The explanation of the methodology set out above has not described in detail the calculations concerning areas but it will be appreciated that the total area related to each student room increases if the rooms are arranged with the

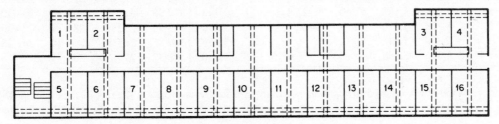

Figure 6.8

Table 6.4
Example of the method applied to a block with rooms of 3,050 mm x 3,660 mm

ADJUSTMENT TO DEPTHS OF ROOMS

mm mm	Cost £	Add Vertical Elements £		Add Horizontal Elements £	Cost £
3,050 x 3,660	221,508	—		—	221,508
3,050 x 3,963	221,508	1,116		2,100	224,724
3,050 x 4,267	221,508	2,232		4,200	227,940
etc.			etc.		etc.
		Ddt. Vertical Elements		Ddt. Horizontal Elements	
3,050 x 3,352	221,508	1,116		2,100	219,292
3,050 x 3,050	221,508	2,232		4,200	215,076
3,050 x 2,743	221,508	3,348		6,300	211,860
etc.			etc.		etc.

ADJUSTMENT TO WIDTH OF ROOMS

mm mm	Cost £	Add Vertical Elements £		Add Horizontal Elements £	£
3,050 x 3,660	221,508	—		—	221,508
3,352 x 3,660	221,508	2,856		3,984	228,348
3,660 x 3,660	221,508	5,712		7,968	235,188
etc.			etc.		etc.
		Ddt. Vertical Elements		Ddt. Horizontal Elements	
2,743 x 3,660	221,508	2,856		3,984	214,668
2,438 x 3,660	221,508	5,712		7,968	207,828
2,133 x 3,660	221,508	8,568		11,952	200,988
etc.			etc.		etc.

Table 6.5
Depth of room at right-angles to corridor

Width of room parallel to corridor

Usable area m² per place

	2,438	2,743	3,050	3,352	3,660
2,438	9·47	10·22	10·96	11·71	12·44
2,743	10·21	11·06	11·89	12·73	13·56
3,050	10·96	11·89	12·82	13·75	14·68
3,352	11·70	12·73	13·75	14·77	
3,660	12·45	13·56	14·68		

Gross area m² per place

	2,438	2,743	3,050	3,352	3,660
2,438	14·21	15·14	15·98	16·81	17·65
2,743	15·33	16·35	17·28	18·21	19·23
3,050	16·44	17·56	18·58	19·60	20·72
3,352	17·55	18·77	19·88	21·08	
3,660	18·77	19·97	21·18		

Cost per place

	2,438	2,743	3,050	3,352	3,660
2,438	4,902	4,962	5,040	5,106	5,178
2,743	5,028	5,094	5,172	5,250	5,322
3,050	5,154	5,226	5,310	5,388	5,466
3,352	5,280	5,358	5,448	5,532	
3,660	5,412	5,496	5,586		

Cost per m²

	2,438	2,743	3,050	3,352	3,660
2,438	344·97	327·74	315·39	303·75	293·37
2,743	327·98	311·56	299·30	288·30	276·76
3,050	313·50	297·61	285·79	274·90	263·80
3,352	300·85	285·45	274·04	262·43	
3,660	288·33	275·21	263·74		

Note: These costs were then adjusted to maintain a constant area for the lavatories at the rear of the building. This entailed a similar exercise in calculating the cost of strips along and across the accommodation marked **AB** on Figure C.1.

long dimensions parallel to the corridor. The construction cost expressed in terms of cost per square foot increases as the size of the rooms is decreased, the combined effect of the two factors of cost and area is to produce a matrix of total costs which show that it is possible to provide a wide range of different room shapes and sizes but within the same overall target cost. Despite the fact that each of these variations has approximately the same study bedroom cost the total usable area, given a constant addition of 3·53 m^2 per room for shared communal areas, i.e. lavatories, bathrooms, kitchen and storage areas, varies between 10·96 m^2 and 12·45 m^2 and the gross area from 16·44 m^2 and 17·65 m^2 per student.

The matrix therefore gives a guide to the designer in assessing the relative alternatives of providing maximum area within a specified cost per place or minimum area at a higher standard of specification, but it is important to recognize that in planning small rooms the relative size and position of elements such as windows, doors and furniture has an important effect on apparent size. The provision of adequate communal space is also important, and the area and cost per study bedroom can vary according to the numbers sharing each group of these facilities.

COMPUTERS

Solving equations and carrying out design exercises are considerably simplified by use of computers or desk-top calculating machines.

Computers are already in extensive use for the production of contract documents, in which dimensions are generally taken off in the normal way but descriptions are coded either manually or semi-automatically by the use of punched cards. The computer and the associated hardware are then used for sorting, calculating, and printing. It is also possible to store information related to standard types of buildings for use in the preparation of approximate estimates. Cost information relating to both capital and recurrent expenditure can be programmed to produce a fully priced estimate. It would be possible to store the data related to a range of specifications and obtain an estimate for work by simply presenting the computer with the leading dimensions of the rooms and suitable information on door and window openings.

However, these systems of estimating do not indicate optimum solutions. If the cost equations developed in this chapter could be combined with these estimating procedures, then it would be possible to indicate the dimensions or the parameters of design that would give the most economic solution.

The valuation of alternative solutions to problems is difficult by traditional surveying methods. It is usually impossible for the architect to produce sufficient information on alternative solutions because so much of the work would be abortive.

The examples in this chapter have been proved using a small programmed calculator. This produced instantaneous solutions to various equations and provided a rapid appraisal of the exercise described above. There remains the problem that even with a large computer it would be difficult to store all the variations in cost that, for example, might arise from changing spans or loadings on a concrete floor. However, this problem can be partly overcome by the use of the techniques of sensitivity analysis i.e. the solution to the cost equation could be found for a range of floor costs increasing at (say) 10 per cent increments. This test would show whether possible errors in costing the floors affected the conclusions drawn from the comparisons. It might also serve to indicate the degree of uncertainty surrounding the final total estimate. The possibility of directing a computer by the use of a light pen, and the facility for the direct production of drawings, suggest that much of the algebraic work could solve the necessary differential equations without the need to formalize the designs as in the simple illustrations used in this chapter.

7

Statistics

Statistics may be studied at two levels. Firstly to understand the methods of organizing numerical information about particular situations or cases, and the procedures by which such information can be examined, represented, and understood. Secondly, to consider sets of data and the procedures that can be followed to decide if they are representative of a wider group and whether deductions made from the data could be considered as applicable to the whole group.

The study of statistics goes beyond that which can be encompassed in this book, but the methods described in this chapter should be sufficient to allow the surveyor to judge whether his conclusions are sensible and at what stage qualified statistical advice should be sought. At the elementary level, the subject is simple mathematics, coupled with the adoption of a number of statistical conventions. At the advanced level the methods are dependent on the theory of probability.

Averages and Representative Figures

The mathematical formula for calculating the average or the arithmetic mean is $\dfrac{x_1 + x_2 + x_3}{n} = x_n$. This is usually written as $\bar{x} = \Sigma \dfrac{x}{n}$. The Greek letter *sigma* is conventionally used to indicate the sum of the observations of the measure

of x. In quantity surveying an average in this form is often used to reduce the number of dimensions that need be written for similar items. For example in calculating the volume of excavation for manholes or column bases, the depths are normally averaged.

On a level site the excavation of a sloping drainage trench may be calculated from the depths of the formation level below the surface at each end of the trench. The average depth calculated in this way is accurate, and the method is, of course, identical to that of calculating the volumes of a regular solid from the normal rules of mensuration (Figure 7.1).

Volume of trench:
$\dfrac{x_1 + x_2}{2} \cdot l \cdot \text{width}$
$= \bar{x} \cdot l \cdot \text{width}$

Areas of:
rectangle $= x_1 l$
triangle $= (x_2 - x_1) \cdot \dfrac{l}{2}$
Total
$\quad$ area $= x_1 l + x_2 \dfrac{l}{2} - x_1 \dfrac{l}{2}$
$\qquad = \dfrac{x_1 l}{2} + \dfrac{x_2 l}{2}$
Volume $= \dfrac{x_1 + x_2}{2} l \cdot \text{width}$

However, if the surface of the ground was uneven, the average depth calculated by adding the depth $x_1 + x_2 + x_3 + x_4$ and dividing by four could not be used for accurate calculations (Figure 7.2).

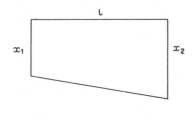

Volume of trench: $\dfrac{x_1 + x_2}{2} \times l \times \text{width}$

$= \bar{x} \times l \times \text{width}$

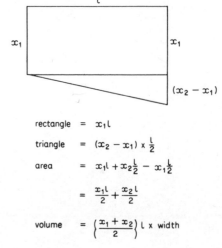

rectangle $= x_1 l$

triangle $= (x_2 - x_1) \times \dfrac{l}{2}$

area $= x_1 l + x_2 \dfrac{l}{2} - x_1 \dfrac{l}{2}$

$= \dfrac{x_1 l}{2} + \dfrac{x_2 l}{2}$

volume $= \left(\dfrac{x_1 + x_2}{2} \right) l \times \text{width}$

Figure 7.1

The method of dealing with the situation is to consider each of the lengths l_1, l_2, and l_3 separately; nevertheless the arithmetic mean $\frac{1}{4}(x_1 + x_2 + x_3 + x_4)$ would be a figure indicative of the general depth of the trench and could be used for descriptive purposes. An average can, therefore, be a precise figure for computing purposes, or it may be a representative figure.

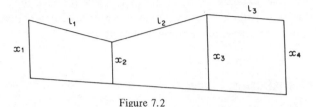

Figure 7.2

Table 7.1 shows the marks awarded to a group of students in an examination. The total of these marks is 4,146, which number, divided by the number of students, 72, gives the arithmetic mean 57·58. It must be noted that this figure,

Table 7.1

46	62	38	45	69	72	54	95	26
61	45	45	69	72	34	90	27	55
60	48	59	70	22	87	51	51	59
51	66	36	49	85	50	56	78	38
62	52	59	82	53	21	57	81	48
62	40	80	42	43	76	60	65	54
65	79	59	57	74	59	64	61	58
59	54	63	56	72	64	53	51	40

although calculated accurately, is not precisely at the centre of the range of results, nor does it represent any particular result, but it can be used as a yardstick to measure the range of results and the general level of attainment.

Median and Interquartile Range

The median is the central observation of a group. For the results shown in Table 7.1 the median lies between 58 and 59. If the median is considered to be 58·5, then half the observations lie above the level and the remaining half below. However, the position of the median is not influenced by very low or very high marks that might be thought to be unrepresentative of the general performance of the group. So it is useful to consider the performance of the moiety of the groups whose results are central about the median. From Table 7.1 there are 18 students with results below 48·5, and a further 18 with results above 65·5, the remaining 36 receiving marks above 48·5 and below 65·5. This latter group is in what is known as the interquartile range. A knowledge of the median and

the interquartile range is more useful in describing both the spread and the general level of a group of observations than the arithmetic mean; but even these figures do not indicate the level of results achieved by the greatest number of students.

Mode

The mode is the observation that occurs most frequently in a series of observations. In Table 7.1 this value is 59.

Harmonic Mean

The formula for the harmonic mean is

$$\frac{n}{\Sigma\left(\frac{1}{x}\right)}$$

It is used when averaging rates. For example, a journey around three sides of an equilateral triangle with sides A miles, at 30, 40, and 50 m.p.h., would take a total of $\frac{A}{30} + \frac{A}{40} + \frac{A}{50}$ hours $= \frac{20A + 15A + 12A}{600} = \frac{47A}{600}$, and the average speed would be $\frac{3A \times 600}{47A} = 38\cdot3$ m.p.h.

By applying the formula, the harmonic mean

$$= \frac{3}{\frac{1}{30} + \frac{1}{40} + \frac{1}{50}}$$

$$= \frac{3}{\frac{20 + 15 + 12}{600}}$$

$$= \frac{1,800}{47}$$

$$= 38\cdot3$$

This mean is only accurate where the value of the numerator is constant, i.e. in the example above the distances covered in each side of the triangle were constant. In examining the cost analysis of tenders, a form of the harmonic mean must be used. As an example Table 7.2 shows the total tender cost, area and cost per square metre for six buildings.

Table 7.2

£	m²	£ per m²
80,000	500	160
80,000	1,000	80
350,000	5,000	70
500,000	10,000	50
720,000	12,000	60
2,100,000	30,000	70
Total 3,830,000	58,500	

31

The simple arithmetic mean of the cost per square metre figures is 81·67. The representative mean in this case is best calculated by dividing the total tender cost of the six schemes by the total area,

$$\frac{3,830,000}{58,500} = 65·47$$

or by taking the cost of each scheme and the cost per square metre rate as below:

$$\frac{80,000 + 80,000 + 350,000 + 500,000 + 720,000 + 2,100,000}{\frac{80,000}{160} + \frac{80,000}{80} + \frac{350,000}{70} + \frac{500,000}{50} + \frac{720,000}{60} + \frac{2,100,000}{70}}$$

$$= 65·47$$

Geometric Mean

The geometric mean is calculated by the formula $\sqrt[N]{(x_1 x_2 x_3 \ldots x_n)}$. It is used to average exponential series, that is a series where the terms are varied by a constant incremental change in the exponent or the power of the numbers, e.g. it could be applied to general formulae for calculating compound interest $A = P(1 + i)^n$, where A = amount, P the principal, i the rate of interest, and n the term of years.

As an example, find the geometric mean of the series between the value of n where i is 10 per cent and the principal £1: for the years 10, 20, 30, and 40 the amount of £1 is given as 2·594, 6·727, 17·445 and 45·259. The geometric mean, which in this case represents the value at 25 years, is found by substitution in the formula:

Geometric mean = $\sqrt[4]{(2·594 \times 6·727 \times 17·449 \times 45·259)}$

$$= 10·83$$

For this particular series the geometric mean is also mathematically identical to the expression of the 25th term. For other exponential series this may not be the case, but this mean will be a more accurate indicator or representative figure than the simple arithmetical mean.

Distribution Curves

Often the number of observations is large, and statisticians adopt standard formal procedures for ordering and simplifying their calculations.

Table 7.3 shows the method of examining and presenting the examination marks in Table 7.1. The range of results has been divided into classes, and the classes have been defined with their boundaries chosen to suit the value of the observations and the mean value indicated. Each result is represented by a tally mark in the appropriate class. It may be noted that the frequency multiplied by the mid-value of the class, which if there had been no approximations would equal the total number of marks awarded, differs from the actual total by only 3.

$$\text{Arithmetic mean} = \frac{4,149}{72}$$

$$= 57·6$$

Table 7.3

Class values		Class boundaries		Mid value of class observations	Tally marks		Frequency	Frequency × mid-value of class	Frequency expressed as percentage
20	24	19·5	24·5	22	11		2	44	2·8
25	29	24·5	29·5	27	11		2	54	2·8
30	34	29·5	34·5	32	1		1	32	1·4
35	39	34·5	39·5	37	111		3	111	4·2
40	44	39·5	44·5	42	1111		4	168	5·5
45	49	44·5	49·5	47	11111 11		7	329	9·6
50	54	49·5	54·5	52	11111 11111 1	11		572	15·2
55	59	54·5	59·5	57	11111 11111 11	12		684	16·6
60	64	59·5	64·5	62	11111 11111	10		620	13·9
65	69	64·5	69·5	67	11111		5	335	7·0
70	74	69·5	74·5	72	11111		5	360	7·0
75	79	74·5	79·5	77	111		3	231	4·2
80	84	79·5	84·5	82	111		3	246	4·2
85	89	84·5	89·5	87	11		2	174	2·8
90	94	89·5	94·5	92	1		1	92	1·4
95	99	94·5	99·5	97	1		1	97	1·4
							72	4,149	100·0

The median occurs in the class 55–59, which has a mid-value of 57.

It is often useful to present the data produced by this form of analysis graphically. The representation of the frequency percentage as a distribution curve is shown in Figure 7.3.

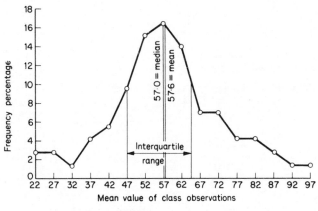

Figure 7.3

Presented in this form it is easy to see the spread of data above and below the median. It is also possible to mark the interquartile range of the central 50 per cent of the observations. In this instance the distribution is evenly spread around the mean, which is also near the centre of the range of possible marks, but if a large number of

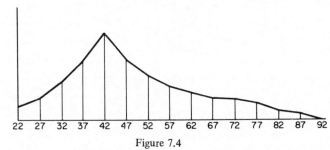

Figure 7.4

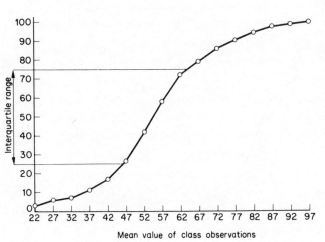

Figure 7.5

candidates had received low marks, perhaps with a mean value of 42, and the remainder had received marks as high as in the table, the distribution curve would have taken the form shown in Figure 7.4. A distribution curve in this form is described as showing positive skew, and the reverse situation is called negative skew.

Another form of graphical presentation is known as an ogive (Figure 7.5). This form allows for immediate readings to be taken of the cumulative frequencies, and for this set of data shows the proportion of the group that achieved certain levels of marks.

The choice of the classes and the boundaries will be related to the amount of data and the conclusions to be drawn. In the example above the analysis has been made within a range of 5 marks. A less detailed analysis could have been made using steps of 10 marks.

Scatter Charts

Another method of presenting data is the scatter chart. For the quantity surveyor this is a useful device for examining data on costs and areas. Table 7.4 is a sample of information related to primary and secondary schools in the year 1957. Figure 7.6 shows the range of costs of both in the form of a distribution curve. Figure 7.7 shows the cost and area per place of the same schools in the form of a scatter graph. As can be seen the scatter graph also illustrates the range of data but it cannot be used directly for measurement in the same fashion as an ordinary graph. It would be difficult, for example, to determine the values of the median for either area or cost. A method of overcoming this difficulty is to count the number of cases that fall into the various 'squares' on the graph, which would give an indication of the 'mode' for area and cost considered as a composite function.

In Figure 7.7 the majority of the values fall to the left of the curves marked P and S. These curves indicate the cost limits, which at that time were £154 for primary schools and £264 for secondary schools. The architects designing these schools have clearly attempted to build as close to the limits as possible, but the graphs indicate that a range of choices in area and specification is possible. The most usual decisions are within a range of 12½ per cent from the median. In most cases the product of the area per place and the rate per square foot gives the cost limit per place. In this example a system of analysis based on the actual values of area or cost taken separately would not give the essential fact that considered together they fall below a particular limiting value. This is a reminder that statistical interpretation must take into account all the known information, and must be studied from various points of view before any definite conclusions can be drawn.

If we suppose that the direct relation between cost and area was not known, it would be possible to determine

Table 7.4

Net Cost of 135 Primary and 108 Secondary Schools started between January and
December 1957

PRIMARY				SECONDARY			
*Exact Limits**	*Mid-point*	*Number*	*%*	*Exact Limits**	*Mid-point*	*Number*	*%*
53·5—56·4	55·0	0	0	53·5—56·4	55·0	1	0·93
56·5—59·4	58·0	1	0·74	56·5—59·4	58·0	1	0·93
59·5—62·4	61·0	3	2·22	59·5—62·4	61·0	2	1·85
62·5—65·4	64·0	6	4·44	62·5—65·4	64·0	6	5·55
65·5—68·4	67·0	14	10·37	65·5—68·4	67·0	14	12·97
68·5—71·4	70·0	30	22·23	68·5—71·4	70·0	17	15·74
71·5—74·4	73·0	30	22·23	71·5—74·4	73·0	38	35·18
74·5—77·4	76·0	25	18·52	74·5—77·4	76·0	24	22·22
77·5—80·4	79·0	19	14·07	77·5—80·4	79·0	4	3·70
80·5—83·4	82·0	4	2·96	80·5—83·4	82·0	1	0·93
83·5—86·4	85·0	1	0·74	83·5—86·4	85·0	0	0
86·5—89·4	88·0	1	0·74				
89·5—92·4	91·0	0	0				
92·5—95·4	94·0	1	0·74				
		135	100·00			108	100·00

* Shillings per square foot of floor area.

an algebraic equation of lines *P* and *S* (i.e. the values of the cost limit at that time) by applying normal algebraic techniques to the information of the scatter graph.

To calculate the formula for line *P* it is necessary to assume an equation for the curve in general terms and to determine at least three co-ordinates through which the curve passes.

Three suitable points for line *P* from Figure 7.7 are as follows:

y	*x*
88s. 0d.	35
77s. 0d.	40
70s. 0d.	44

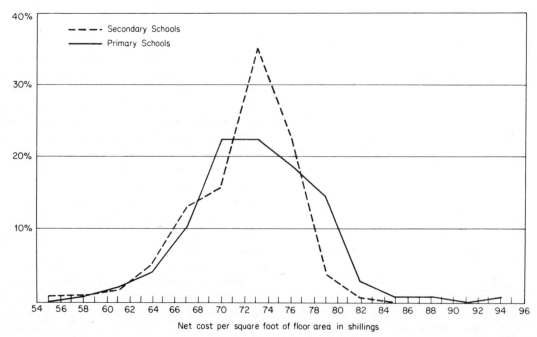

Figure 7.6

The general expression for a quadratic equation is $y = ax^2 + bx + c$, where x and y are dependent variables and a, b, and c are constants. The first step is to substitute the values of x and y in the equation and solve simultaneously the three resulting equations to determine a, b and c:

$$88 = 1{,}225\,a + 35b + c \qquad \text{(Eq. 7.1)}$$
$$77 = 1{,}600\,a + 40b + c \qquad \text{(Eq. 7.2)}$$
$$70 = 1{,}936\,a + 44b + c \qquad \text{(Eq. 7.3)}$$

Taking Equation 7.1 from 7.2

$$-11 = 375a + 5b \qquad \text{(Eq. 7.4)}$$

Taking Equation 7.2 from 7.3

$$-7 = 336a + 4b \qquad \text{(Eq. 7.5)}$$

Taking Equation 7.4 from 7.5 after multiplying 7.4 by 4 and 7.5 by 5 to eliminate b we obtain:

$$9 = 180a$$
$$\therefore a = 0{\cdot}05$$

Substituting in 7.4, $\quad -11 = 18{\cdot}75 + 5b$
$$b = -5{\cdot}95$$

Substituting in 7.1, $\quad 88 = 61{\cdot}25 - 208{\cdot}25 + c$
$$c = 235$$

Therefore $y = 0{\cdot}05\,x^2 - 5{\cdot}95\,x + 235 \qquad \text{(Eq. 7.6)}$

A line plotted to this equation will pass through the three points and will closely follow line P on Figure 7.7.

Outside the range of these three pairs of co-ordinates the line will be found to diverge from line P. It is, therefore, evident that this calculation has produced a result which is only correct over a limited range. The next stage would be to investigate the possibility that the curve is of a different form from a parabola. For example, the general equation for a hyperbola is as follows:

$$y = \frac{a}{x} + b$$

where x and y are variables and a and b constants. Substituting the values from the table as before in the general equation gives three further equations.

$$88 = \frac{a}{35} + b \qquad \text{(Eq. 7.7)}$$

$$77 = \frac{a}{40} + b \qquad \text{(Eq. 7.8)}$$

$$70 = \frac{a}{44} + b \qquad \text{(Eq. 7.9)}$$

$$\text{or: } 3{,}080 = a + 35b \qquad \text{(Eq. 7.10)}$$

$$3{,}080 = a + 40b \qquad \text{(Eq. 7.11)}$$

$$3{,}080 = a + 44b \qquad \text{(Eq. 7.12)}$$

Taking Equation 7.10 from Equation 7.11 gives:

$$0 = 5b$$

$$0 = b$$

$$y = \frac{3{,}080}{x} \text{ or } xy = 3{,}080$$

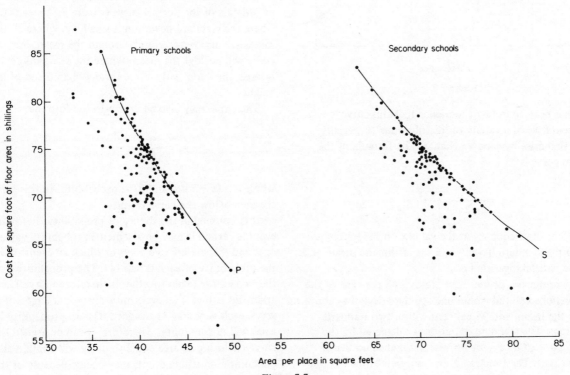

Figure 7.7

The value of y measured on the graph is in shillings per square foot, so the answer is given in shillings. The product of the area per place and the cost per unit area gives the cost per place, in this instance £3,080/20 = £154. The data and the form of the scatter chart might well have suggested that the formula would be of this type, but the method described for calculating an equation in the form of a parabola would still hold as a basic procedure for other examples.

Properties of Distribution Curves

In the introduction to this chapter it was noted that one of the basic statistical studies is the determination of whether patterns contained within a sample range of data are likely to be representative of a complete community of observations. For this it is necessary to examine the properties of the 'normal' distribution curve. Figure 7.8 shows a standard curve against which other distributions can be compared.

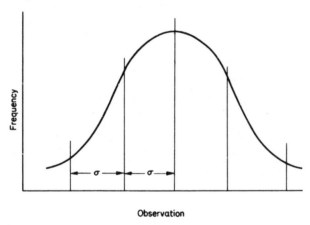

Observation

Figure 7.8

It has been found by experience that this curve is representative of a variety of 'distributions', especially those that arise by random chance. The formula of the normal curve is

$$y = \frac{1}{\sigma\sqrt{2\pi}} e^{\frac{-(x-\bar{x})^2}{2\sigma^2}}$$

where y is the frequency at the value x on the horizontal axis, σ the standard deviation, $\bar{x}$ the arithmetic mean, and e is the natural logarithm base.

The properties of the curve are that 68 per cent of the observations will fall within one standard deviation above or below the mean, and 95 per cent within two standard deviations. The standard deviation is calculated by the formula $\sigma = \sqrt{(\Sigma(x-\bar{x})^2)/n}$ where n is the number of observations. The function $\Sigma(x-\bar{x})^2/n$ is known as the variance.

For an understanding of the importance of the variance and the standard deviation it is useful to look at a model situation. Table 7.5 shows at 'A' the values of a series of observations. The arithmetic mean is 6. The problem is to find a way of describing and measuring the degree of scatter above and below the mean. One method that might be used is to calculate a simple arithmetic mean of the differences between each observation and the arithmetic mean of the observations. The same table shows at 'B' a similar set of observations, but the values have been chosen to give a different range and a different distribution, though the amount of the mean of the differences is identical to that calculated for 'A'. Therefore, although the mean of differences, which is known as the mean deviation, is an indicator of the degree of scatter, it does not necessarily react to changes in the range.

If the difference between the observations and the arithmetic mean is squared and the total divided by the number of observations, the value obtained is the variance as described above.

In this example the variance for Table A is 2·50 and for Table B 2·25. The higher number reflects the increased range of Table A compared with Table B, i.e. (9 − 3) = 6 against (8 − 4) = 4. The variance is, therefore, a more useful indicator of the degree of scatter around the mean than the mean deviation. In addition, in calculating the mean deviation, the sign of $(x - \bar{x})$ was ignored, which is mathematically unsatisfactory. In calculating the variance this problem does not arise because the differences are squared.

The fact that the standard deviation is one of the major parameters of the normal curve (Figure 7.8) means that where the standard deviation is small, i.e. where all the values are discovered closely around the mean, the normal curve will peak at the mean. Where the standard deviation is large, the curve will be more widely based and of less height.

The curve may also be drawn to the formula

$$y_1 = \frac{1}{\sqrt{2\pi}} e^{-\frac{1}{2}u^2}$$

where $u = (x - \bar{x})/\sigma$, and y_1 = probability. In this form the area below the curve is unity.

It is assumed in the theory of probability that if an event is certain it may be assigned a probability value of one, and if there are two ways in which an event may occur the probability of each is half ($\frac{1}{2}$). The probabilities of the two events taken together is therefore unity. The general argument is that if an event may occur in a large number of ways, each way may be assigned its own probability but the total will remain unity. Therefore, it can be argued that a curve enclosing an area equal to unity will contain all the possibilities in which events may occur. Because of the standardization implicit in this version of the curve, tables

Table 7.5

A		B	
(n = 16)			
Observations	*Differences from mean*	*Observations*	*Differences from mean*
(x)	$(x - \bar{x})$	(x_1)	$(x_1 - \bar{x}_1)$
3	3	4	2
4	2	4	2
4	2	4	2
5	1	4	2
5	1	5	1
5	1	5	1
6	0	6	0
6	0	6	0
6	0	6	0
6	0	6	0
7	1	7	1
7	1	7	1
7	1	8	2
8	2	8	2
8	2	8	2
9	3	8	2

$\Sigma x = 96 \qquad \Sigma(x - \bar{x}) = 20$

Arithmetic means:

$$\frac{\Sigma x}{n} = 6 \qquad \frac{\Sigma(x - \bar{x})}{n} = 1{\cdot}25$$

$\Sigma x_1 = 96 \qquad \Sigma(x_1 - \bar{x}_1) = 20$

Arithmetic means:

$$\frac{\Sigma x_1}{n} = 6 \qquad \frac{\Sigma(x_1 - \bar{x}_1)}{n} = 1{\cdot}25$$

$(x - \bar{x})^2$	$(x_1 - \bar{x}_1)^2$
9	4
4	4
4	4
1	4
1	1
1	1
0	0
0	0
0	0
0	0
1	1
1	1
1	4
4	4
4	4
9	4

$\Sigma(x - \bar{x})^2 = 40$

$\Sigma(x_1 - \bar{x}_1)^2 = 36$

$$\text{Variance} = \frac{\Sigma(x - \bar{x})^2}{n} = 2{\cdot}50$$

$$\text{Variance} = \frac{\Sigma(x_1 - \bar{x}_1)^2}{n} = 2{\cdot}25$$

$$\text{Standard deviation} = \sqrt{2{\cdot}50} = 1{\cdot}58$$

$$\text{Standard deviation} = \sqrt{2{\cdot}25} = 1{\cdot}50$$

can be drawn up to show the areas under the curve at various points (Table 7.6 and Figure 7.9).

Table 7.6
Area of One Tail of a Normal Curve

u	Probability
0·00	0·5
0·25	0·401
0·50	0·309
0·75	0·227
1·00	0·159
1·25	0·106
1·50	0·067
1·75	0·040
2·00	0·023
2·25	0·012
2·50	0·006
2·75	0·003
3·00	0·001

Table 7.6 can, therefore, be used to decide the probability that an event may occur or an observation may fall, within a particular range of values. For example, there is a 0·5 probability that a value will fall above or to the right of the mean value of the range, a 0·159 probability that it will fall above $u = +1$, i.e. a standard deviation above the mean, or that for a value to fall within $u = +1$ and $u = +2$, the probability will be $0·159 - 0·023 = 0·136$.

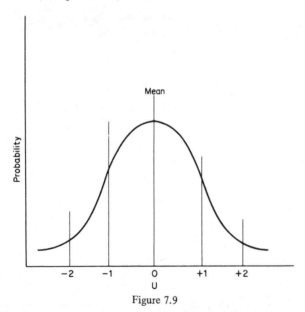

Figure 7.9

This facility is useful in the examination of sample groups drawn from a general population. For example, any particular value or observation may occur anywhere within the range of values, but if a large sample is taken, it would be expected that the mean value of the sample would be close to the mean value of the whole population. In fact it would be possible to hypothesize a distribution curve for the mean values of samples within a population, since, because each sample will contain high and low values that will be self-cancelling, it would be expected that the value of the means will fall in a tight peak distribution curve, as in Figure 7.10.

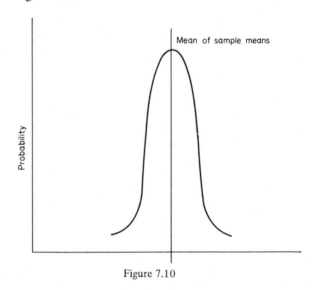

Figure 7.10

If it then appeared that the mean of the sample fell (say) into an area of the curve that had a probability of less than 1 per cent, i.e. the mean falling over 1·25 standard deviations away from the mean (Table 7.6), it might be assumed that the sample exhibited some special condition and was not part of the main population. The standard deviation used here would be the standard deviation of the sample means around the population mean. The argument followed is that there would be less than one chance in 100 (i.e. less than 1 per cent) that the value of the sample mean would occur in the main population. This would also be less than one chance in 100 that the range of values in the sample would be found. It follows that if the range of values were not likely to happen by chance, the sample must be affected by some other influence, which might be significant.

This is a brief explanation of the most important application of statistics to scientific research. The study of sample size and what deviations from the normal curve may be regarded as significant should properly be left to the statistician, and readers wishing for more details are referred to standard textbooks.

Linear Regression Equations

The most useful application for the quantity surveyor of the theory of probability is the calculation of regression equations. A regression equation is the mathematical

expression of an association between two variable quantities. Experimental data often suggests that a relation exists between two variables, but the individual observations exhibit a range of values and the problem is to determine a line that is the 'best fit' between them.

The graphical representation of the situation is given in Figure 7.11.

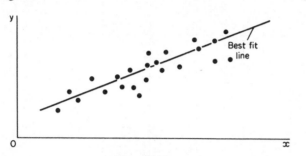

Figure 7.11

A reasonably close analogy would be the problem of determining a navigable channel between marker buoys, as in Figure 7.12. The buoys may be affected by tidal currents and may not be placed directly over the edges of the channel. If we wished to follow a safe course, it would be imperative to follow the line offering the best probability of deep water. It might be assumed that the probable position of the channel would be halfway between the buoys.

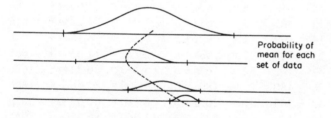

Probability of mean for each set of data

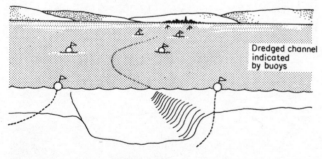

Dredged channel indicated by buoys

Figure 7.12

Statistically the buoys represent information probably resulting from the relation between two variables, a relation that could be represented by a trend line. To achieve this, the squares of the differences between the value that would be predicted from the trend line and the actual observations are calculated to be as small as possible. Calculating the square of the difference between the actual

and predicted value for a trend line is clearly a similar operation to calculating the variance described in the section dealing with distribution curves (p. 35). Indeed, the trend line may be considered as joining the mean values of a series of distribution curves. The trend line shown on Figure 7.11 can be given the general expression $y = ax + b$. This means that the value of y at the point x_1 is expected to be $ax_1 + b$. If the observed value is y_1, the difference between the observed and the expected value would be $ax_1 + b - y_1$. The square of this difference is $a^2x_1^2 + 2abx_1 - 2ax_1y_1 + b^2 - 2by_1 + y_1^2$.

Table 7.7 sets out for four values of x, the differences squared, and the sum of the squares of the differences.

Table 7.7

Value	Square of differences
x_1	$a^2x_1{}^2 + 2abx_1 - 2ax_1y_1 + b^2 - 2by_1 + y_1{}^2$
x_2	$a^2x_2{}^2 + 2abx_2 - 2ax_2y_2 + b^2 - 2by_2 + y_2{}^2$
x_3	$a^2x_3{}^2 + 2abx_3 - 2ax_3y_3 + b^2 - 2by_3 + y_3{}^2$
x_4	$a^2x_4{}^2 + 2abx_4 - 2ax_4y_4 + b^2 - 2by_4 + y_4{}^2$

$$a^2\Sigma x^2 + 2ab\Sigma x - 2a\Sigma xy + nb^2 - 2b\Sigma y + \Sigma y^2$$
$$= S = \text{sum of differences squared} \qquad \text{(Eq. 7.13)}$$

By applying the principles of differentiation as described in Chapter 6, it is possible to devise equations which will give the values of a and b (the coefficient of x and the constant) that will ensure this sum will be a minimum, i.e.

$$\frac{dS}{da} = 2a\Sigma x^2 + 2b\Sigma x - 2\Sigma xy$$

At the minimum value $dS/da = 0$ then $\Sigma xy = a\Sigma x^2 + b\Sigma x$

$$\frac{dS}{db} = 2a\Sigma x + 2nb - 2\Sigma y.$$

At the minimum $dS/db = 0$ then $\Sigma y = a\Sigma x + nb$.
The minimum value of S will be found when:

$$\Sigma y = a\Sigma x + nb \qquad \text{(Eq. 7.14)}$$

and $$\Sigma xy = a\Sigma x^2 + b\Sigma x \qquad \text{(Eq. 7.15)}$$

If the values of Σx, Σy, Σxy, and Σx^2 are determined for the sample and substituted in the equations above, the values of a and b can be found by solving the simultaneous equations. The application of this theory can be best explained in relation to a numerical example.

Table 7.8 shows the numbers of staff and students in a small group of university departments. The problem is to decide whether the figures show a predictable relationship between the two variables. The data is also plotted in Figure 7.13.

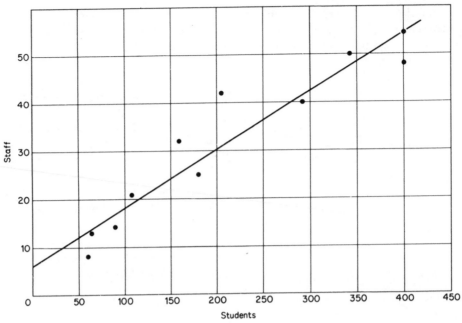

Figure 7.13

Table 7.8

y	x
Staff	*Students*
8	60
13	65
14	92
21	106
32	162
25	180
42	205
40	294
50	344
48	402
$\Sigma y = 293$	$\Sigma x = 1,910$

Table 7.9

y	x	$y =$	$ax + b$	$xy =$	$ax^2 +$	bx
8	60	$8 =$	$60a + b$	$480 =$	$3,600a +$	$60b$
13	65	$13 =$	$65a + b$	$845 =$	$4,225a +$	$65b$
14	92	$14 =$	$92a + b$	$1,288 =$	$8,464a +$	$92b$
21	106	$21 =$	$106a + b$	$2,226 =$	$11,236a +$	$106b$
32	162	$32 =$	$162a + b$	$5,184 =$	$26,244a +$	$162b$
25	180	$25 =$	$180a + b$	$4,500 =$	$32,400a +$	$180b$
42	205	$42 =$	$205a + b$	$8,610 =$	$42,025a +$	$205b$
40	294	$40 =$	$294a + b$	$11,760 =$	$86,436a +$	$294b$
50	344	$50 =$	$344a + b$	$17,200 =$	$118,336a +$	$344b$
48	402	$48 =$	$402a + b$	$19,296 =$	$161,604a +$	$402b$

$293 = 1,910a + 10b$ $71,389 = 494,570a + 1,910b$

$\Sigma y = a\Sigma x + nb$ $\Sigma xy = a\Sigma x^2 + b\Sigma x$

The first step is to set out the figures so that the values of Σy, Σx, Σxy, and Σx^2 required for substitution in Eq. 7.14 and Eq. 7.15 can be calculated.

Table 7.9 shows one form of presentation. The values of x and y for each set of data are substituted in the equation $y = ax + b$; thus where $y = 8$ and $x = 60$, $y = ax + b$ becomes $8 = 60a + b$. The second equation $xy = ax^2 + bx$ can be found by multiplying the figures substituted in $y = ax + b$ by the value for x i.e. $60(8) = 60(60a + b)$ becomes $480 = 360a + 60b$

It is next necessary to solve the simultaneous equations:

$$293 = 1,910a + 10b$$
$$71,389 = 494,570a + 1,910b$$

It will be found that $a = 0 \cdot 12$ and $b = 6 \cdot 59$
i.e. $y = 0 \cdot 12x + 6 \cdot 59$.   (Eq. 7.16)

This equation may be drawn as a graph by substituting values for x and calculating the corresponding values for y (Table 7.10 and Figure 7.14).

40

The interpretation of this equation is that the smallest department has a nucleus of between 6 and 7 staff members and that one extra member of staff is required for approximately each additional group of 9 students. The minimum number of staff members is given by the intercept on the y axis when $x = 0$; the incremental addition is given by the slope of the graph and corresponds to the coefficient of x, i.e. the ratio of the increase in y compared to the increase in x is 0·12 to 1 or approximately 1 to 9.

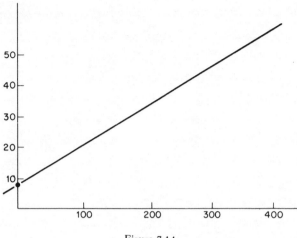

Figure 7.14

Table 7.10

x	y
0	6·59 (7)
100	18·59 (19)
200	30·59 (31)
300	42·59 (43)
400	54·50 (55)

REGRESSION EQUATIONS BY FORMULAE

The equations for the coefficient of x and the constant, Equations 7.14 and 7.15 above, can be solved to produce a formula for calculating a and b directly:

If
$$\Sigma y = a\Sigma x + nb \quad \text{(Eq. 7.14)}$$

and
$$\Sigma xy = a\Sigma x^2 + b\Sigma x \quad \text{(Eq. 7.15)}$$

it follows that
$$\Sigma y \Sigma x = a(\Sigma x)^2 + nb\Sigma x$$

and
$$n\Sigma xy = na\Sigma x^2 + nb\Sigma x$$

then
$$\Sigma y \Sigma x - n\Sigma xy = a(\Sigma x)^2 - na\Sigma x^2$$

$$a = \frac{\Sigma y \Sigma x - n\Sigma xy}{(\Sigma x)^2 - n\Sigma x^2} \quad \text{(Eq. 7.17)}$$

also
$$\Sigma y \Sigma x^2 = a\Sigma x^2 \Sigma x + nb\Sigma x^2$$

$$\Sigma xy \Sigma x = a\Sigma x^2 \Sigma x + b(\Sigma x)^2$$

then
$$\Sigma xy \Sigma x - \Sigma y \Sigma x^2 = b(\Sigma x)^2 - nb\Sigma x^2$$

$$b = \frac{\Sigma xy \Sigma x - \Sigma y \Sigma x^2}{(\Sigma x)^2 - n\Sigma x^2} \quad \text{(Eq. 7.18)}$$

Substituting in these formulae the values of Σx, Σxy, Σy, and Σx^2 found in Table 7.9, the values of a and b can be found as follows:

$$a = \frac{293 \times 1,910 - 10 \times 71,389}{1,910 \times 1,910 - 10 \times 494,570} = 0·12 \quad \text{(Eq. 7.17)}$$

$$b = \frac{71,389 \times 1,910 - 293 \times 494,570}{1,910 \times 1,910 - 10 \times 494,570} = 6·59 \quad \text{(Eq. 7.18)}$$

These formulae need not be remembered, but, of course, they are essential for programming a computer or when using a desk-top calculating machine for statistical work.

CODED VARIABLES FOR LINEAR EQUATIONS

It is obvious that the numerical value of the functions can be very large and even a simple statistical exercise can be extremely demanding if calculating machines are not available. One method of reducing the size of the functions is to relate the observed values to their mean value, and proceed as before but with figures that have now been 'coded' and reduced in size. In the following example the table of staff/student numbers used before (Table 7.8) has been used again, but the figures (Table 7.11) are now expressed in terms of tens of staff and hundreds of students.

The equation used to find the values in the regression equation using coded variables is:

$$Y = \frac{(\Sigma XY)}{(\Sigma X^2)} \cdot X \quad \text{(Eq. 7.19)}$$

Substituting values from Table 7.11:

$$Y = \frac{15·427}{12·977} \cdot X \quad \text{(Eq. 7.20)}$$

$$Y = 1·189 \, X$$

but since $Y = (y^1 - 2·93)$ and $X = (x^1 - 1·91)$ then:

$$y^1 - 2·93 = 1·189 \, (x^1 - 1·91)$$

$$y^1 = 1·2x^1 + 0·659 \quad \text{(Eq. 7.21)}$$

41

Table 7.11

y^1	x^1	Y	X	YX	X^2
0·8	0·60	−2·13	−1·31	2·790	1·716
1·3	0·65	−1·63	−1·26	2·054	1·588
1·4	0·92	−1·53	−0·99	i·515	0·980
2·1	1·06	−0·83	−0·85	0·706	0·723
3·2	1·62	0·27	−0·29	−0·078	0·084
2·5	1·80	−0·43	−0·11	0·047	0·012
4·2	2·05	1·27	0·14	0·178	0·020
4·0	2·94	1·07	1·03	1·102	1·061
5·0	3·44	2·07	1·53	3·167	2·341
4·8	4·02	1·87	2·11	3·946	4·452
				15·427	12·977

$$\frac{\Sigma y^1}{n} = \frac{29\cdot3}{10} \quad \frac{\Sigma x^1}{n} = \frac{19\cdot10}{10}$$

$$\bar{y}^1 = 2\cdot93 \quad \bar{x}^1 = 1\cdot91$$
$$Y = y^1 - \bar{y}^1 \quad X = x^1 - \bar{x}^1$$

The symbols $x^1 y^1$ are used to indicate that they represent a coded form of the data xy from Table 7.8.

This equation can be tabulated for various values of x^1 and the scales corrected as Table 7.12.

Table 7.12

Students	Staff	Students	Staff
x^1	y^1	$x^1 \times 100 = x$	$y^1 \times 10 = y$
0	0·659	0	7
1	1·859	100	19
2	3·059	200	31
3	4·259	300	43
4	5·459	400	55

Non-Linear Regression Equations

The regression equations 7.16 and 7.21 are in a linear form. It would be equally possible to calculate a regression equation in a non-linear form which would meet the same condition that the squares of the differences should be a minimum. Using the scaled dimensions from the previous examples (Table 7.11), the values required can be set down as in Table 7.13.

As was explained on p. 34 one form of a curvilinear regression equation is a parabola with the general equation,

$$y = ax^2 + bx + c$$

The values of a, b and c can be calculated from solutions of the following simultaneous equations

$$\Sigma y = a\Sigma x^2 + b\Sigma x + nc \quad \text{(Eq. 7.22)}$$

$$\Sigma xy = a\Sigma x^3 + b\Sigma x^2 + c\Sigma x \quad \text{(Eq. 7.23)}$$

$$\Sigma x^2 y = a\Sigma x^4 + b\Sigma x^3 + c\Sigma x^2 \quad \text{(Eq. 7.24)}$$

These equations have been derived from the same basic argument used to find the minimum sum of the square of the differences for the linear solution at Table 7.8 et seq. The square of the difference between an observed value y_1 and a predicted value would be $(ax_1^2 + bx_1 + c - y_1)^2$. The total of this function is differentiated with respect to the three constants a, b and c.

Table 7.13

y^1	x^1	$(x^1)^2$	$x^1 y^1$	$(x^1)^3$	$(x^1)^2 y^1$	$(x^1)^4$
0·8	0·60	0·360	0·480	0·216	0·288	0·130
1·3	0·65	0·423	0·845	0·275	0·550	0·179
1·4	0·92	0·846	1·288	0·778	1·184	0·716
2·1	1·06	1·124	2·226	1·191	2·360	1·262
3·2	1·62	2·624	5·184	4·251	8·397	6·887
2·5	1·80	3·240	4·500	5·832	8·100	10·498
4·2	2·05	4·203	8·610	8·616	17·653	17·663
4·0	2·94	8·644	11·760	25·413	34·576	74·714
5·0	3·44	11·834	17·200	40·709	59·170	140·039
4·8	4·02	16·160	19·296	64·963	77·568	261·151
29·3	19·10	49·458	71·389	152·244	209·846	513·239

Substituting the values from Table 7.13:

$$29 \cdot 3 = 49 \cdot 458\,a + 19 \cdot 10\,b + 10\,c$$
$$71 \cdot 389 = 152 \cdot 244\,a + 49 \cdot 458\,b + 19 \cdot 10\,c$$
$$209 \cdot 846 = 513 \cdot 239\,a + 152 \cdot 244\,b + 49 \cdot 458\,c$$

it can be shown that

$$a = -0 \cdot 326$$
$$b = +2 \cdot 639$$
$$c = -0 \cdot 496$$

and therefore

$$y^1 = -0 \cdot 326(x^1)^2 + 2 \cdot 639 x^1 - 0 \cdot 496 \qquad \text{(Eq. 7.25)}$$

Table 7.14

x^1	y^1
1	1·817
1·5	2·729
2	3·478
2·5	4·064
3	4 489
3·5	4·747
4	4·844

Figure 7.15 shows both regression equations (Eqs. 7.21 and 7.25). Between the values of $x = 1$ and $x = 3 \cdot 5$, where they are running more or less parallel, the largest difference is about 15 per cent, but the curves diverge outside this

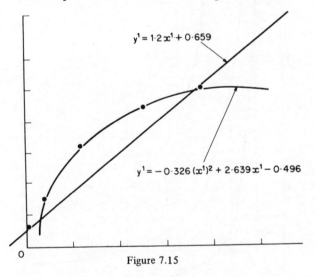

$$y^1 = 1 \cdot 2 x^1 + 0 \cdot 659$$

$$y^1 = -0 \cdot 326 (x^1)^2 + 2 \cdot 639 x^1 - 0 \cdot 496$$

Figure 7.15

range. This emphasizes the point that it is dangerous to extrapolate equations outside the range on which they have been calculated. The curve is also probably less representative of the relation between the variables. For example, at low value of x^1, the student numbers, and the value of y^1, the staff numbers, could be negative and at higher values than $x^1 = 4$ the staff numbers will drop.

Both these results are unlikely, and suggest that in this instance the linear form is a better indication of the relation. However, if there was reason to believe that a curve was the proper relation, other non-linear functions could be tried — for example, the hyperbole (xy = constant) or a logarithmic equation.

Correlation

The fact that values for the constants in a regression equation can be obtained by substituting data in standard formulae (i.e. Eqs. 7.14, 7.15, 7.17, 7.18, 7.19, and 7.20 or Eqs. 7.22, 7.23, and 7.24) does not in itself guarantee that there is any true relation between the variables.

It is, therefore, essential to devise tests to judge whether a regression equation represents a true relation between the observations. If there is an association between two variables, it is said that there is a correlation. The appearance of the graph showing staff numbers plotted in relation to the student numbers in Figure 7.13 suggests that there is an association, an increase in student numbers being matched by a proportional increase in staff numbers. If the points had scattered over the graph then it would be expected that correlation was low or even non-existent.

The correlation is measured by using the 'product moment coefficient'. This is a function with a value which will vary from 0 where there is no association to 1, where there is a direct relation. In addition, the algebraic sign of function indicates either positive correlation, where the values on both axes of the graph increase, or negative correlation where one value increases while the other decreases.

One form of the equation for calculating the coefficient of correlation, which can be used for the coded variables shown in Table 7.11, is as follows:

$$r \text{ (the coefficient of correlation)} = \frac{\Sigma XY}{\sqrt{\Sigma X^2 \cdot \Sigma Y^2}}$$

$$\text{(Eq. 7.26)}$$

From that example $\Sigma XY = 15 \cdot 427$, $\Sigma X^2 = 12 \cdot 977$. The value of ΣY^2 is 21·022 from the following:

Y^2	
4·537	
2·657	
2·341	
0·689	
0·073	
0·185	
1·613	
1·145	
4·285	
3·497	
$\Sigma Y^2 = 21 \cdot 022$	

Thus

$$r = \frac{15\cdot427}{\sqrt{12\cdot977 \times 21\cdot022}} = \frac{15\cdot427}{\sqrt{272\cdot802}} = \frac{15\cdot427}{16\cdot517} = 0\cdot934$$

A second form, which can be used in conjunction with the data calculated in Table 7.9, is as follows:

$$r = \frac{n\Sigma xy - \Sigma x\Sigma y}{\sqrt{[n\Sigma x^2 - (\Sigma x)^2]}\,\sqrt{[n\Sigma y^2 - (\Sigma y)^2]}} \quad \text{(Eq. 7.27)}$$

The values from that example together with the values of Σy^2 calculated at 10,687 (see below) may be substituted in this equation to give r.

$$r = \frac{10 \times 71,389 - 293 \times 1,910}{\sqrt{(10 \times 494,570 - 1,910^2)}\sqrt{(10 \times 10,687 - 293^2)}}$$

$$= \frac{154,060}{\sqrt{1,297,600}\,\sqrt{21,021}}$$

$$= 0\cdot933$$

The value of Σy^2 for this equation is computed as follows:

y^2
64
169
196
441
1,024
625
1,764
1,600
2,500
2,304
Σy^2 = 10,687

In this example the coefficient of correlation is impressively high but the number of observations is quite low. The next consideration is, therefore, to decide how much data is necessary before we can be certain that the calculated equation is representative. Using the framework of this example, it would be expected that local variations in staff and student numbers would prevent an exact correspondence between the data plotted on the graph and a line corresponding to the calculated equation. However, if there were a large number of observations showing a correlation, we would be more confident of the validity of the equation than if we were dealing with only a few sets of data. On the other hand, if the degree of correlation was relatively higher in respect of a smaller set of data, we could be confident of a close association between the variables.

This argument may also be expressed in reverse, in the sense that if we had a 'true' relation expressed for a small group, the more observations that were taken the more likely it would be for appearance of extreme random variations from the 'normal' situation. It follows that the higher the number of observations, the lower would be the degree of correlation that would be necessary to provide the same degree of confidence in the relation.

It is, therefore, necessary to test the correlation by further statistical techniques, which relate the sample size and probability levels. The formula for this test (t-test) is

$$t = \frac{r\sqrt{(n-2)}}{\sqrt{(1-r^2)}} \quad \text{(Eq. 7.28)}$$

Applying this test to the coefficient of correlation calculated from Eq. 7.26

$$t = \frac{0\cdot93\sqrt{(10-2)}}{\sqrt{(1-0\cdot93^2)}}$$

$$\therefore \qquad t = 7\cdot15$$

Appendix F shows the function t tabulated for various sample sizes and for various probabilities. In this table the sample size minus 2 is known as the 'degree of freedom' or ν value. For the data in Table 7.8 at $\nu = 8$ a t value of 7·15 considerably exceeds the 0·1 per cent level and is, therefore, highly significant. This means that such a value would have only occurred by chance once in over 1,000 times.

If the table for t is plotted as a graph (Figure 7.16), it can be shown that to be significant the value of t must be much higher if samples are small.

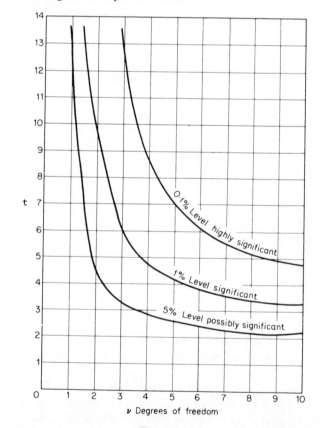

Figure 7.16

A final point to be considered in connection with regression equations is how far an observed value may vary from the predicted line and still be considered part of the population represented by that line.

To consider the range of values that we might expect at the value $x_1 = 1.5$ in the equation $y = 1.2x + 0.659$, first substitute in the equation $x_1 = 1.5$, giving a value for y of 2.459. The next step is to calculate the spread of the y values using the formula

$$S^2xy = \frac{1}{n-2}\left[\Sigma Y^2 - \frac{(\Sigma XY)^2}{\Sigma X^2}\right] \quad \text{(Eq. 7.29)}$$

$$= \frac{1}{8}\left[21.02 - \frac{15.427^2}{12.977}\right] = 0.335$$

This numerical value is then used in the formula to calculate the variance of y about y^1 when $x = x_1$

$$= S^2(y_1^1) = S^2yx\left[1 + \frac{1}{n} + \frac{X_1^2}{\Sigma X^2}\right] \quad \text{(Eq. 7.30)}$$

X_1 is the coded value for x_1 given by subtracting the mean of x from the required value of x (i.e. $x_1 - \bar{x}$),

$$X_1 = 1.5 - 1.91$$

$$= -0.41$$

$$S^2(y_1) = 0.335\left[1 + \frac{1}{10} + \frac{0.168}{12.977}\right]$$

$$= 0.373$$

$$S(y_1^1) = \sqrt{0.373} = 0.611$$

Since the number of observations is 10, it is taken that there are $10 - 2 = 8$ degrees of freedom.

The next step is to relate the t value for a given confidence limit and degree of freedom to the value of y:

$$t = \frac{y - y_1}{S(y_1^1)} \quad \text{(Eq. 7.31)}$$

$$t = \frac{y - 2.459}{0.611}$$

$$\text{or} \quad y = 0.611t + 2.459 \quad \text{(Eq. 7.32)}$$

Referring to t table, where the degree of freedom is 8, we can be 95 per cent confident that t will not lie outside ± 2.31. Substituting this value in Eq. 7.32

$$y = 0.611t + 2.459$$

$$y = 0.611(\pm 2.31) + 2.459$$

$$y = 3.873 \text{ or } 1.045$$

We can, therefore, expect with 95 per cent confidence that the values of y expected where $x = 1.5$ will fall within these two values. This range is equal to about 60 per cent above or below the value predicted by the regression equation at this point, and illustrates the degree of dispersion that might be met even when the equation exhibits a high numerical correlation.

The following examples illustrate research studies combining mathematical analysis and statistical methods applied to the preparation of approximate estimates. The objective is to show applications of the procedures developed in this chapter but also to suggest that useful results may follow quite small-scale investigations. The advantages that follow from more accurate estimates or improved cost research in the early stages of design may lead to savings to the client that will far outweigh the expenditure of professional time and resources.

Quantity Factors for Partitions

This example examines the proposition that the areas of partitions will have some predictable relationship to the schedule of accommodation supplied as the brief. Figure 7.17 shows a simple rectangular building of conventional design providing rooms numbering r. Since the total area of the floor is $a(2b + c)$ the average area per room will be $a/r(2b + c)$. If the storey height is h the average area of partitions per room will be

$$\frac{h}{r}\left[2a + 2b\left(\frac{r}{2} - 1\right)\right]$$

which simplifies to

$$\frac{2h}{r}(a - b) + bh.$$

Supposing that the relationship will be linear these two functions can be incorporated in the equation $y = Mx + N$, where y is the average area of partitions and x the average room size thus

$$\frac{2h}{r}(a - b) + bh = \frac{Ma}{r}(2b + c) + N.$$

From inspection of this equation it is apparent that if the number of rooms is large then $N = bh$ and it follows that M will equal

$$\frac{2h(a - b)}{a(2b + c)};$$

substituting these functions in the basic equation gives a final version

$$y = \frac{2h(a - b)}{a(2b + c)}x + bh.$$

tested in a simple numerical example.

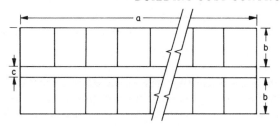

Figure 7.17

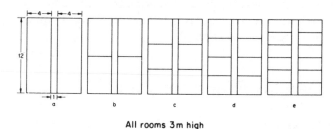

All rooms 3m high

Figure 7.18

Table 7.16

y	x	yx	x²	y²
29·24	40·39	1,176·21	1,625·67	850·99
40·50	47·38	1,919·15	2,244·88	1,640·68
83·24	132·01	10,988·91	17,427·73	6,928·97
41·52	39·57	1,643·50	1,566·29	1,724·52
45·80	92·06	4,216·70	8,476·17	2,097·72
39·29	71·72	2,818·45	5,143·84	1,544·30
46·26	43·47	2,011·54	1,890·36	2,140·48
53·14	84·44	4,487·58	7,131·50	2,823·87
61·22	69·86	4,277·16	4,880·77	3,748·20
48·03	65·40	3,141·34	4,277·58	2,306·92
66·05	91·13	6,019·92	8,305·97	4,363·06
27·49	21·64	595·25	468·56	756·20
28·89	28·89	834·78	834·78	834·78
34·83	52·02	1,812·47	2,706·63	1,213·71
35·39	41·06	1,453·45	1,686·15	1,252·86
57·13	77·01	4,400·30	5,931·46	3,264·40
37·16	35·12	1,304·98	1,233·20	1,380·93

Σy 775·18 Σx 1,033·17 Σyx 53,101·69 Σx^2 75,831·54 Σy^2 38,872·59

Table 7.15

Plan	Rooms	Average room area	Partition area	Average partition area
a	2	x = 54	72 + 0	y = 36
b	4	27	72 + 24	24
c	6	18	72 + 48	20
d	8	13.5	72 + 72	18
e	12	9	72 + 120	16

In Table 7.15 the average room and partition areas are calculated for the five examples in Figure 7.18. If the dimensions are substituted in the equation it will be found that the average partition area can be calculated directly from the average room size i.e. where $a = 12, b = 4, c = 1$ and $h = 3$ then

$$y = \frac{2.3\,(12 - 4)}{12\,(2.4 + 1)}\,x + 4.3 \text{ or } y = \tfrac{4}{9}x + 12.$$

In real buildings extra space will be required for lavatories, cleaners' stores and plant rooms. If the average area of rooms is computed by dividing the total area by the number of rooms on the schedule, the space occupied by corridors, stairs, lift shafts and the lavatories, etc. and the area of partitions surrounding these spaces must introduce factors which will complicate the simple formula. A regression equation deduced from analysis of actual designs will include the effect of these factors, but, because of the variability between buildings, it is necessary to check that any result has statistical significance.

Table 7.16 sets out the average areas of rooms and partitions for seventeen university buildings. The regression equation is calculated by substituting the totals of the columns in the two Eqs. 7.14 and 7.15,

$$775 \cdot 18 = 1,033 \cdot 17a + 17b$$

$$53,101 \cdot 69 = 75,831 \cdot 54a + 1,033 \cdot 17b$$

giving $a = 0 \cdot 46$ and $b = 17 \cdot 68$ and thus $y = 0 \cdot 46x + 17 \cdot 68$.

It is interesting that the coefficient of x is close to the value found in the simple example described in Table 7.15, however the value of the constant is considerably increased for the reasons described above.

The values in Table 7.16 can also be substituted in Eq. 7.27 to check the correlation

$$r = \frac{(17 \cdot 53,101) - (1,033 \cdot 775)}{\sqrt{17 \cdot 75,831 - 1,033^2}\,\sqrt{17 \cdot 388,72 - 775^2}}$$

$$= 0 \cdot 88.$$

This is a high coefficient of correlation but as described

previously must be checked against the number of observations by the use of Eq. 7.28

$$t = \frac{0.88\sqrt{17-2}}{\sqrt{1-0.88^2}}$$

$$= 7.18.$$

Reference to the table in Appendix F shows that this degree of correlation is highly significant and would be a reasonable basis for preparing an approximate estimate.

Similar equations could be developed for the relationship between room area and the external walls, or the room areas and the combined area of all the walls, in addition it would be possible to predict the range of room sizes that might be expected in buildings serving varying functions.

Structure Frames

The following example investigates aspects of the cost of a prefabricated steel structural frame designed within a system for use in educational buildings. This element is often the most expensive in an analysis. It is also one of the most difficult to examine in relation to its function within the structure.

Design decisions will affect the spacing of the columns, the direction of the spans, the storey heights, and the loading conditions. The cost of the components will be primarily controlled by the cost of the materials, factory overheads, and the relation between factory and on-site labour. In a systemized frame the permutations of the various components are, to some degree, limited and predictable. This is of course in marked contrast to a concrete frame or a traditional steel frame which because the designers' range of choice is so extensive can exhibit extremely wide ranges of beam and column sizes that cannot be predicted.

Table 7.17 shows the areas and elemental costs of the frame for a group of six storey buildings.

The gross floor areas of the buildings ranged from 960 m² to 1,200 m² and the scatter of costs per square metre of floor area within this range of floor area was very erratic, making it impossible to establish a regular cost trend founded on the base of the gross floor area of building.

Projects 17 and 21 were the cheapest and most expensive respectively, although of equal area.

All twenty-one projects were using the same industrialized building system, so it might have been expected that the costs per square metre would show a close relationship. When producing a cost plan, it might seem reasonable to have a 'suggested cost target', a single figure recommended by the developer of the system. Cost analysis of the system in use, however, as evidenced by this table, showed that it was not possible to use a single figure and a more detailed examination was necessary.

Table 7.17

Project	Floor area, m²	Cost per m² of floor area, £
1	960	8·33
2	960	8·45
3	1,000	8·50
4	1,000	8·75
5	1,000	8·96
6	1.040	8·21
7	1,040	8·57
8	1,070	9·55
9	1,100	8·20
10	1,100	8·62
11	1,100	9·17
12	1,100	9·39
13	1,120	8·30
14	1,120	9·12
15	1,120	9·78
16	1,110	8·23
17	1,200	7·92
18	1,200	8·30
19	1,200	8·77
20	1,200	9·34
21	1,200	10·88

Table 7.18

Project	Floor area carried per column, m²	Cost per m² of floor area, £
21	x = 8·64	y = 10·88
8	10·22	9·55
4	11·33	8·75
15	14·40	9·78
20	15·05	9·34
5	15·61	8·96
11	17·28	9·17
14	18·12	9·12
10	18·39	8·62
3	18·58	8·50
19	18·58	8·77
1	18·58	8·33
18	18·86	8·30
7	20·07	8·57
9	20·44	8·20
12	20·44	9·39
13	21·55	8·30
2	21·92	8·45
17	22·30	7·92
16	22·30	8·23
6	24·80	8·21

Examination of the bay sizes produces another criteria against which costs can be set. Bay sizes described in terms of span and column spacing are difficult to use as a basis for analysis. A more practical yardstick proves to be cost related to 'density of columns' expressed as the average number of square metres of floor area served per column. The density is obtained by dividing the total gross floor area of building by the total number of columns of the building.

This yardstick when set against the cost of frame per square metre of floor area and collated in order of the density of columns is shown in Table 7.18.

It can be seen from Table 7.18 that costs per square metre seem to be higher when the density of columns is greatest (i.e. less floor area per column).

It is possible to produce a graph (Figure 7.19) of the figures in Table 7.18 and to draw a reasonable trend line. A formula can be calculated from this line giving the relationship between cost and column density, though a better fit can be calculated by applying basic statistical methods. To check whether the inverse relationship that appears to hold between area and cost is real it is necessary to test, as before, for correlation.

The degree of correlation (r) is measured by the product moment correlation coefficient, using the formula

$$r = \frac{n\Sigma xy - \Sigma x\,\Sigma y}{\sqrt{[n\Sigma x^2 - (\Sigma x)^2]}\ \sqrt{[n\Sigma y^2 - (\Sigma y)^2]}} \quad \text{(Eq.7.27)}$$

where n = number of observations

x and y = the original values given in Table 7.18.

To simplify the arithmetic coded variables, u and v for x and y can be used in the formula to obtain the value of r. The coded values from Table 7.18 are shown in Table 7.19.

It is usual for a set of figures to give a value of r below 1 because of the imperfections in the sets.

$$\therefore\ r = \frac{21\,(-4{,}526) - 0{\cdot}09\,(-1)}{\sqrt{[21\,.\,349{\cdot}8 - (0{\cdot}09)^2]}\ .\ \sqrt{[21\,.\,93{,}119 - (-1)^2}}$$

$$= \frac{-95{,}046 + 0{\cdot}09}{\sqrt{[7{,}346 - 0{\cdot}008]}\ .\ \sqrt{[1{,}955{,}499 - 1]}}$$

$$= \frac{-95{,}046}{\sqrt{7{,}346}\ .\ \sqrt{1{,}955{,}498}}$$

$$= \frac{-95{,}046}{85{\cdot}6\,.\,1{,}398{\cdot}4}$$

$$r = -0{\cdot}79$$

To assess the significance of the resulting value of r it is necessary to apply a t test of significance as before.

If the result exceeds the value given by the t table for the 1 per cent level, it can be stated that correlation exists with only 1 in 100 chance (i.e. 1 per cent chance) of being wrong.

Test for significance

$$t = \frac{r\sqrt{(n-2)}}{\sqrt{(1-r^2)}} = \frac{-0{\cdot}79\,\sqrt{19}}{\sqrt{(1-0{\cdot}62)}} \quad \text{(Eq. 7.28)}$$

$$= \frac{-0{\cdot}79\,.\,4{\cdot}36}{\sqrt{0{\cdot}38}} = \frac{-3{\cdot}44}{0{\cdot}62}$$

$$= 5{\cdot}55$$

degrees of freedom $\qquad v = n - 2 = 19$

Reference to the t table in Appendix F shows that with 19 degrees of freedom the t values which must be reached or exceeded for significance are as follows:

% level	50	25	10	5	2·5	1	0·1
t value required	0·69	1·19	1·73	2·09	2·43	2·86	3·88

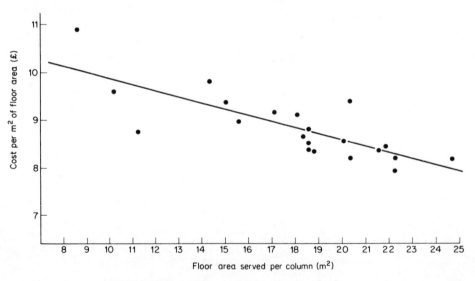

Figure 7.19 Cost of frame related to density of columns.

Table 7.19

$x =$ m² floor area per column	$y =$ cost per m² of floor area	$u =$ $x - 17.97$	$v =$ $y - 885$	uv	u^2	v^2
8·64	1,088	−9·33	+203	−1,894	87·05	41,209
10·22	955	−7·75	− 70	− 543	60·06	4,900
11·33	875	−6·64	− 10	+ 10	44·09	100
14·40	978	−3·57	+ 93	− 332	12·74	8,649
15·05	934	−2·92	+ 49	− 143	8·53	2,401
15·61	896	−2·36	+ 11	− 26	5·57	121
17·28	917	−0·69	+ 32	− 22	0·48	1,024
18·12	912	0·15	+ 27	+ 4	0·02	729
18·39	862	0·42	− 23	− 10	0·18	529
18·58	850	0·61	− 35	− 21	0·37	1,225
18·58	877	0·61	− 8	− 5	0·37	64
18·58	883	0·61	− 2	− 1	0·37	4
18·86	830	0·89	− 55	− 49	0·79	3,025
20·07	˙857	2·10	− 28	− 59	4·41	784
20·44	820	2·47	− 65	− 161	6·10	4,225
20·44	939	2·47	+ 54	+ 133	6·10	2,916
21·55	830	3·58	− 55	− 197	12·82	3,025
21·92	845	3·95	− 40	− 158	15·60	1,600
22·30	792	4·33	− 93	− 403	18·75	8,649
22·30	823	4·33	− 62	− 268	18·75	3,844
24·80	821	6·83	− 64	− 437	46·65	4,096
Σ377·46	Σ18,584	Σ0·09	Σ− 1	Σ−4,526	Σ349·80	Σ93,119

$$\bar{x} = \frac{377.46}{21} \qquad \bar{y} = \frac{18,584}{21}$$

$$= \quad 17.97 \qquad = 885$$

This means that with a value of 5·55 correlation is indicated below the 0·1 per cent level, i.e. less than a 1 in 1,000 chance of being wrong if we assume that cost and area of floor served per column are associated.

Since this correlation is good and it is reasonable to accept that y does vary in direct relation to x, the next step is to find the coefficient m and c in formula $y = mx + c$.

The least squares method using coded variables u and v for x and y, which means that Σu and Σv approximately equal 0, provides the simplified formula

$$v = \left(\frac{\Sigma uv}{\Sigma u^2}\right) u \qquad \text{(Eq. 7.34)}$$

From Table 7.19

$$\Sigma uv = - 4,526$$

$$\Sigma u^2 = 349 \cdot 8$$

$$\therefore v = \left(\frac{-4,526}{349 \cdot 8}\right) u$$

$$= 12 \cdot 94\, u$$

Hence reversing the coding

$$y - 885 = - 12 \cdot 94\, (x - 17 \cdot 97)$$

$$y = 1,117 - 13x \text{ approximately}$$

∴ cost in pence per m² of floor area = $1,117 - 13$ times floor area per column in m².

It is known that the cost of the frame will vary around the predicted value calculated by the above formula, and it is useful to know the amount by which the value is likely to vary. The t table can be used to estimate the range of values within which the costs will fall, with a given probability. These values are called the confidence limits for the predicted cost.

It is necessary to calculate the standard error of estimate, which is given by the formula

$$\frac{t\sigma}{\sqrt{n}}, \text{ where } \sigma = \text{the standard deviation}$$

The standard deviation (or root mean square deviation of x from $\bar{x}$) for coded values is equivalent to

$$\left[\frac{\Sigma v^2}{n} - \left(\frac{\Sigma v}{n} \right)^2 \right]$$

In this example

$$\sigma_v = \left[\frac{93119}{21} - \left(\frac{-1}{21} \right)^2 \right]$$

$$= \sqrt{[4,434 - 0]}$$

$$= 66 \cdot 7$$

Hence by formulae standard error

$$= \frac{t\sigma}{\sqrt{n}}$$

$$= \frac{66 \cdot 7 t}{\sqrt{21}}$$

$$= 14 \cdot 37 t$$

As tables of t show that 5 per cent of all cases lie outside $t = \pm 2 \cdot 09$ when $v = 19$ we can say that 95 per cent of all cases are likely to lie within the limits $t = \pm 2 \cdot 09$.

The range of values for y becomes

$$y \pm 14 \cdot 37 \, (2 \cdot 09)$$

$$= y \pm 30 \cdot 03.$$

8

Cost in Use—Theory

The cost of building described in a cost analysis is based on the contract sum paid by the building owner. This cost, although it will normally be paid by instalments over the period of the contract, may be considered as a single capital charge in contrast to expenditure on fuel and maintenance that will occur throughout the life of the building. The full economic effect of the various design decisions taken by the architect can only be examined if capital and long-term costs can be represented together. Similarly, the decisions which must be made on buildings for commercial development must be based on the comparison of capital costs of land, construction and fees with long-term running costs, maintenance and the returns of income through rents.

Techniques for making such calculations developed by valuation surveyors and accountants are based on the principle of compound interest. Formulae derived from this principle, although mathematically simple, have a complicated form and are difficult to use in everyday calculations. Therefore, the results have been calculated for various numerical values and presented in tabular form. However, the arithmetic of the derivation of the tables is a useful aid to the understanding of their use. The development of the most frequently used tables is described below as a preliminary to an explanation of their practical use in Chapter 9. Tables themselves are provided in Appendix E.

Compound Interest

In the simplest application interest is calculated at the end of each year as a percentage of the amount deposited at the beginning of the year. If the interest is not withdrawn, it is added to the amount deposited and becomes the principal on which the interest is calculated in the following year.

$$P = \text{principal}$$

$$i = \text{rate of interest}$$

$$n = \text{number of years}$$

At the end of the first year the amount equals the principal plus the interest on the principal.

$$\text{Amount (first year)} = P + iP$$

$$= P(1 + i)$$

At the end of the seond year interest must be calculated on the total figure:

$$\text{Amount (second year)} = P(1 + i) + iP(1 + i)$$

$$= P(1 + i)(1 + i)$$

$$= P(1 + i)^2$$

$$\text{Amount (after } n \text{ years)} = P(1 + i)^n \qquad \text{(Eq. 8.1)}$$

This is the basic formula for calculating compound interest, and tables are available to show, after a specified number of years and for various rates of interest, the amount where the principal equalled £1, or alternatively what the principal or present value would be if the amount is to equal £1.

AMOUNT OF £1

This table is calculated using the formula

$$\text{Amount (after } n \text{ years)} = £1 . (1 + i)^n \qquad \text{(Eq. 8.2)}$$

To calculate how a certain principal will increase over a term of years when invested at a certain rate of interest, use the Table E.1 for 'Amount of £1' at Appendix E. The principal is multiplied by the figure from the table appropriate to the term of years and the rate of interest.

PRESENT VALUE OF £1

This table is calculated using the formula

$$\text{Amount (after } n \text{ years)} = £1 = P . (1 + i)^n$$

or

$$P = \frac{£1}{(1 + i)^n} \qquad \text{(Eq. 8.3)}$$

This formula for the present value is the reciprocal of the formula for calculating the amount of £1. To find what principal would need to be invested to achieve a certain amount, use the Table E2 for 'Present Value of £1'; the amount required is multiplied by the figure from the table appropriate to the term of years and the rate of interest. These two applications of the formulae are used to relate two capital sums, one at the beginning of the term of years and one at the end. The formulae can be extended to relate a capital sum invested at the beginning of the period to an annual income.

PRESENT VALUE OF £1 PER ANNUM

The principal that must be invested to give a certain amount after one year, designated by $P_{(1)}$, would be given by the equation:

$$P_{(1)} = \frac{\text{Amount}}{(1 + i)} \qquad \text{(Eq. 8.3)}$$

The principal necessary to provide the same amount after two years, designated $P_{(2)}$, would be given by:

$$P_{(2)} = \frac{\text{Amount}}{(1 + i)^2}$$

To provide equal annual sums for each of two years it would be necessary to invest

$$P_{(1)} + P_{(2)} \text{ or } \frac{\text{Amount}}{(1 + i)} + \frac{\text{Amount}}{(1 + i)^2}$$

To provide for an annual income for each of n years it would be necessary to invest a single sum equal to

$$\frac{\text{Income}}{(1 + i)} + \frac{\text{Income}}{(1 + i)^2} \cdots + \frac{\text{Income}}{(1 + i)^{(n-1)}} + \frac{\text{Income}}{(1 + i)^n}$$

$$\text{(Eq. 8.4)}$$

This is a geometric series and the sum may be found by multiplying both sides of the equation by $(1 + i)$:

Total principal $\times (1 + i) =$

$$\text{Income} + \frac{\text{Income}}{(1 + i)} + \frac{\text{Income}}{(1 + i)^2} \cdots + \frac{\text{Income}}{(1 + i)^{(n-1)}} \qquad \text{(Eq. 8.5)}$$

If Equation 8.4 is subtracted from Equation 8.5, all intermediate terms disappear and the result is

Total principal $. (1 + i) -$ total principal

$$= \text{Income} . \left(1 - \frac{1}{(1 + i)^n}\right)$$

Total principal $. i$

$$= \text{Income} . \frac{(1 + i)^n - 1}{(1 + i)^n}$$

Total principal

$$= \text{Income} . \frac{(1 + i)^n - 1}{i(1 + i)^n} \qquad \text{(Eq. 8.6)}$$

By substituting the value of £1 for the income, the formulae can be used to calculate the present value of £1 per annum. In this form the calculation is known as the Years Purchase (Single Rate). A table based on the formulae would show what capital sum, invested at the beginning of a term of years, would be equivalent to an annual return of £1 throughout the period at a particular rate of interest. (*See* Table E.3 in the appendixes.) The year's purchase is sometimes quoted in isolation (i.e. year's purchase equals 17).

This practice is based on the assumptions that certain classes of property can be expected to return a particular rate of interest for a period of time and that the calculated value for the present value of £1 per annum would be 17. Such approximations are possible because the figures for years purchase are reasonably constant after thirty to forty years for the remaining useful life of a building. If an unlimited term of years is considered, a perpetuity, the years purchase is equivalent to 100 divided by the rate of interest.

Equation 8.6 can also be used to determine the annual payments necessary to redeem a loan. In this instance the value of £1 is substituted for the principal and the formula is rearranged to show the repayment instalments.

$$\text{Repayment (annual)} = £1 \text{ (i.e. the loan)} . \frac{i(1 + i)^n}{(1 + i)^n - 1}$$

$$\text{(Eq. 8.7)}$$

Normally, for domestic loans, repayments are required monthly and valuers will use a table showing the amount necessary to redeem a loan of £100 in monthly instalments. This is based on equation 8.7 modified as follows:

$$\text{Repayment (monthly)} = \frac{£100}{12} . \frac{i(1 + i)^n}{(1 + i)^n - 1}$$

In this form it is known as the mortgage instalment table.

ANNUAL SINKING FUND

Equations 8.1 to 8.7 relate capital invested at the beginning of a period to capital or annual sums during or at the end of the period. It is often necessary to calculate the sum produced at the end of a term of years by annual payments throughout the period — an annual sinking fund. In deriving this formula it is assumed that the principal is invested in equal instalments at the end of each year and no interest accrues on the final payment.

Amount (end of 1st year) = Annual sinking fund instalment
$$= s$$

Amount (end of 2nd year) $= s + s(1 + i)$

Amount (end of n years) $= s + s(1 + i) + s(1 + i)^2 \cdots$

$$\cdots s(1 + i)^{n-1} \qquad \text{(Eq. 8.8)}$$

The sum of this series may be calculated by multiplying both sides of the equation by $(1 + i)$, giving:

Amount (end of n years) $. (1 + i) = s(1 + i) + s(1 + i)^2 \cdots$

$$\cdots s(1 + i)^n \qquad \text{(Eq. 8.9)}$$

Subtracting 8.8 from 8.9 gives:

Amount (end of n years) $\times i$

$$= s(1 + i)^n - s$$

$$\text{Amount} = s\left(\frac{(1 + i)^n - 1}{i}\right) \qquad \text{(Eq. 8.10)}$$

The valuation tables will normally show the value of s necessary to give £1 at the end of the period and are, therefore, based on the equation

$$s = \frac{£1 \cdot i}{(1 + i)^n - 1} \qquad \text{(Eq. 8.11)}$$

See Table E.4 in the appendixes for example figures

In many situations a person making a loan may be willing to receive only the interest on the loan year by year with a full repayment at the end of the period. To service the debt and to build up a fund sufficient to redeem the loan, the borrower must set aside a sum equal to the interest and a sinking fund instalment each year. For a loan of P, the annual cost will be

$$\text{Repayment (annual)} = Pi + \frac{Pi}{(1 + i)^n - 1}$$

$$= \frac{Pi(1 + i)^n - Pi + Pi}{(1 + i)^n - 1}$$

$$= \frac{Pi(1 + i)^n}{(1 + i)^n - 1} \qquad \text{(Eq. 8.12)}$$

If the loan was for £1, this equation would equal

$$\frac{£1 \times i(1 + i)^n}{(1 + i)^n - 1}$$

This is identical to the equation derived at 8.7 for the mortgage instalment table.

Table 8.1

Number of Years n	Present Value of £1 (Note 1)	Present Value of £1 per annum (Note 2)	Annual Sinking Fund (Note 3)	Reciprocal of Present Value of £1 per per annum
	£	£	£	£
1	0·952	0·952	1·000	1·050
2	0·907	1·859	0·488	0·538
3	0·864	2·723	0·317	0·367
4	0·823	3·546	0·232	0·282
5	0·784	4·329	0·181	0·231
6	0·746	5·076	0·147	0·197
7	0·711	5·786	0·123	0·173
8	0·677	6·463	0·105	0·155
9	0·645	7·108	0·091	0·141
10	0·614	7·722	0·080	0·130
11	0·585	8·306	0·070	0·120
12	0·557	8·863	0·063	0·113
13	0·530	9·394	0·056	0·106
14	0·505	9·899	0·051	0·101
15	0·481	10·380	0·046	0·096
20	0·377	12·462	0·030	0·080
25	0·295	14·094	0·021	0·071
30	0·231	15·372	0·015	0·065
35	0·181	16·374	0·011	0·061
40	0·142	17·159	0·008	0·058
45	0·111	17·774	0·006	0·056
50	0·087	18·256	0·005	0·055
55	0·068	18·633	0·004	0·054
60	0·054	18·929	0·003	0·053

Note 1. The amount that must be invested now to produce £1 at the end of a period of x years.
Note 2. Years Purchase (Single Rate): the amount that must be invested now to produce £1 at the end of each of a period of x years.
Note 3. The amount to be invested at the end of each of x years to produce £1 at the end of a period of x years.

Repayment figures are given in Table E.5 in the appendixes.

The last calculation showed that the mortgage instalment was equal to the sinking fund instalment plus the rate of interest. Since the mortgage instalment is the reciprocal of the present value per annum, the latter will equal the reciprocal of the sinking fund plus the interest rate.

It may be helpful at this point to review the valuation tables, which are most useful for studying the relation between capital expenditure and running costs. Table 8.1 is calculated at an interest rate of 5 per cent.

For a period of 20 years at 5 per cent the present value of £1 is £0·377, which means that

£0·377 invested now will produce £1 at end of 20 years

or

£1 invested now will produce £1/0·377 at end of 20 years

£1 invested now will produce £2·653 at end of 20 years

The figure of £2·653 could be found in the table for 'the amount of £1', for the appropriate interest rate and period of years. This table is, therefore, simply the reciprocal of the table for the present value.

The present value of £1 received at the end of one year is given as £0·952, and to produce the same sum at the end of a period of two years it is necessary to invest £0·907. The sum of these figures, £1·859, if invested at 5 per cent will, therefore, give £1 at the end of each of the two years. It is the figure which is found in the table for the present value of £1 per annum where $n = 2$.

For a period of 20 years an investment of £12·462 will produce £1 in each year. This means that:

£12·462 invested now will produce £1 at the end of each of 20 years

£12·462 borrowed now must be repaid at £1 for each of 20 years

£1 borrowed now must be repaid at £1/12·462 for each of 20 years

£1 borrowed now must be repaid at £0·080 for each of 20 years

The figure of £0·080 could be found in the mortgage instalment table, but it will be given in terms of a loan of £100 and for monthly repayments, i.e. £0·668.

It is common experience that a loan may either be repaid in annual instalments or by the payment of interest in each year and a final repayment of the whole sum at the end of the period. To find the amount that must be set aside to repay the loan reference is made to the table for the annual sinking fund instalment. For each £1 borrowed for a period of 20 years the annual instalment would be £0·030. The interest on the loan would be £0·05 for each

£1 borrowed and, therefore, the total annual cost would be £0·080. Reference to Table 8.1 will show that this sum is identical to the reciprocal of the present value of £1 per annum for the same period, illustrating that the value per annum or the year's purchase figure is equal to

$$\frac{1}{\text{annual sinking fund instalment} + \text{rate of interest}}$$

It may be noted that this expression is frequently quoted as the definition of Years Purchase. Its chief use is in situations where the rates of interest for the loan and the sinking fund might vary.

Dual-Rate Tables

In the calculation of Equation 8.12 it was assumed that the rate of interest paid on the loan and the rate of interest invested in the sinking fund were the same.

In practice the rate of interest paid on a loan and the interest that can be obtained to build up a sinking fund will differ. The formula used to find the annual payments to redeem a loan assuming two rates of interest will be calculated as follows:

Amount of loan	P
Number of years	n
Interest rate on loan	$i_{(1)}$
Interest rate on sinking fund	$i_{(2)}$
Annual interest	$= P \cdot i_{(1)}$
Annual sinking fund instalment	$= \dfrac{P \cdot i_{(2)}}{(1 + i_{(2)})^n - 1}$

$$\text{(Eq. 8.11)}$$

Total annual payments

$$= P \left[i_{(1)} + \frac{i_{(2)}}{(1 + i_{(2)})^n - 1} \right] \qquad \text{(Eq. 8.13)}$$

This equation may also be expressed in the form

$$\text{Present value } (P) = \frac{\text{Annual payments}}{i_{(1)} + \dfrac{i_{(2)}}{(1 + i_{(2)})^n - 1}} \qquad \text{(Eq. 8.14)}$$

This equation gives the present value of annual payments to provide a particular rate of interest and allow for a sinking fund at a given rate to replace the invested capital. This is known as the Dual Rate Year's Purchase.

In valuing a leasehold interest the problem is to calculate the capital value of annual payments, which must be divided

between the sinking fund instalment to replace the equity and the annual return, i.e. the interest on the capital.

Capital value of investment P

Interest rate on capital value $i_{(1)}$

Interest rate on sinking fund $i_{(2)}$

Annual income from lease A

$$\text{Annual sinking fund instalment} = \frac{P \cdot i_{(2)}}{(1 + i_{(2)})^n - 1}$$

(Eq. 8.11)

$$\text{Actual annual income} = A - \left[\frac{P \cdot i_{(2)}}{(1 + i_{(2)})^n - 1} \right]$$

$$\text{Interest on capital value} = \frac{\text{Actual annual income}}{\text{Capital value of investment}}$$

$$i_{(1)} = \frac{A - \left[\dfrac{P \cdot i_{(2)}}{(1 + i_{(2)})^n - 1} \right]}{P}$$

or

$$P \cdot i_{(1)} + \frac{P \cdot i_{(2)}}{(1 + i_{(2)})^n - 1} = A$$

or

$$P = \frac{A}{i_{(1)} + \dfrac{i_{(2)}}{(1 + i_{(2)})^n - 1}}$$

(Eq. 8.15)

Valuation tables are available to show the present value (P) for various rates of interest where the annual income equals £1:

i.e.
$$\text{Present value} = \frac{£1}{i_{(1)} + \dfrac{i_{(2)}}{(1 + i_{(2)})^n - 1}}$$

(Eq. 8.16)

In practice, income tax is levied on the annual income from a leasehold. The tax is not simply calculated on the actual annual income, which is the direct return to the investor, but also on the sinking fund instalment. The calculation above shows the sinking fund instalment that must be invested to replace the capital value over the term of years. This annual instalment must be found after tax has been paid, and, therefore, if the tax were £0·25 in the pound, the actual deduction from the sinking fund must be £1·00/(£1·00 − £0·25) multiplied by the instalment. In general terms, where t is the rate of tax, the equation to find the present value of an annual leasehold interest will be

$$P = \frac{£1·00}{i_{(1)} + \dfrac{£1·00}{£1·00 - t} \cdot \dfrac{i_{(2)}}{(1 + i_{(2)})^n - 1}}$$

(Eq. 8.17)

Income tax will, in fact, affect all compound interest calculations and a similar adjustment must be made to the calculation of the present value of £1, mortgage instalment table and calculations for the annual sinking fund; tables suitably adjusted for various rates of tax will be found in the standard reference books.

The effect of taxation will depend on the individual circumstances of the client and for the remainder of this book calculation of cost in use comparisons will ignore this factor. Similarly, for simplicity of working, it has been assumed that single rate years purchase can be considered.

Conclusion

The derivation of the various tables described above shows the common relation to the basic formula for compound interest, and the commonly used tables have a relation expressed as follows:

Present value of £1

$$= \frac{1}{\text{Amount of £1}}$$

Present value of £1 per annum (years purchase)

$$= \frac{1}{\text{Mortgage instalment per annum}}$$

Mortgage instalment per annum

$$= \frac{\text{Interest on loan + annual}}{\text{sinking fund instalment}}$$

Present value of £1 per annum (years purchase)

$$= \frac{1}{\text{Interest on loan + annual sinking fund instalment}}$$

There is an additional table published for the amount of £1 per annum. This is the reciprocal of the annual sinking fund table and represents the amount, that is the total fund, which would result from annual investments of £1 made at the end of each year.

In the following section a series of problems are solved, firstly by the substitution of numerical values in the appropriate formulae, and secondly by application of data from valuation tables. In the first example the application of the data from the valuation table has been repeated to show the effect of using the reciprocal table.

Examples using Valuation Tables

AMOUNT OF £1

What is the amount of £200 invested for five years at an interest rate of 5 per cent?

from (Eq. 8.1)

$$\text{Amount} = £200 \left(1 + \frac{5}{100}\right)^5$$

$$= £200 \times 1 \cdot 276$$

$$= £255 \cdot 20$$

From tables for Amount of £1

£1 invested at 5 per cent will accumulate in 5 years to

£1·276

£200 invested will accumulate to £200 × 1·276

£200 invested will accumulate to £255·20

From table for Present Value of £1

£0·784 invested at 5 per cent will accumulate in 5 years to

£1

£1 invested will accumulate to $\dfrac{£1}{0 \cdot 784}$

£200 invested will accumulate to $\dfrac{£200}{0 \cdot 784}$

£200 invested will accumulate to £255·20

PRESENT VALUE OF £1

What is the present value or the sum which must be invested now to accumulate to £300 in 6 years at an interest rate of 7 per cent?

from (Eq. 8.3)

$$P = \frac{£300}{\left(1 + \dfrac{7}{100}\right)^6}$$

$$= £199 \cdot 80$$

From table for Present Value of £1

0·666 invested now at 7 per cent will accumulate in 6 years to £1

£300 × 0·666 invested will accumulate to £300

£199·80 invested will accumulate to £300

PRESENT VALUE OF £1 PER ANNUM

What is the present value of an annual income of £500 for ten years at an interest rate of 4 per cent? from (Eq. 8.6)

$$\text{Present Value} = 500 \left[\frac{\left(1 + \dfrac{4}{100}\right)^{10} - 1}{\dfrac{4}{100} \left(1 + \dfrac{4}{100}\right)^{10}} \right]$$

$$= 500 \left[\frac{1 \cdot 479 - 1}{0 \cdot 05917} \right]$$

$$= \frac{500 \times 0 \cdot 479}{0 \cdot 05917}$$

$$= £4048$$

From table for Present Value of £1 per annum, i.e. Single Rate Years Purchase

£8·111 invested now at 4 per cent will provide an annual income of £1 for 10 years.

£4,055 (i.e. £500 × 8·111) invested will provide £500 per annum

MORTGAGE INSTALMENT TABLE

What will be the monthly instalment to redeem a loan of £200 at 5 per cent in a period of five years? from (Eq. 8.7)

Repayment =

$$\frac{£200}{12} \left[\frac{\dfrac{5}{100} \times \left(1 + \dfrac{5}{100}\right)^5}{\left(1 + \dfrac{5}{100}\right)^5 - 1} \right]$$

$$= \frac{12 \cdot 76}{12 \times (1 \cdot 276 - 1)}$$

$$= £3 \cdot 854$$

From Mortgage Instalment table

1·925 is the monthly sum in £ to redeem £100 at 5 per cent in a period of 5 years

2 × 1·925 is the sum to redeem £200

£3·85 is the sum to redeem £200

ANNUAL SINKING FUND

What will be the annual sinking fund instalment to provide a fund of £50,000 at 5 per cent over 40 years? (Eq. 8.11)

$$\text{Annual instalment} = \frac{£50,000 \times \frac{5}{100}}{\left(1 + \frac{5}{100}\right)^{40} - 1}$$

$$= \frac{2,500}{7 \cdot 047 - 1}$$

$$= £413 \cdot 50$$

£0·008 is the annual sum invested to amount to £1 at 5 per cent over 40 years

£50,000 × 0·008 is the annual sum invested to amount to £50,000

£400 is the annual sum invested to amount to £50,000

PRESENT VALUE OF ANNUAL PAYMENTS, i.e. DUAL-RATE YEARS PURCHASE

What is the present value of an annual income of £1,000 at a rate of interest of 6 per cent after allowing for a sinking fund at a rate of 3½ per cent for a period of 30 years?

$$\text{Present Value} = \frac{£1,000}{\frac{6}{100} + \left[\frac{\frac{3½}{100}}{\left(1 + \frac{3½}{100}\right)^{30} - 1}\right]} \quad \text{from (Eq. 8.14)}$$

$$= \frac{1,000}{0 \cdot 06 + \left[\frac{0 \cdot 035}{2 \cdot 799 - 1}\right]}$$

$$= \frac{1,000}{0 \cdot 06 + 0 \cdot 01945}$$

$$= £12,590$$

From table for Year's Purchase (dual-rate principal)

£12,590 invested produces an annual income of £1 at 6 per cent after allowing for a sinking fund at 3½ per cent

£1,000 × 12·590 invested produces £1,000

£12,590 invested produces £1,000

9

Cost in Use—Application

Application of Valuation Tables to 'Cost in Use' Problems

Tables for use in this chapter will be found in Appendix E to the book.

EXAMPLE 1

Life of building: 80 years
Component 'A': initial and replacement costs £4,000
Life 20 years
Component 'B': initial and replacement costs £6,000
Life 40 years
Rate of Interest: 5 per cent

Component 'A' will be replaced after 20, 40, and 60 years. The cost of each replacement can be related to a value at the beginning of the period. The relation is between the amount, the cost of replacement at the various times in the future, and the present value or the principal in the formula:

$$\text{Principal} = \frac{\text{Amount}}{(1 + i)^n} \quad \text{from (Eq. 8.3)}$$

The value of the initial cost and the replacement at the start of the period will be

$$\text{Initial Cost} + \frac{\text{Replacement Cost}}{(1 + i)^{20}} + \frac{\text{Replacement Cost}}{(1 + i)^{40}}$$
$$+ \frac{\text{Replacement Cost}}{(1 + i)^{60}}$$

$$\text{or } £4,000 \left(1 + \frac{1}{1 \cdot 05^{20}} + \frac{1}{1 \cdot 05^{40}} + \frac{1}{1 \cdot 05^{60}}\right)$$

$$= £4,000 \,(1 + 0 \cdot 377 + 0 \cdot 142 + 0 \cdot 054)$$
$$= £4,000 \times 1 \cdot 573 = £6,292$$

Using published valuation tables the calculation may be set out as follows:

Present value of £1 at 5 per cent at 20 years 0·377

	40 years 0·142
	60 years 0·054
	0·573
Initial Cost	1·000
	1·573

Present value of £4,000

$$= £4,000 \times 1 \cdot 573$$

$$= £6,292$$

The calculation for Component 'B' would be

Present value of £1 at 5 per cent at 40 years 0·142

Initial Cost	1·000
	1·142

Present value of £6,000 = £6,852

The relationship between the initial and replacement costs of Components 'A' and 'B' = 1:1·089

The calculation in this form is only possible where the life of the building and the number of replacements are known. Where the life of the building is not known, an alternative approach, based on annual costs, must be used. If it is assumed that the initial cost of the Components is borrowed as if it were a mortgage and repaid during the life of the Component, the annual cost of such repayments can be compared to measure the financial implications of the choices.

EXAMPLE 2

Components 'A' and 'B', data as before.

The calculation for Component 'A'. From the mortgage instalment table the monthly sum in £s to reduce £100 at 5 per cent over a period of 20 years = £0·669.

Annual Cost:	$\frac{£4,000}{£100} \times 12 \times 0 \cdot 669 = £321$
For Component 'B':	monthly sum at 5 per cent over a period of 40 years = £0·486
Annual Cost:	$\frac{£6,000}{£100} \times 12 \times 0 \cdot 486 = £350$

Relationship between annual costs of Components 'A' and 'B' = 1:1·089

Since the replacement costs have been taken to be identical to the initial costs and the repayments must be paid throughout the life of the building, the ratio between the annual costs will be constant at all times.

It is often necessary to base the choice between specifications on both the initial costs and the subsequent maintenance costs, or, for a service installation, on the initial and running costs. Where annual running costs are to be considered, it will usually be easier to translate the initial and replacement capital costs into annual costs, as described in Example 2, as it reduces the number of references to the tables. However, it is possible to translate annual costs into capital value and this method is shown in the following example.

EXAMPLE 3

Life of building: 80 years
Installation 'A': initial and replacement costs £4,000
Life 20 years
Annual running costs £300
Installation 'B': initial and replacement costs £6,000
Life 40 years
Annual running costs £250
Rate of Interest: 5 per cent

The present value of initial and replacement costs, as in Example 1 is £6,290.

The present value of £1 per annum at 5 per cent over a period of 80 years = £19·596. Therefore the present value of £300 per annum = £300 x 19·596 = £5,879.

Total present value for Installation A = £12,169.

For Installation 'B' the present value of the initial and replacement costs was £6,852, as in Example 1.

Present value of running costs at 5 per cent over a period of 80 years

£250 x 19·596 = £4,899.

Total present value: £11,751.

Relationship between initial, replacement, and running costs of Installation 'A' and 'B' = 1:0·96.

EXAMPLE 4

Installations 'A' and 'B', data as before.
Annual cost of Installation 'A', as Example 2   £321

Annual running cost	£300
	£621
Annual cost of Installation 'B'	£350
Annual running cost	£250
	£600

Relationship between initial, replacement, and running costs of Installations 'A' and 'B' = 1:0·96.

The forms of calculation described above can be used to quantify the effect of design or specification decisions, but the techniques can also be used to show what decisions on specification must be made to produce some particular cost pattern or result. For example, there are many building techniques of proved efficiency. The method of financial analysis can be used to find what limit should be placed on the capital cost of alternatives to traditional solutions that might have a different life and different maintenance costs.

EXAMPLE 5

Find the maximum initial cost of an alternative to a traditional roof design with a life of 15 years and the same annual equivalent cost.

Traditional design and specification: tiled roof on timber substructure £50·00 per m^2 of roof area.

Expected life: 75 years
Rate of Interest: 5 per cent

The first step is to determine the annual equivalent cost of the roof:

Present value of £1 per annum at 5 per cent over a period of 75 years = £19·485 i.e. £19·485 invested gives an annual income of £1 for 75 years.

£50·00 invested or expended is equivalent to an annual sum of £50·00/19·485 for 75 years = £2·56.

The equivalent annual cost of the traditional roof is therefore £2·56.

The initial cost of an alternative design with a life of only 15 years and the same annual cost, is found as follows:

Present value of £1 per annum over 15 years = £10·380 i.e. £10·380 invested gives an annual income of £1 for 15 years.

It follows that 10·380 x £2·56 or £26·64 invested is equivalent to £2·56 for 15 years. The £2·56 can be regarded as the repayment of a loan of £26·64 and this payment throughout the whole life of the building and covers the four subsequent replacements.

If there is to be a financial advantage in building a temporary building, the roof with a short life must have a maximum initial cost of £26·64 per m^2 compared with the permanent structure with a cost of £50·00 per m^2, assuming the annual costs are to be the same.

EXAMPLE 6

If it is supposed that the life of the second alternative might be extended by annual maintenance work, this could be taken into account in the calculation. Check if the life could be extended by a factor of two by expending 20 per cent of annual cost on maintenance.

$$\text{Initial cost} = (\text{years purchase 30 years}) \times \frac{80}{100} \times \text{£2·56}$$

$$= 15·372 \times \frac{80}{100} \times \text{£2·56}$$

$$= \text{£31·48}$$

This means that an alternative with a life extended to 30 years by annual maintenance of £0·51 per m² (i.e. 20% of £2·56) would show a financial advantage if it could be designed for less than £31·48.

Comparison of Alternative Methods

In the examples above, the alternative approaches have been made to examine the financial balance between choices, and it has been shown that in any situation these different methods demonstrate the same ratio of costs. Example 1 showed that the present value of initial and replacement costs of Component 'A' was £6,292 over an 80-year period. Example 2 showed that the annual cost of the same Component was £321. These costs are related, and the figure of £6,292 must be the present value of an annual expenditure of £321. The present value of £1 per annum at 5 per cent over an 80-year period is £19·596, which, multiplied by an annual cost of £321 equals £6,292.

Where it is necessary to find the ratio of costs between alternatives, as in Examples 1 and 2, it is possible to devise a formula to give a direct comparison. The formula for the present value per annum is

$$\text{Annual cost} \frac{(1 + i)^n - 1}{i (1 + i)^n} \quad \text{from (Eq. 8.6)}$$

or Annual Cost =

$$\frac{\text{Present value (i.e. cost of Component)} \times i (1 + i)^n}{(1 + i)^n - 1}$$

If we are to compare two Components with costs C_1 and C_2 and with respective lives of X and Y years, the annual cost of the first Component would be

$$\text{Annual cost}_1 = \frac{C_1 \cdot (1 + i)^X i}{(1 + i)^X - 1}$$

The cost of the second alternative will, of course, be the same, but with the substitution of C_2 and Y. The ratio of the cost of the two Components will be, therefore,

$$\frac{\text{Annual Cost}_1}{\text{Annual Cost}_2} = \frac{C_1 (1 + i)^X i}{(1 + i)^X - 1} \times \frac{(1 + i)^Y - 1}{C_2 (1 + i)^Y i}$$

$$= \frac{C_1}{C_2} \left[\frac{(1 + i)^{(X + Y)} - (1 + i)^X}{(1 + i)^{(X + Y)} - (1 + i)^Y} \right]$$

$$\text{(Eq. 9.1)}$$

EXAMPLE 7

Components 'A' and 'B', data as Example 1.

$$\frac{\text{Annual Cost A}}{\text{Annual Cost B}} = \frac{4,000}{6,000} \times \frac{1 \cdot 05^{(40 + 20)} - 1 \cdot 05^{20}}{1 \cdot 05^{(40 + 20)} - 1 \cdot 05^{40}}$$

$$= \frac{2}{3} \times \frac{18 \cdot 68 - 2 \cdot 65}{18 \cdot 68 - 7 \cdot 04}$$

$$= \frac{2}{3} \times \frac{16 \cdot 03}{11 \cdot 64}$$

$$= \frac{1}{1 \cdot 089}$$

Examples 1–5 above compared alternatives that were similar in character, but the method can also be applied to design problems, which may have quite different solutions, or to the problems of relating the capital costs of development to rents, running costs, site values, etc.

EXAMPLE 8

Alternative A

Gross floor area of building: 3,000 m². Structural cost:

£300 per m²

Lighting cost: £5·00 per m² per annum. Heating and cleaning costs, etc.: £20·00 per m² per annum.
Building's life 100 years
Interest rate: 5 per cent.

Present value of £1 per annum at 5 per cent over a period of 100 years = £19·848. If the capital cost or present value is £900,000, this will produce an annual cost of

$$\frac{£900,000}{19 \cdot 848} = £45,344$$

	£
Annual cost	45,344
Lighting costs: 3,000 m² @ £5·00	15,000
Heating and cleaning costs: 3,000 m² @ £20	60,000
Total annual cost of Alternative A	£120,344

Alternative B

Based on the assumption that the introduction of mechanical ventilation and permanent artificial lighting makes it possible to use an alternative design with a lower floor area and reduced structural costs due to a more favourable wall to floor ratio, etc.

Building gross floor area: 2,500 m². Structural cost: £250 per m²
Lighting cost: £10 per m² per annum. Heating and cleaning cost: £20 per m² per annum
Mechanical ventilation: 1,500 m². Capital cost: £100 per m²
Installation Life: 25 years. Annual running cost: £12 per m²
Building life 100 years. Interest rate 5%

Building structure annual costs: $\dfrac{£625,000}{19·848}$ = £31,489

Lighting costs: 2,500 m² at £10 = £25,000

Heating and cleaning costs: 2,500 m²
    at £20 = £50,000

    £106,489

Mechanical Ventilation:
Present value of £1 per annum at 5 per
    cent over a period of 25 years: £14·094

Annual cost: $\dfrac{£100 \times 1,500}{14·094}$ = £10,642

Running cost: 1,500 m² at £12 = £18,000

Total annual cost of Alternative B = £135,131

EXAMPLE 9

Cost of site: £500,000
Net usable floor area: 8,000 m². Circulation space, plant
    rooms, etc. 1,000 m²
Building cost: £400 per m². Annual running costs,
    heating, etc.: £600,000
Fees, etc.: 20 per cent
Building life: 100 years. Interest rate: 5 per cent
Capital cost of building: £400 x 9,000 m² = £3,600,000
Present value of £1 per annum at 5 per cent over a
    period of 100 years: £19·848

Annual cost: $\dfrac{£3,600,000}{19·848}$ = £181,378

Fees, etc.: 20 per cent = £36,275
Running costs: £600,000
Assuming initial cost of site is borrowed at
    5 per cent and the loan will be redeemed
    by the sale of the site at the end of the
    period
Annual cost: £25,000

    £842,653

The annual cost of the net usable floor area from this calculation would be about £105 per m², and this figure would be the yardstick by which to measure the cost of leasing the alternative building.

The factors taken into consideration in this example are, of course, far simpler than would be found in practice. It might be more realistic to suppose that the capital cost of the building might be borrowed as a mortgage, with a short repayment period, and that a sinking fund was invested to replace the building at the end of its useful life.

If we assumed that this was an office building erected as an investment and could command a net rent of £125 per m², giving an annual income of £1,000,000 the profitability of the scheme should be judged by comparing this sum to the annual cost and not by comparing the annual return to the actual capital outlay at the beginning of the contract.

Where investment is concerned, it will normally be necessary to establish what the return will be after putting aside a contribution to a sinking fund to provide for replacement of the investment at the end of the period.

EXAMPLE 10

Capital building cost: £3,600,000
Sinking fund for replacement over 80 years at 3 per cent
Expected return on capital: 10 per cent

To find the annual rent necessary to provide a return of 10 per cent, the dual rate years purchase table is used. The present value of £1 per annum after allowing for a sinking fund at 3 per cent and with a return of 10 per cent over 80 years is £9·698. The annual rent should, therefore, be

$$\frac{£3,600,000}{9·698} = £371,210$$

This result can be checked as follows:

Annual sinking fund instalment to amount to £1 over a
    period of 80 years at 3 per cent = 0·003
Annual instalment to amount to £3,600,000 = 0·003
    x £3,600,000 = £10,800

If this figure is deducted from the gross rent calculated above, the remainder, £360,410, is the net return on the capital and equals a return of 10 per cent.

Conclusion

There are a number of general comments applicable to all the examples described above. Firstly, it has been assumed that it is possible to predict the life of the building accurately. For a building on a leasehold site, there will be a predetermined date at which it will cease to have any value to the leaseholder, and there may be other cases where the useful life of the building will be determined by some external factor. For example, the life of buildings associated with an airport might be determined by the growth in air traffic, which might make them unsuitable or redundant. For most other buildings the structure is likely to outlast the time span of the processes for which it is designed: there must be many industrial buildings whose use has changed several times during the life of the structure. The determining factors in deciding when a building will be demolished are the value of the site, the cost of adaptation or replacement, the changing standards of safety and welfare for the occupants, and other considerations that can be described as the 'social climate of opinion'. In short, buildings may be said to have a 'physical' and an 'economic' life span, and the only practical procedure is to work on the assumption that buildings are likely to be replaced at the end of the latter period. Since the calculations are little affected by the

change in the period where this exceeds 40–50 years, the accuracy of this prediction is not of great importance.

Similarly it is difficult to predict the life of materials; most materials used in building, provided that they are protected from the weather, will have an almost indefinite life. The only real exceptions to this are wearing surfaces such as floors, mechanical devices such as ironmongery, service installations, and possibly specific elements of the building such as the roof, which are subject to the risk of storm damage. It is again necessary, therefore, to base assumptions on experience of what has happened in the past, though it is equally certain that expenditure on maintenance may extend the life of even 'temporary' materials well beyond the purposes for which the building was designed. In these circumstances calculations cannot give a completely accurate prediction of cost, only an indication of an order of advantage.

The next problem is whether it is necessary to take into account future increases in building costs, which will affect maintenance and replacement. It would not be difficult to include some arbitrary factor for price increases in the basic calculations, though obviously there would be considerable difficulty in deciding what the factor should be. The answer to this problem is that, although these procedures are related to the rate of interest, the interest is not the only 'profit' made on an investment. In an expanding or inflating economy the value of investment will show a capital increase, an increase that is likely to be of the same magnitude as rises in the cost of building. For example, if we consider the simple instance of an industrial building, the processes carried out in the new building should add to the prosperity of the firm and to their ability to meet higher costs in the future. Again, there is the fact that companies and individuals can, in general, afford to maintain their premises and expand and redevelop on new sites despite the rising cost of building. This expansion is financed by the past or the prospective growth of their business, and the increased cost of building is met by the greater monetary value of their turnover and higher income they receive.

The problem of inflation is closely bound to the rate of interest, which may be considered to contain three components – risk, profit and inflation. Where there is a high rate of inflation, there will, of necessity, be a high rate of interest. As the interest rate is raised, the present value of a future payment, either annual or intermittent, is reduced, and, therefore, if it is assumed that future costs will be inflated, the higher costs will be counterbalanced by a correspondingly high interest rate. The assessment of cost-in-use calculations depends on the accuracy of the data that is used, and it is natural that quantity surveyors should be concerned that future costs are computed as carefully as

is possible. These calculations are, in fact, better considered as an examination of probabilities than as an accurate evaluation. In any case inflation will affect the cost of all the alternative solutions, and in most circumstances would not affect the order of advantage between one proposal and another.

The rate of interest is determined by the financial situation of the client. It may represent the rate of interest he must pay to borrow capital, or the return that he normally expects on his capital investments. A public body may use the bank rate, or a test rate of interest that may be established from time to time by the Treasury. It will usually be sensible to carry out cost-in-use calculations using a range of interest rates. This is known as a sensitivity analysis. If a range of possibilities is to be considered, the sensitivity analysis will show whether the order of preference changes at some point on the range, and it can then be considered whether this critical interest rate is relevant to the circumstances of the client. For example, if such an analysis showed that out of a range of choices a particular solution was advantageous at an interest rate of below 5 per cent and another at over 12 per cent, both might be discarded, since it is more likely that the client will borrow, or request a rate of return, within this range of interest rates.

There are other ways in which the data used in the calculations may be adjusted to deal with the future expenditure. In the examples earlier in this chapter it has been assumed that maintenance or replacement costs will be incurred at precise intervals of time. In practice, apart from planned preventative maintenance, it is unlikely that such a regular pattern would occur. The solution to this problem is to use probability theory (*See* Chapter 7). If an event is certain, it has a probability value of 1; if it is unlikely to happen, the value is zero. It might be thought certain that a particular component would have a maximum life of 50 years and a possible life pattern expressed in terms of probability as follows:

0–10	0
10–20	0·2
20–30	0·4
30–40	0·3
40–50	0·1
	1·0

The present value at each period could be calculated by multiplying the figure from the tables by the value of the replacement and the value of the probability at that time. By this means it would be certain the replacement costs of all the components would have been taken into account within a period of 50 years, but would also have taken into consideration the fact that some would have needed replacement after a life of only 10 to 20 years.

10
Economics of Planning

Development in Design

The architect's problem in designing a building is to relate his client's brief to the requirements of the site, available forms of construction, and statutory planning requirements in the light of his experience and his personal inspiration. In the course of this process his decisions may be controlled by a cost limit imposed by the brief, and he should be conscious of the cost implications of every choice of design and specification that he makes. The cost of the building is determined by every decision made and, just as initial design decisions will affect a continuing series of inter-related developments throughout the design period, decisions on costs will also affect and be affected by the development of his ideas.

Given a brief, the architect can start to design the building. During the early stages he will formulate his ideas and decide upon the disposition of the accommodation, the shape of the building, and the general form of construction and specification. This is a complex activity; interplay of one factor with another and the interaction of design and specification render it impracticable to consider separately the various factors affecting building costs. The effect of building shape cannot, for example, be divorced from that of differing forms of construction. It is convenient, however, to consider basic problems, initially at least, under two headings:

1. Design or quantity decisions, which govern general and detailed planning and the ultimate appearance of the building
2. Specification decisions, which concern the quality of the material used in the building and the standard of work-manship required.

Under both headings it is necessary to distinguish between 'key' decisions – those which have irreversible effect on a building or project, say its basic plan shape or height – and 'incidental' decisions, which can be changed up to the time of construction without any fundamental effect on the building design, as, for instance, the specification of tiling in bathrooms.

Advice in the early design stages will usually relate to 'key' decisions. One of the earliest the architect will have to resolve will be the shape of the building, since this decision may well influence more than any other the final cost of the building.

Plan Shape of Building

The plan shape of a building will affect not only the external cladding elements, i.e. external walls, windows and external doors, but also the internal vertical elements such as partitions and the services, both heating and plumbing.

The full effect of plan shape is not always easy to establish, but a simple method can be devised of relating the amount of external cladding elements to the superficial floor area of the building so as to reveal the effect of different plan shapes. The relation can be expressed as a ratio of the area of the external cladding elements to the floor area of the building, and is commonly referred to as the external cladding to floor ratio.

In Figure 10.1, A, B, and C represent the outlines of three buildings of a constant height of 3 metres, each containing 225 square metres of floor area. Plan A is a compact plan with a perimeter of 60 metres; Plan B, a less compact plan with a perimeter of 74 metres; and Plan C a plan with a perimeter of 84 metres.

Table 10.1

Example	Area of External Cladding Elements, m^2	Floor Area, m^2	Ratio of External Cladding Elements to Floor Area	Base Plan A 100
Plan A	180	225	0·80	100
Plan B	222	225	0·99	124
Plan C	252	225	1·12	140

This example (Table 10.1) demonstrates that the more compact the plan can be made and the nearer it is kept to the square, the more economic it will be in terms of the area (and, therefore, the cost) of the external cladding elements – Plan A being the square, Plan B is 24 per cent and Plan C 40 per cent more expensive.

It is necessary to consider size in relation to plan shape. Small buildings will require a higher proportion of external cladding elements to floor area than large buildings, and it will not always be possible to reduce the proportions, even though they may appear on initial examination to be high. Consider building A, size 15 metres by 15 metres, and

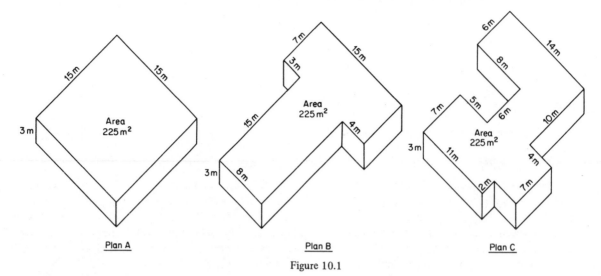

Figure 10.1

compare this with a similarly shaped building D, size 150 metres by 150 metres, as in Table 10.2.

Building A is, therefore, proportionately more expensive so far as the amount of external cladding is concerned by

$$\frac{0.72 \times 100}{0.08} = 900 \text{ per cent}$$

Table 10.2

Example	Area of External Cladding Elements, m^2	Floor Area, m^2	Ratio of External Cladding Elements to Floor Area	Base Plan A 100
Plan A	180	225	0.8	100
Plan D	1,800	22,500	0.08	10

From this second example we can conclude that where the choice exists between enclosing an area in one large building or in two or more smaller buildings, it will almost certainly be more economical to choose to provide the accommodation in the larger building. If we were considering only external cladding elements, this would be absolutely true, but other factors such as servicing and lighting requirements must serve to qualify this conclusion. It is also worth noting that an external corner column will only be carrying a quarter of a bay and will be eccentrically loaded, this being less economical than an internal column. It follows, therefore, that a rectangular plan shape with only four external corner columns will be more economical than an irregular plan shape with numerous corner columns.

Storey Height

Storey height will largely be determined by the needs of the user of the building. A greater height than is necessary to provide comfortable conditions may be required to accommodate large machinery or equipment, overhead cranes, etc. Like the plan shape, the storey height will affect the vertical elements of the building both internally and externally, and will also have some effect on the costs of services, particularly heating, due to the increased volume of the building.

The effect on the external cladding elements can be simply demonstrated if the diagrams of buildings A, B, and C are re-examined and a comparison made between the original height of 3 metres and an alternative height of 4 metres.

Table 10.3 sets out the results of this comparison and reveals the importance of examining both plan shape and storey height, together with the area of the building, before concluding that a particular design is economic or otherwise. A high-storeyed building will cost more per square metre of floor area than one with a lower storey height, other factors being equal, and will also have a higher external cladding to floor area ratio. The cost of the vertical elements will be affected in direct relation to the change in storey height. For example, if the vertical elements totalled £80 per square metre of floor area on a building with a storey height of 3 metres, the total analysed cost of which was, say, £280 per square metre of gross floor area, it could be expected that a similar building planned to a 4 metres height would cost

$$£280 - £80 + \left(\frac{4m}{3m} \times £80\right)$$

$$= £200 + £106.66$$

$$= £306.66$$

This calculation will apply only if the change is confined to storey height, the building being similar in all other respects. Quantity factors, however, can be employed,

regardless of whether the change occurs to plan shape or storey height, as shown by the following examples based on the buildings illustrated in Figure 10.1.

analyses, which will give costs expressed per square metre of gross floor area of the building. The client is primarily interested in the total floor area that can be put to use for

Table 10.3

Example	Area of External Cladding, m²		Floor Area m²	Ratio of External Cladding Elements to Floor Area		Relative Cost: Base Plan A x 3m high = 100	
	3m high	4m high		3m high	4m high	3m high	4m high
Plan A	180	240	225	0·80	1·07	100	134
Plan B	222	296	225	0·99	1·32	124	165
Plan C	252	336	225	1·12	1·49	140	186

Analysis – Building Plan A – storey height 3m
   Total cost £280 per square metre
   Cost of external cladding elements £80 per square metre
   Ratio of external cladding elements to floor area = 0·80

Required – Cost of Building Plan A but storey height 4m

$$£200 + \left(\frac{1·07}{0·80} \times £80\right) = £307·00$$

Required – Cost of Building Plan C with storey height 4m

$$£200 + \left(\frac{1·49}{0·80} \times £80\right) = £349·00$$

These examples illustrate the use of quantity factors and the importance of stating the quantity factor against the analysed costs per square metre of floor area of the building if maximum value is to be obtained from the analysis in any future cost-planning exercise.

Single and Multi-Storey Building

Generally the cost of a building per square metre of floor area can be expected to increase with the addition of extra storeys. The introduction of a frame, the necessity to hoist materials, the need to meet regulations on fire escapes, and the introduction of lifts, etc. will add to costs, although the extra costs may be partially offset by savings on service layouts, repetitive planning, efficient use of tower cranes, etc.

GROSS AND NET FLOOR AREAS

The cost relation between single and multi-storey building will not always be revealed by the simple examination of cost

his own purposes, and the area occupied by toilet accommodation, plant rooms, corridors, staircases, entrance halls, etc., while being necessary for the proper functioning of the building, are of little real value to the client. It is possible to consider a building in terms of the gross floor area and also the net usable area, the building client being much more interested in the net usable floor area, though the architect will be restricted by various planning regulations based on the gross floor area. The best value for money will be obtained by keeping the difference between these two areas to the absolute minimum.

Before considering costs, it is necessary to examine the effect of an increase in the number of storeys on the relation between net and gross areas.

In Figure 10.2 plans F and G show two buildings with identical plan areas, F being single-storey and G two-storey. While the gross area of building G is double that of building F, the introduction of a staircase has caused a severe reduction in the net usable area, and even though the total cost per m² of the two buildings may be similar, the cost of providing the net usable area may be very different.

This can be examined as follows: assume an analysed cost for both buildings of £250 per square metre of gross floor area. The cost per square metre of net usable area would be

Single-storey building F = $\frac{240 \times £250}{210}$ = £285·71 per square metre of usable area

Two-storey building G = $\frac{480 \times £250}{367·5}$ = £326·53 per square metre of usable area

It will be seen in Chapter 13 that office rents are assessed on the lettable, i.e. usable area of a building, and if the above example is related to an office block, then a higher capital charge would have to be deducted from the rent and therefore the client would clearly consider building F the better value for money. The effect on the relation between net usable and gross floor areas of changes above two-storeys would probably not be as great as the change illustrated in the above example, as a staircase would then be a constant feature of the plan.

As a general rule, the best plan ratios will be obtained from single-storey building, but the local planning authority will advise the architect on permitted site density, plot ratio, or the maximum number of persons to be housed per acre; and in these days of high site costs the architect will endeavour to make the maximum use of the land, which may lead to multi-storey building.

A commercial building will receive a plot ratio figure — for example, 4:1, which means that if the site is 1,000 square metres in area, then the maximum total floor area permitted is 4,000 square metres, which can be provided in any number of storeys.

The illustrations in Figure 10.3 show alternative ways in which the area can be provided.

The four-storey design may be cheaper structurally but the depth of building will probably call for permanent artificial lighting and ventilating systems, whereas the eight-storey design may avoid the latter two items but require a frame and a lift installation. The twelve-storey design will certainly be more expensive because, although avoiding the lighting and ventilating problems, other requirements such as fire escape provisions, extensive lift installation, etc. will become necessary. The twelve-storey design may, however, be the best solution for aesthetic reasons, and it may also have advantages from the letting viewpoint if, for example, market research has shown that prospective tenants for the particular building require between 500 and 1,000 square metres. If the choice of a particular number of storeys conveniently divides a building into floors of a convenient usable or lettable area, then advantages for letting may outweigh the extra building costs.

How are costs likely to vary with the number of storeys? Costs can again be considered against the elements of the building and if the costs in terms of the unit rate of the element are assumed to be constant, i.e. the specification remains unaltered, the changes in cost can easily be appreciated by examination of the element quantity factors. The changes will vary in different proportions depending upon (1) whether the total floor area of the building remains constant, as building (1) in Figure 10.4; or (2) whether the plan area remains constant with the additional floors adding to the total floor area, as building (2) in Figure 10.4; and this can be illustrated by examining each of the elements in turn.

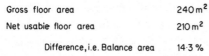

Single storey

Gross floor area	240 m²
Net usable floor area	210 m²
Difference, i.e. Balance area	14·3 %

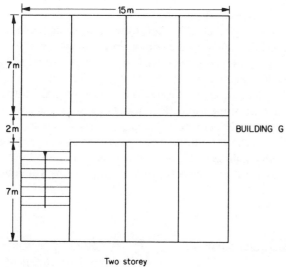

Two storey

Gross floor area	480 m²
Net usable floor area	367·5 m²
Difference, i.e. Balance area	30·6 %

Figure 10.2

Foundations

The sizing of foundation bases or load-bearing strips will vary in proportion to the load being carried, which will increase as more upper floors are introduced. The foundation slab will have a constant unit rate and its cost, in terms

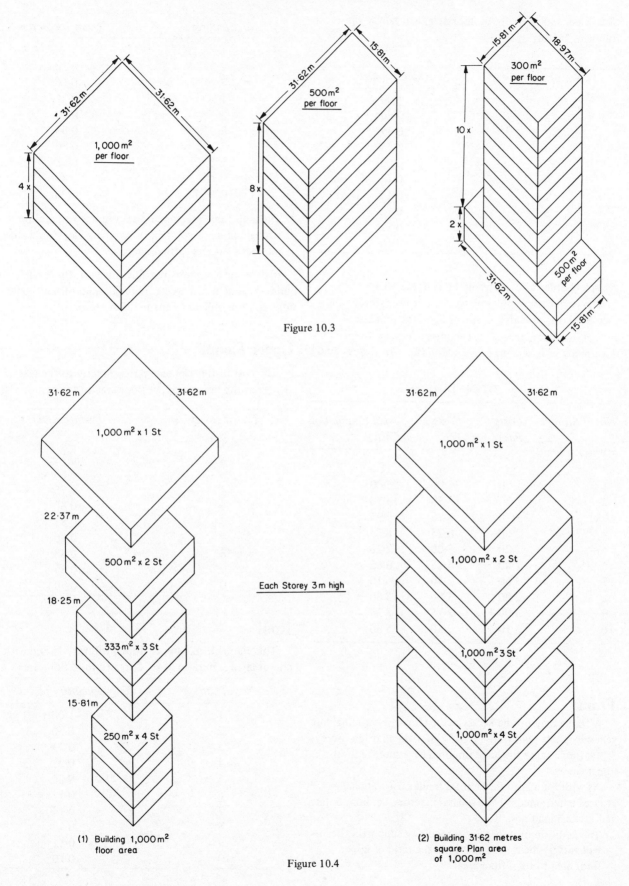

Figure 10.3

Each Storey 3m high

(1) Building 1,000 m² floor area

(2) Building 31·62 metres square. Plan area of 1,000 m²

Figure 10.4

of cost per square metre of floor area, will fall by the following factor:

No. of storeys	Quantity factor
1	1·00
2	0·50
3	0·33
4	0·25
5	0·20
6	0·17
7	0·14
8	0·12
9	0·11
10	0·10

A typical order of costs would be as Table 10.4.

The costs drop rapidly up to three or four storeys and then level off, probably to rise again as the number of storeys increases, or when it becomes necessary to introduce piling or basement construction (*see also Appendix C*).

Table 10.4

No. of Storeys	Costs: Bases	Costs: Slab	Total Foundation Cost
	£	£	£
1	1·00	25·00	26·00
2	1·20	12·50	13·70
3	1·70	8·25	9·95
4	2·00	6·25	8·25
5	2·20	5·00	7·20
6	2·40	4·25	6·65
7	2·60	3·50	6·10
8	2·80	3·00	5·80
9	3·00	2·75	5·75
10	3·10	2·50	5·60

Frame

A frame may not be necessary in a low-rise building, but generally costs tend to rise rapidly over the first few storeys as the frame takes the loads imposed by a succession of upper floors.

As with foundations, the total frame cost will change at rates determined by two separate factors, i.e. horizontal and vertical loadings.

1. The addition of upper floors requiring supporting beams will vary at the rate of change in the ratio of upper floor area to total floor area:

No. of storeys	Quantity factor
1	—
2	0·50
3	0·66
4	0·75
5	0·80
6	0·83
7	0·86
8	0·88
9	0·89
10	0·90

2. The additional loading on the columns will require strengthening of columns or reducing bay sizes as the number of floors carried increases.

If the total floor area remains constant, the smaller building on plan will create more perimeter frame conditions and this will add a further cost factor.

Upper Floors

The cost of this element varies directly to the rate of change in the ratio of upper floor area to total floor area:

No. of storeys	Quantity factor
1	—
2	0·50
3	0·66
4	0·75
5	0·80
6	0·83
7	0·86
8	0·88
9	0·89
10	0·90

Roof

This element, like upper floors, will vary in line with the rate of change in ratio of roof area to total floor area:

No. of storeys	Quantity factor
1	1·00
2	0·50
3	0·33
4	0·25
5	0·20
6	0·17
7	0·14
8	0·12
9	0·11
10	0·10

Staircases

Obviously, no staircases are necessary in a single-storey building, but at least one staircase will be required in a two-storey building, and the need for fire escapes in three storeys will make two staircases mandatory. Examination of existing buildings in categories of type of building indicates that the cost of staircases is reasonably constant for two storeys and above, economic planning providing a reasonably constant level of utilization of each staircase.

External Walls, Windows and External Doors

The cost of these elements will vary according to the size and plan shape of the building, the number of storeys, and storey height. The nature of the variation in these elements in particular will depend mainly on the two factors: (1) whether the total floor area remains constant; and (2) whether the total floor area changes while the plan area remains constant.

If the first factor applies, the ratio of the area of the element to floor area will change appreciably because of the principle discussed earlier, i.e. small buildings will require a higher proportion of external cladding elements to floor area than large buildings, the size being related to plan area. If, however, the second factor applies, the change in the ratio of the element to floor area will be minimal, if in fact it changes at all, only a change in storey height having any appreciable effect.

An indication of the changes is given in the following table based on the buildings illustrated in Figure 10.4, for (1) a building with 1,000 square metres of floor area; and (2) a building 31·62 metres square with a plan area of 1,000 square metres:

| No. of storeys | Quantity factors | |
	1. Constant area	2. Constant plan area
1	0·38	0·38
2	0·54	0·38
3	0·65	0·38
4	0·76	0·38
10	1·20	0·38

Partitions

Partitions will be the internal element most affected by changes in plan shape, although the nature of the effect is difficult to assess with any accuracy, as it depends a great deal upon the type of building being considered.

If we examine detailed cost analyses for domestic buildings, we find that as the enclosing wall to floor ratio changes so also does the internal partition to floor ratio, but in the opposite direction, often to the extent that the costs to all intents and purposes exactly compensate each other; we can say, therefore, that differences of plan shape in the structure have little to no effect. This arises because of the very high density of internal partitioning called for in a domestic building in order to provide a large number of small rooms.

On the other end of the scale we can consider a factory type of building, which will have a very small amount of internal partitioning. In this case the enclosing wall to floor ratio value will have its maximum effect, and as the building perimeter moves further from the square so the cost will increase.

Internal Doors

The cost of this element will be controlled by the same factors as the partitions.

Wall, Floor and Ceiling Finishes and Decorations

Wall finishes and decorations applied to the external walls and internal partitions will be affected similarly to those two elements. Floor and ceiling elements, being horizontal in the building, are directly related to the floor area and will, therefore, only change as floor area changes.

Services

The effect of planning changes on heating services is discussed in Chapter 12, but it can be noted here that service costs will increase with a jump at three or four storeys when it becomes necessary to install a lift. The effect will lessen as additional storeys are added, provided the area per floor is economically served. For example, if a lift will serve say 800 square metres of floor area per floor, then changes in the number of storeys that reduce the area below 800 square metres will cause the installation to appear more expensive when related to a cost per square metre of floor area.

11

Economics of Construction

During the design stages the Architect or Engineer will have to make decisions on the form of construction to be employed to meet the various elemental requirements.

Structural Frame

If a multi-storey framed building is under consideration, an early decision will be required whether to use structural steel or reinforced concrete. A number of considerations may influence the choice. The most important of these will be the suitability of the structure to its purpose but other factors, such as the influence of the frame on the construction programme, the influence that it will have on the design of other components, and the effect on the cost of the building must be taken into account. The fact that the two materials can exist side by side indicates that the balance of advantage is small and it would be unwise to suggest that either method will have economic advantages without a thorough investigation of all the circumstances.

The structural engineer's advice will obviously take into account all the factors that affect the choice between two systems, but his main responsibility will be the suitability of the system for the building design. On an irregularly shaped site or for a building with irregular loading conditions it may be easier to design a frame using steel and to accept the disadvantages of irregularly sized columns and beam casings. Such a design would also be possible in concrete, but the irregularity may result in high costs for the formwork. Conversely, in a building with a regular plan and constant concrete sections, repetition of formwork sizes may produce economies that will allow a concrete frame to show positive advantages.

Reinforced concrete design also allows a certain amount of flexibility in that various loading conditions may be accommodated within a design by adjusting the quantity of reinforcing steel and keeping the column and beam sizes constant. The extra expense of using rather more concrete than might structurally be necessary is often offset by the repetition of wall or window units.

The engineer will be well aware of the necessity of protecting a multi-storey steel structure against fire. It is probable that a simple pre-cast steel structure would be cheaper than reinforced concrete to meet the same loading conditions, but this advantage may be lost when the steel is cased for fire protection. Similarly, the advantage of speed of erection of the steel frame may be lost if the time to erect column and beam casings providing in-situ concrete fire protection is taken into account.

The architect will have to consider the effect that the choice of frame will have on the general design of the building and of the details of particular elements. The most obvious effect, apart from the size of frame members and casings, will be the design of the floors. With a steel frame these are likely to be some form of precast concrete unit or a composite hollow tile in-situ floor. If this is the case, it is unlikely that the designer will be able to assume that the floor will provide any structural strength to the building. In a concrete frame the floor and beam design may be considered together, and this will almost certainly reduce the depth of beams, and, with some systems of design, the beams may be omitted altogether. This may lead to a number of economies: (i) a much more simple structure, which will allow speedier building; (ii) it may be much easier to accommodate services; (iii) it may permit the omission of suspended ceilings; and (iv) there may be a general saving in height on each storey level of the building, with consequent savings on the internal walls.

From the contractor's point of view there are advantages and disadvantages in both systems. A steel-framed structure can usually be erected more quickly than an in-situ concrete frame, but it will usually be impossible for any general site work to be carried out while the steel is being erected and plumbed. This means that the contractor is faced with a break in his structural programme between completing the foundations and starting to erect the floors and cladding the building. This may result in a loss of impetus on the site and possible labour difficulties, which will be avoided if continuity can be maintained. With a concrete frame constructional work can be programmed to allow erection of the frame, floors and cladding, floor level by floor level, and as soon as proper time has been allowed for the concrete to obtain its working strength, work on partitions and finishes can be started.

The problem of working on site is further complicated by the question of cranes and hoists. Where a complete steel frame has been erected, it may be difficult to arrange the cranes to allow materials to be brought to various floor levels and to the enclosed sections of the building. This problem will not usually arise in reinforced concrete frame.

Further factors that have a bearing on the choice of frame are the local conditions of access to the site, availability of labour and materials, etc. For example, it may be possible to obtain steel sections from local suppliers at reasonable rates and with minimum transport charges, but on a site remote from steelworks the cost of haulage may prove too expensive. Similarly, the size and position of the site must be considered. It might be that the access is so constricted that it is impossible to bring in large steel members, but site restriction may make it difficult to find room for a concrete plant.

The amount of labour available must also be taken into account. If there is a shortage of carpenters, the consequent delays on formwork might make the use of an in-situ concrete system impossible. Although this difficulty might affect the use of steel, the delays in forming beam casings might not have a great effect on the progress of the work, and, in any case, may be overcome by using prefabricated casings.

All the above points have to be taken into account in making a choice between a steel and an in-situ concrete frame; a different range of possibilities would be open if the choice lay between steel and a precast concrete frame, or if the building was a type that did not call for fire protection of the steel.

Roof Construction

A further example is provided by consideration of roof structure.

A roof may be flat or pitched and covered with felt, asphalt, zinc, aluminium copper, lead, tiles, etc.

The following quote is taken from a paper prepared by an architect who occupies the position of a client with many years of experience of his building in use.

'In a large proportion of the new buildings, the architectural design has resulted in a flat roof form. This can entail disproportionately high costs in heat insulation, concrete roof slabs, screeds and surfacing materials, roof drainage and in providing support in the structure for the heavy materials used in the roof treatment. If one accepts that the roof is the main defence against the rigours of an English climate, it follows that capital expenditure related to incidence of maintenance is of paramount importance. Many proprietary surfacing media for flat roofs are in use, but almost all entail specialist attendance when maintenance work becomes necessary and at high cost.

Many roofs of this type are also formed without proper regard to the treatment of roof surfacing materials at abutments and at eaves of buildings where roof surfacing is often finished with specialist flashing pieces in place of the more orthodox and time-proved methods

imposing almost insoluble problems for those engaged in subsequent maintenance.

A further maintenance problem arising from the provision of flat roofs as compared with pitched roofs, affects the services within the building. One of the greatest problems in the maintenance of a heavily serviced laboratory building is to carry out regular maintenance inspection and work, and at the same time limit the inconvenience to the occupying departments as much as possible. With the provision of a pitched roof, it is possible to take rising mains for the services involved directly into the roof space from which points they can be taken with complete freedom to the points at which they should drop to the laboratories concerned. Maintenance personnel can operate in the roof voids quite divorced from the work going on in any particular laboratory, and alterations to the disposition of services can be effected without interfering with decorations or laboratory fitments below. This is to be compared with the inflexible vertical ducts from ground level to each laboratory, often formed with a minimum of access facilities and at increased cost, necessary when roof voids are not available. Where flat roof construction in heavily serviced buildings is adopted, it is not unusual to find an additional floor at the top of the building constructed at high cost to provide perhaps in a more luxurious form, conditions which could, to a very large extent, be achieved by pitched roof construction'.

The difficulties of carrying out maintenance and repair work and the inconvenience to the client should not be ignored, although these factors may be difficult to quantify.

Roof structure is one of the elements more easily dealt with, as life periods of the various materials used in the roofs are now well established, making it possible for the quantity surveyor to present a 'value for money' report to the architect and client to assist them in making their final decision.

Table 11.1 provides an indication of the order of initial capital costs for a range of roof finishings, and in the lower half of this table the effect of the need to maintain and renew certain of these materials has been taken into account to give the 'costs in use' for the various finishes, which in turn have been calculated against a range of periods of 'economic life of building'.

Two points arising from Table 11.1 highlight the value of carrying out this sort of exercise. The first is the change in ratios between the costs of various finishes, as the shorter life and cheaper finishes are used on the longer life building. The second is the alternative approach to the felt roof finish. Felt roofs if left alone, apart from repairing any leaks that may occur, will probably last about 20 years and the 'costs in use' for this approach is shown in the first column. If, on the other hand, a planned maintenance programme is

Table 11.1

'Costs in Use' of Various Roof Finishes (excluding Effect on Heating Costs)

(Costs in £ per square metre)

FLAT ROOFS:

Roof Structure	Cost	Initial Capital Cost of Roof Finishes						
		3-layer felt 19 mm Asphalt BS 988	19 mm Asphalt BS 1162	Zinc 14G	Aluminium 20G	Copper 24G	Lead 4 lb	
Timber construction joists and boarding	21·00							
Reinforced concrete with cement and sand screed	25·00	7·50 9·25	12·50	25·00	26·00	35·00	40·00	
Predicted Life (years) (Minimal periodic maintenance except *)		20 30* 40	40	40	100+	100+	100+	

PITCHED ROOF:

Roof Structure	Cost	Finish	Cost
Timber construction TRADA truss, battens and felt	25·00	Tiles	22·00
Predicted Life (years)			70

'COSTS IN USE' (Interest rate 5%)

Capitalized Initial and Running Costs of Roof Finishes

Economic Life of Building	3-layer felt	19 mm Asphalt BS 988	19 mm Asphalt BS 1162	Zinc 14G	Aluminium 20G	Copper 24G	Lead 4 lb	Tiles
20 years	7·50	8·30	9·25	12·50	25·00			22·00
40 years	10·33	10·35	9·25	12·50	25·00	26·00		22·00
60 years	11·37	10·52	10·55	14·30	28·55	35·00	40·00	22·00
80 years	11·77	10·93	10·55	14·30	28·55			22·73
100 years	11·94	11·04	10·75	14·50	29·05			22·73

(The values 26·00, 35·00 and 40·00 are braced as constant capitalized values across the economic lives.)

* Substantial maintenance every 5 years.

72

followed and the roof is given a complete bitumen treatment every 5 years, the life will probably be extended by 10 years to about 30 years. It can be seen from the table that the second approach is likely to provide the better value for money once the economic life of the building extends beyond the 40-year period.

12
Economics of Services—Heating

Heating Installations

The Ministry of Public Buildings and Works Research and Development Paper, published in 1967, entitled *Heating Installations* points out that, under cost control during design, the cost of a heating installation is the product of two factors:

1. Quantity of heat required, which is largely dependent on the architect's design skill.
2. Cost per unit, which is largely dependent on the engineer's design skill.

The quantity of heat required to maintain a comfortable temperature level inside a building will depend on a number of factors:

1. The shape and size of the building.
2. The thermal transmittance, i.e. U value, of the external surfaces.
3. The orientation and degree of exposure.
4. The amount of ventilation.

A change in any of these factors will affect the capital cost of the heat source (for example, boiler plant and boiler house) and distribution system (for example, pipes and radiators), and also the maintenance and running costs, particularly the fuel costs.

The inclusion of a specialist heating engineer in the design team is essential if the full effects of design decisions are to be assessed and the results used to produce an economic building solution.

Cost advice available to the design team will necessarily rely on information from past schemes and reasonably accurate assessing.

Analysed costs are often expressed in terms of (1) total cost, (2) the cost per kilowatt, and (3) the cost per square metre of floor area, divided between cost of heat source, distribution cost and emission cost. Information given in this form can be used when considering cost plans and the use of quantity factors.

When more detailed costings are required, it may be necessary to approach nearer to first principles, especially when advice is required on the cost affect of a change in specification.

At the design stage a key decision will have to be taken concerning the plant layout and type of fuel to be used.

Space heating, ventilation, and hot-water requirements will need to be estimated, and for this purpose the following formulae will produce a reasonably accurate result:

Max. rate of Heat Loss $= A \times U \times \Delta t$ (watts)

Max. hourly Heat Demand $= A \times U \times \Delta t \times \dfrac{3600}{1000}$ (kJ)

$$\text{(Eq. 12.1)}$$

A = total surface area of structure (m^2)
U = thermal transmittance of structure (W/m^2 deg. C)
Δt = difference between internal and external design temperatures (deg. C)

(*Note:* watts = joules/second.)

Max. hourly Heat $= s \times d \times V \times N \times \Delta t$ (kJ) (Eq. 12.2)
Demand for Ventilation

$s \times d$ = specific heat air × density of air
(kJ/kg × kg/m^3 = kJ/m^3)

(*Note:* A value of 0·7 can be used for approximation.)
V = volume of building (m^3)
N = number of air changes per hour

The sum of equations 12.1 and 12.2 plus, say, 5 per cent for hot water supplies gives the maximum hourly demand on the installation and therefore determines the boiler capacity.

The U (i.e. thermal transmittance) value can be calculated or taken from tables such as those in the guide published by the Institution of Heating and Ventilating Engineers. In a building consisting of areas of different construction the average U value will be found by totalling the sum of the areas multiplied by U values of the different forms of construction and dividing by the total area:

$$\text{i.e. Average } U \text{ value} = \frac{\text{Sum of areas} \times U \text{ values}}{\text{total area}}$$

The orientation and degree of exposure of the site will significantly affect the thermal transmittance of the structural component. Three grades of exposure are the following:

1. Sheltered – which includes the first two storeys above ground level of buildings within towns.
2. Normal – which includes the third, fourth and fifth storeys of buildings within towns and most suburban and country premises.

74

3. Severe – which includes the sixth and higher storeys of buildings within towns and buildings situated on exposed hill sites or close to the coast.

A range of typical thermal transmittance values, i.e. U values, for windows is given in Table 12.1.

Table 12.1
Typical Thermal Transmittance Values (W/m² deg. C)

Orientation	Exposure		
	Sheltered	Normal	Severe
Window: single glazed	4·00	4·50	5·00
double glazed	2·65	2·85	3·05

The value of Δt will be $16°C$ if it is assumed that the maximum heating load placed on a system will occur when the outside design temperature is $0°C$ and the inside design temperature is $16°C$.

An inside design temperature of $16°C$ will satisfy most requirements. The Offices, Shops, and Railway Premises Act of 1963 requires a temperature of not less than $16°C$ to be maintained inside a building, and the Parker Morris report on Housing recommends $12·5°C$ for kitchen and circulation areas up to $18°C$ in living areas. Using $0°C$ as the outside temperature may mean that on about fifteen days of the year, when the outside temperature drops below $0°C$, the heating plant would not have the capacity to maintain the internal temperature, but the ability of structures to store and release heat slowly, rather like night storage heaters, would render this apparent deficiency acceptable. The Parker Morris report on Housing recommends working from an outside temperature of $-1°C$, which would reduce the deficiency period to about ten days. It is questionable, however, whether the effect of this $1°C$ difference reflected in the cost of plant is justifiable.
(*See footnote on p. 81 on the effect of Building Regulations 1976.*)

Internal Design or 'Base' Temperature

It has been found by experiment that no heating is required to maintain an inside temperature approximately $2°C$ above the outside temperature, and for this reason the internal design or base temperature can be taken at $2°C$ below the desired room temperature.

A large development project totalling 200,000 m² may produce an estimated requirement for a heating installation capable of meeting a peak demand of 25,000 kW.

Knowledge of the peak demand will enable alternative ways of meeting the demand to be examined. Boiler sizes can be established, and the alternatives of locating the boilers in a central boiler house or in a number of localized boiler houses can be examined.

Boilers, whether fired by coal, oil or gas, will have similar space requirements, and it may be possible on a project to locate the heat source in (1) a single central boiler house, or (2) four zoned boiler houses, or (3) boiler houses located in each building to be served. Assuming an oil-fired system the estimated capital costs may amount to:

1. *Central boiler-house system*
	£
8 x 3,500 kW boilers	280,000
Oil storage tanks and compound	120,000
Boiler house, including chimneys	200,000
Plant and installation	100,000
Site distribution mains and ducts	350,000
	£1,050,000

   $$\frac{£1,050,000}{200,000 \text{ m}^2} = £5·25 \text{ per m}^2$$

2. *Four zoned boiler-house system*
	£
12 x 2,500 kW boilers	240,000
Oil storage tanks and compounds	150,000
Boiler houses, including chimneys	260,000
Plant and installation	175,000
Site distribution mains and ducts	325,000
	£1,150,000

   $$\frac{£1,150,000}{200,000 \text{ m}^2} = £5·75 \text{ per m}^2$$

3. *Local boiler houses in buildings to be served*
	£
60 x 500 kW boilers	750,000
Oil storage tanks and compounds	350,000
Boiler houses, including chimneys	700,000
Plant and installation	400,000
	£2,200,000

   $$\frac{£2,200,000}{200,000 \text{ m}^2} = £11·00 \text{ per m}^2$$

The boiler ratings are higher than the estimated requirements to allow for stand-by facilities in the event of breakdowns and a design margin.

If alternatives (1) or (2) are considered, it is necessary to estimate the cost of the calorifiers and calorifier rooms that would be required in the buildings to be served. The cost of this provision is estimated at £4·00 to make the comparative costs.

	£ per m² of floor area served
1. Central boiler-house system	9·25
2. Four-zoned boiler-house system	9·75
3. Local boiler-house system	11·00

The advantages of the central boiler-house system are
1. Capital costs are less.
2. Less standby equipment is required.
3. Less labour is required to operate and maintain the system
4. Greater boiler efficiency is achieved by better utilization of capacity.
5. Atmospheric pollution is reduced to a minimum, since centralized plant under skilled supervision can be controlled efficiently.
6. Bulk storage of fuel in fewer tanks is cheaper and fuel delivery is facilitated.
7. A single chimney is easier to treat architecturally.

Annual Fuel Consumption

Before choosing the most economic fuel, it is necessary to estimate the total amount consumed per annum.

SPACE HEATING

The sum of heating and ventilation loads gives the peak demand required in respect of space heating. To use this peak demand to estimate the annual fuel consumption, it is necessary to extend the formula by applying factors to take into account the boiler efficiency, and the length of time the boilers will be in operation.

Two methods are commonly used.

Equivalent Hours

This method uses the equivalent number of hours per annum it is estimated that the heating plant would need to run at the maximum designed rate to satisfy the total annual heat demand. The number of 'equivalent hours' is not the number of hours during which the heating plant is working per annum or per heating season, but the number of hours it is calculated it would be necessary to operate at the maximum boiler capacity to satisfy the total annual heat demand.

Tables giving the number of 'equivalent hours', calculated according to the type of heating and period of use for any set of circumstances and geographical location, are published and generally available. For example the tables of 'equivalent hours' give 2,856 for a building heated by an intermittent firing method for 7 days a week, 40 weeks a year, and 15 hours per day plus 2 hours pre-heating. If a building was heated for 5½ days a week, 40 weeks a year and 9 hours per day plus 3 hours pre-heating, the figure would be 1,668 'equivalent hours'.

To obtain the total heat required per annum, the formula would be adjusted to read

$$\text{Annual heat required (kJ)} = A \times U \times \Delta t \times E \times \frac{3{,}600}{1{,}000} \quad \text{(Eq. 12.3)}$$

where E' = 'equivalent hours', as given by standard tables.

Degree Days

This method uses meteorological observations over the period 1945 to 1955. One degree day is a period of twenty-four hours when the average outside temperature is 1°C below the base temperature. If the average temperature is 2°C below the base temperature for twenty-hour hours, then this is counted as two degree days, and by adding up the daily totals the number of degree days per annum or heating season is obtained.

A typical range of degree day values for various circumstances is given in Table 12.2.

To obtain the total heat required per annum by this method, it is necessary also to take into account the type of heating by applying a factor according to the efficiency of the system proposed.

An average efficiency of about 80 per cent should be obtained if the installation is controlled by an experienced engineer.

Similarly, if the twenty-four hours degree day table is used, it is necessary to take account of the load factor — i.e. the percentage of a twenty-four hour day during which the boilers are considered to be working at full capacity, or the total daily output divided by the boiler capacity and expressed as a percentage of twenty-four hours.

The total heat required per annum using the degree day method would be obtained by adjusting the formula to read

Annual heat requirement (kJ) =

$$\frac{\text{degree day} \times 24 \text{ hours} \times \text{load factor} \times \text{boiler capacity}}{\Delta t \times \text{overall efficiency}}$$

$$\text{(Eq. 12.4)}$$

HOT WATER SUPPLY

The calculation for consumption of fuel for hot water would be based on the hourly load for hot water supplies multiplied by the hours and number of days of occupation.

Table 12.2
Degree Days
Heating period to maintain 18°C internal temperature

	24 hours	24 hours but reduction to 13° C at night and weekends	Daytime only; Complete shutdown night and weekends
	1 Sept–31 May	1 Oct–31 May	1 Oct–31 May
London	2,008	1,193	650
Southampton	1,932	1,192	637
Bristol	2,076	1,254	673
Birmingham	2,219	1,443	745
Durham	2,404	1,360	744
Glasgow	2,474	1,433	750

Suppose for the project considered previously, which had a peak heat loss of 25,000 kW, it was found by the operation of equations 12.3 and 12.4 that the annual requirement for space heating and hot water is 250,000,000 MJ. This must then be expressed as quantity of fuel.

The comparative calculations for the alternative fuels coal, oil and town gas, assuming a choice of the central boiler-house system, would be as follows:

Coal

A. *Capital Costs*

	£
Cost of Boilers = 8 @ £40,625 each	325,000

Cost of incidental boiler plant, etc.

	£	
Storage hopper	25,000	
Ash handling plant	17,500	
Circulating pumps and starter	5,000	
Pressurization plant	25,000	
Pipework in boiler house	12,500	
Horizontal flues	15,000	
Smoke control equipment	10,000	
Insulation	15,000	
Control panel and instrumentation	15,000	140,000

Cost of boiler-house building and chimney:

Area of boiler house = 35 m x 25 m =	875 m²	
Area of fuel store = 15 m x 25 m =	375 m²	
	1,250 m²	

	£	
1,250 m² @ £250 per m² =	312,500	
Cost of chimney =	67,500	380,000

Carried forward £845,000

Brought forward £845,000

Cost of radiators and piping system based on gross area of 200,000 m² @ £17·50 per m² say	3,500,000
	4,345,000
Site distribution mains	150,000
Total Capital Cost	£4,495,000

B. *Running Costs*

Fuel:
  Calorific value – 26 MJ/kg
  Annual coal consumption

$$\frac{250{,}000{,}000 \text{ MJ}}{26 \text{ MJ/kg}} = 9{,}615{,}385 \text{ kg} = 9{,}615 \text{ tonnes}$$

Cost at £40 per tonne =	£384,600

Labour. It is assumed that with a fully mechanized boiler house the plant could be operated by:
One man on a mechanical shovel to trim fuel for two 8 hr shifts 7 days a week
Two men to supervise boiler and feed plant for three 8 hr shifts 7 days a week
One man to remove ash etc. for one 8 hr shift 7 days a week.
∴ total labour = equivalent to approx. 500 man-hours per week during winter 30 weeks period, and say 250 hours per week in 20 week summer period.

Assume wages of £3 per hour inclusive of overheads.

30 winter weeks @ £1,500 =	£45,000	
20 summer weeks @ £750 =	£15,000	£60,000

Maintenance. Approx 2½ per cent of boiler-room plant costs £11,500

The above figures apply to boiler and fuel handling.

Oil

A. *Capital Costs*   £

Cost of Boilers = 8 @ £32,500 each   260,000
Cost of incidental boiler plant, etc.

	£	
Plant as for coal excluding Ash handling plant and storage hopper	97,500	
Oil storage	72,500	170,000

Cost of boiler house (as for coal)   380,000
Cost of radiators and pipework
(as for coal) say   3,500,000

                                                          4,310,000

Sit distribution mains   150,000

Total Capital Cost   £4,460,000

B. *Running Costs*
Fuel
Calorific Value — 38 MJ/litre
Annual oil consumption

$$\frac{250,000,000 \text{ MJ}}{38 \text{ MJ/litre}} = 6,580,000 \text{ litres}$$

Cost at £0·15 per litre =   £987,000

Labour. It is assumed that with a fully automatic boiler house the plant can be supervised by:

One man per 8 hr shift, 2 shifts per day
Total hours per week = approx. 120
Cost per annum at £3·50 per man-hour
= 120 x 50 x £3·50   £21,000

Maintenance. For boiler plant and fuel system approx.

2½ per cent plant cost   £10,750

Gas

It is anticipated that a supply could be obtained straight from the mains, so that no storage is involved.
Delivery — by pipeline.
Methods of Firing — by Gun-type burners, similar to oil burners.

A. *Capital Cost*   £
Cost of Boilers (same as for oil)   260,000
Incidental boiler plant, etc.

	£	
Circulating pumps and starters	5,000	
Increment of cost to bring in larger gas main	32,000	
Pressurization Unit	25,000	
Horizontal Flues	15,000	
Carried forward	£77,000	£260,000

Brought forward	£77,000	£260,000
Smoke Control Equipment	10,000	
Insulation	15,000	
Control panel and instrumentation	15,000	
Pipework in boiler house	7,500	124,500

Cost of boiler-house building and chimney

900 m² @ £250 per m²	225,000	
Chimney	60,000	285,000

Cost of radiators and pipework (as for oil)   3,500,000

                                                          4,169,500
Site distribution mains   150,000

Total Capital Cost   £4,319,500

B. *Running Costs*
Fuel
Calorific value — 100 MJ/therm
Annual gas consumption

$$\frac{250,000,000 \text{ MJ}}{100 \text{ MJ/therm}} = 2,500,000 \text{ therms}$$

Cost at £0·30 per therm =   £750,000

Labour. It is assumed that with a fully automatic boiler house the plant can be supervised by:

One man per 8 hr shift, 2 shifts per day, total hours per week = approx. 120
Cost per annum of say £3·50 per man-hour
= 120 x 50 x £3·50   £21,000

Maintenance. Approx. 2½ per cent of boiler-room and plant costs   £9,600

The technique discussed in Chapter 8 dealing with 'cost in use' can be applied to these calculations to put them on a comparative basis. The period over which capital costs should be amortized must be considered.

In the commercial field the client will probably assess a project's profitability on the basis of obtaining a return on capital over 15 years at a high rate of interest, whereas with non-commercial projects the estimated full life of plant and materials should be considered and a lower rate of interest is usually taken as more appropriate.

Considering the commercial field, taking a 15 year period and an 8 per cent rate of interest, the comparisons, with costs expressed on an equivalent annual cost basis, would be as follows:

1. *Coal*   *£ per annum*

Capital	— £4,495,000 x 0·117	526,000
Running Costs	— Fuel	384,600
	— Labour	60,000
	— Maintenance	11,500
		£982,100

2. *Oil*

		£
Capital	– £4,460,000 x 0·117	521,800
Running Costs	– Fuel	987,000
	Labour	21,000
	Maintenance	10,750
		£1,540,550

3. *Gas*

Capital	– £4,319,500 x 0·117	505,400
Running Costs	– Fuel	750,000
	Labour	21,000
	Maintenance	9,600
		£1,286,000

Considering the non-commercial field, taking the estimated full life of materials and a 5 per cent rate of interest, the comparisons would be as follows:

1. *Coal*

		£ per annum
Capital	– Boilers (life 20 years) £325,000 x 0·080	26,000
	Incidental plant, boiler-house, radiator system etc. (life 60 years subject to regular maintenance) £4,170,000 x 0·053	221,010
		247,010
Running Costs	– Fuel	384,600
	Labour	60,000
	Maintenance	11,500
		£703,110

2. *Oil*

Capital	– Boilers (life 20 years) £260,000 x 0·080	20,800
	Incidental plant, boiler-house, radiator system etc. as for coal £4,200,000 x 0·053	222,600
		243,400
Running Costs	– Fuel	987,000
	Labour	21,000
	Maintenance	10,750
		£1,262,150

3. *Gas*

Capital	– Boilers (life 20 years) £260,000 x 0·080	20,800
	Incidental plant, boiler-house, radiator system etc. as for coal £4,059,500 x 0·053	215,153
	Carried forward	£235,953

	Brought forward	£235,953
Running Costs	– Fuel	750,000
	Labour	21,000
	Maintenance	9,600
		£1,016,553

The foregoing calculations are sufficient to enable a choice of system and fuel to be made. The significance of the price of the fuel should be noted, although it is important that this example should not be taken as applicable to projects in general. The rates quoted for fuels will vary considerably between various consumers, and it is necessary to obtain quotations for each project considered before carrying out a cost exercise of this nature.

Effects of Varying Specifications

The building client and design team often require advice on the cost implications of the choice of various alternative forms of construction and specification of a building structure, e.g. single or double glazing or the use of more expensive materials providing better insulation. In these cases it is necessary to consider not only the capital and running costs of the proposed alternatives, but also the effects the alternatives may have on other elements of the building, and in particular the heating installation.

A change in the U value of a component will affect the heat losses from the building and consequently the annual fuel consumption. Changes to the size of plant installed are unlikely unless the alternatives considered produce a very large change in U-values and also form a very significant part of the building structure. From the earlier calculations it will be seen that the size of boiler plant is determined by assessing the peak demand on the heating system. The type of change considered here will generally have little effect on peak demand, having more of a long-term effect, and the advice given is usually sufficiently accurate if the calculations are confined to the effects on emission costs, e.g. cost of providing the necessary radiator surface area and the effects on fuel consumption.

It is often sufficient to have the fuel costs available in terms of a cost per useful megajoule (MJ), which can be calculated by the following formula once the cost of fuel from the supplier and the efficiency of the heating system are established.

Cost per useful MJ (£) =

$$\frac{\text{Cost of fuel (£)}}{\text{Calorific value x efficiency of system}}$$

For the project considered so far in this chapter the cost of the three fuels in terms of cost per useful MJ would be

Coal $\dfrac{£40}{26,000 \times 0·8} = £0·0019$ per MJ

Oil $\dfrac{£0 \cdot 15}{38 \times 0 \cdot 8}$ = £0·0049 per MJ

Gas $\dfrac{£0 \cdot 30}{100 \times 0 \cdot 8}$ = £0·0038 per MJ

EXAMPLE 1

What would be the annual cost or saving resulting from the use of double glazing in place of single glazing in an office block of 2,500 m² gross floor area with 750 m² of window area situated on a site where exposure conditions were normal? The office is assumed to operate on a normal working week and the inside design temperature is 16 deg C.

Calculation

Extra capital cost of double glazing

$$750 \text{ m}^2 \text{ @ £30 per m}^2 = \underline{£22,500}$$

Saving on heating –

U values from tables in W/m² deg C:

Single vertical glazing   4·50

Double vertical glazing   2·85

Heating Plant, etc. Maximum hourly heat loss.

– Single glazing (750 x 4·50 x 16) W

– Double glazing (750 x 2·85 x 16) W

– ∴ Difference = 4·50 – 2·85 (750 x 16) W
        = 1·65 (12,000) W
        = 19,800

If the radiator cost was £30 per m² of heating surface and the radiators supply 500 W per m² of heating surface, the saving in capital cost would be

$$\frac{19,800}{500} \times £30 = \underline{£1,188}$$

Fuel consumption. The equivalent hours at maximum heat loss for the system used in the office block obtained from published tables might be 1,147, and the annual saving of heat would then be

$$\frac{19,800 \times 3,600 \times 1,147}{1,000,000} = 81,758 \text{ MJ}$$

Assuming that the method of heating is by oil costing £0·0049 per useful MJ, the annual fuel saving would be worth

$$81,758 \text{ MJ} \times £0 \cdot 0049 = £400$$

In this example, therefore, there is an extra capital cost of £22,500 if double glazing is installed in place of single glazing, against which figure there is an offsetting saving on heating of a capital cost on radiators of £1,188 and an annual saving on the fuel costs of £400.

'Cost in use' techniques can be employed to place these figures on a comparable basis.

The equivalent capital cost saving of the fuel saving of £400 per annum over a building life period of 60 years @ 5 per cent per annum rate of interest would be

$$£400 \times 18 \cdot 929 = £7,572$$

Result

The cost effect of introducing the double glazing would be as follows:

	£	£
Extra capital cost of double glazing		22,500
Less saving of radiators	1,188	
saving of fuel	7,572	8,760
Net extra equivalent capital cost of double glazing in lieu of single glazing.		£13,740

EXAMPLE 2

Consider a similar problem to Example 1, but this time related to a domestic dwelling of 120 m² gross floor area with 25 m² of window area with normal exposure conditions.

Calculation

Extra capital cost of double glazing

$$25 \text{ m}^2 \text{ @ £35 per m}^2 = \underline{£875}$$

Saving on heating –

U values from tables in W/m² deg. C:

Single vertical glazing   4·50

Double vertical glazing   2·85

Heating plant etc. Maximum hourly heat loss.

Single glazing (25 x 4·50 x 16) W

Double glazing (25 x 2·85 x 16) W

∴ Difference = 4·50 − 2·85 (25 × 16) W

$\qquad$ = 1·65 (400) W

$\qquad$ = 660 W

If the radiator cost was £35 per m^2 of heating surface and the radiators supply 500 W per m^2 of heating surface the saving in capital cost would be

$$\frac{660}{500} \times £35 = £46$$

Fuel consumption

The 'equivalent hours' at maximum heat loss for the system used in this building might be 2,147 and the annual saving of heat would then be

$$\frac{660 \times 3,600 \times 2,147}{1,000,000} = 5,100 \text{ MJ}$$

Assuming that the method of heating is coal for which the quotation is £120 per tonne delivered, and having a calorific value of 26,000 MJ/tonne and a boiler efficiency of 60 per cent, the fuel cost per useful MJ would be

$$\frac{£120}{26,000 \times 0·6} = £0·0077 \text{ per MJ}$$

The annual fuel saving would, therefore, be

5,100 MJ × £0·0077 = £40

The equivalent capital cost of this annual saving for a building life period of 60 years @ 5 per cent per annum rate of interest would be

$$£40 \times 18·929 = £760$$

Result

The cost effect of introducing the double glazing would be as follows:

	£	£
Extra capital cost of double glazing		875
Less saving of radiators	46	
saving of fuel	760	806
Net extra equivalent capital cost of double glazing in lieu of single glazing.		£ 69

These two examples highlight the need to consider every project or situation individually, taking the different sets of factors into account.

The figures and calculations used in this chapter are affected by The Building Regulations 1976 section F. This requires that the external walls should have a thermal conductivity (W/m^2 deg C) not exceeding 1·0 and the average of walls and windows not exceeding 1·8. Other rules relate to roofs, floors and party walls etc. The conductivity for double glazing is to be taken as 2·8 and single glazing as 5·7.

13
Budgeting for Development

Before embarking on a building project a developer will carry out a financial feasibility exercise, equating the cost of carrying out the development and the costs of maintaining and operating the building after completion with the new capital value created by the development.

Items appearing in a developer's budget will include capital costs and annual charges.

Capital Costs

1. First is the acquisition of land, which includes the purchase price of the site, and also expenses arising from the purchase transaction such as legal fees and stamp duties. If the site is subjected to restrictive covenants or rights of way, the cost of discharging these will add to the site costs.
2. Then there is the physical preparation of the site, which includes the cost of clearing it of existing buildings, trees or other obstructions before new construction work can begin.
3. Development work, in addition to the construction cost of the new building, is another capital cost and includes the cost of site works such as roads, sewers and other site services, landscaping, and the fees payable for architect, quantity surveyor and other professional services.
4. Interest on capital used during the period of carrying out the construction work must be considered. It is usually calculated as interest on the total construction cost required for the equivalent of half the estimated construction period.
5. Profit on development is important, since it is the profit the developer requires if he is to undertake the work of development. The amount will usually be about 10 per cent of the cost of the work but will vary according to the type of development and the risk involved.
6. Finally, there are disposal expenses, including the cost of arranging the leasing or sale of the completed development.

Annual Charges

1. First is return on investment, calculated as a percentage of the capital invested in the development. The percen-

tage will be based on that for an investment of a similar nature and risk.
2. Depreciation on buildings – a provision made by way of a sinking fund for reproducing the development when it has reached the end of its estimated life span – is a regular charge. This provision is calculated on the capital costs of the wasting or depreciating items of expenditure only, and, therefore, excludes certain capital cost items such as land, site preparation work, and profit.
3. Occupation expenses, such as rates, insurances, repairs, and services costs must be taken into account.
4. Finally there are ownership expenses, which are the costs of management of the completed development, such as the collection of rents, and arranging for maintenance work to be carried out.

Typical Developer's Budget, Example 1

A town site is on offer for £1 million with outline planning approval for the erection of fifteen shops and 4,000 m^2 gross area of office accommodation over the shops. Car parking is available nearby and need not be provided as a part of this development.

The prospective developer requires a 10 per cent development profit, and it is anticipated that the construction will take two years to complete.

ESTIMATE OF CAPITAL COSTS

		£	£
1.	Acquisition of land	1,000,000	
	Legal fees and other expenses	100,000	1,100,000
2.	Physical preparation of site		60,000
3.	Development work		
	Site works	70,000	
	Building construction costs	1,370,000	
	Professional fees	180,000	1,620,000
4.	Interest on capital during construction, 16 per cent of (2) and (3), i.e. £1,680,000 for one year, say		269,000
5.	Profit on development 10 per cent of (1) to (4) i.e. £3,049,000		305,000
6.	Disposal expenses		10,000
			£3,364,000

ESTIMATE OF ANNUAL CHARGES

	£
1. Return on investment 7 per cent on £3,059,000, i.e. £3,364,000 less development profit of £305,000	214,000
2. Depreciation on buildings 5 per cent sinking fund = 0·003 – 60 year period on £1,899,000, i.e. (3), (4), and (6) from Estimate of Capital Costs	5,700
3. Occupation expenses, say	125,000
4. Ownership expenses, say	10,000
	£354,700

The proposed development can be appraised financially by comparing the cost of development with the value created by the development.

Value created can be calculated by using the Valuation method of applying the 'Years Purchase in Perpetuity' multiplier to the money yield from a development. 'Years Purchase' is the multiplier used to convert an annual income into its equivalent capital value. With a perpetual income, i.e. 'Years Purchase in Perpetuity', the multiplier is obtained by dividing the rate of interest into 100. For example, for a perpetual income at 5 per cent rate of interest the 'Years Purchase in Perpetuity' would be 20,

i.e. $\dfrac{100}{5 \text{ per cent interest}} = 20$

therefore, £1 per annum = £20 capital value

The rate of interest taken when calculating the multiplier to be used to convert money yield to capital value will depend on the return on investment considered appropriate to a particular development, but a range of possible values would be that shown in Table 13.1.

Table 13.1

Type of Development		Return on Investment	
		Rate of Interest, per cent	Years Purchase in Perpetuity
Residential:	Houses	10	10·0
	Flats	8	12·5
Factories:	Modern	8	12·5
	Old	12	8·3
Shops:	Large	6	16·7
	Single trader	10	10·0
Offices:	Large	6	16·7
	Small	8	12·5

Money yield from a development is the annual value left after deduction of amounts necessary to cover depreciation, occupation and ownership expenses. The money yield for this proposed development if each of the shops produces a net rent of £5,000 per annum and the offices produce a net rent of £45 per square metre per annum (net rents being gross rents less £140,700 per annum, i.e. (2), (3), and (4) in Estimate of Annual Charges apportioned between shops and offices), would be as follows;

BUDGET ESTIMATE – MONEY YIELD/MARKET VALUE

			£
Shops			
15 No. @ £5,000 net rent p.a.	= £75,000 @ say 8 per cent	= 12·5 Y.P.	937,500
Offices			
3,250 m² @ £45 per m² net rent p.a.	= £146,250 @ say 6 per cent	= 16·7 Y.P.	2,442,375
Total net rent p.a.	£220,250		£3,379,875

The area of 3,250 m² is taken as the lettable office space as it is estimated that 750 m² will be required for balance area accommodation, i.e. entrance halls, corridors, staircases, toilets, etc.

Assuming the developer is using his own capital to finance the project, his method of appraisal would be to set the market value created by the development – £3,379,875 against the capital costs – £3,364,400. If the comparison shows that the market value is greater than capital cost, then the profit on development will be realised and the project considered worthwhile financially.

It should be noted that the annual charges have been taken into account in the Money Yield/Market Value calculation by subtraction of depreciation, occupation, and ownership expenses from gross rent to give a net rent value; and the return on investment in the development, which reflects the profit required from the investment, has been taken into account when deciding the rate of interest/'Years Purchase' value.

An alternative method would be to compare the annual net yield in rents with the required annual return on investment – £220,250 net rent per annum compared with the required £214,000 return on investment (*see* Estimate of Annual Charges 1). Both methods show this particular development proposal to be profitable.

If the developer is borrowing some of the capital required to carry out the development, the method of appraisal will be similar, except that the profit will be considered in relation to the amount of capital the developer himself puts into the project.

For example, if two-thirds of the cost of development were borrowed for this project, the developer's profit would appear to be very high, at approximately 30 per cent,

but excluded from this calculation is the cost of repaying the borrowed monies out of taxed income. This cost of repayment depends on the tax position and financial standing, in the money markets, of the borrower, and it would fall to the developer's accountant to advise on this aspect.

This example of a typical developer's budget reveals how important it is for the professional team of architect, quantity surveyor, and engineers to keep final costs within the figure budgeted for the building, any excess costs inevitably reducing the developer's profit margin.

In recent years it has become more common for the professional team to be consulted when a developer is preparing his development budget. The architect's advice is required on the feasibility of providing a certain amount of accommodation on a site, and the Quantity Surveyor's on the cost of providing that accommodation.

Such advice demands high professional expertise in building economics and cost planning.

Often a developer will find land for sale upon which a particular type and quantity of accommodation can be built, and, although he may be reasonably certain of the income available from the development in rent, he needs to know how much the building will cost. The common question is 'Can a building of the necessary size and quality be erected for the amount of money available?'

Developer's Budget, Example 2

CAPITAL AVAILABLE FOR BUILDING

A developer has found for £500,000 a site upon which he can obtain planning permission to erect an office block containing a gross area of 5,000 square metres. A budget has been prepared, and advice is sought on the feasibility of providing the accommodation at a cost which must be financed from a rental that cannot exceed £45 per square metre per annum, and provide a profit on development of at least 10 per cent.

DEVELOPMENT VALUE

The architect, from sketch drawings, estimates that it will be possible to provide 4,200 m² of lettable accommodation within the gross building area of 5,000 m² permitted on the site.

	£
Therefore, net annual rental 4,200 m² @ £45	189,000
Y.P. in perpetuity @ 7 per cent = 14·3	
Capital value equals annual rental x years purchase = £189,000 x 14·3	
∴ Capital value of development (say)	£2,702,700

CAPITAL COSTS – EXCLUDING BUILDING

	£	£
1. Acquisition of land	500,000	
Legal fees and other expenses	25,000	525,000
2. Physical preparation of site		10,000
3. Profit on development – minimum of 10 per cent required: therefore take one-eleventh of £2,702,700, say		245,700
4. Disposal expenses		10,000
		£790,700

Therefore, amount available for building is	£
Capital value of development	2,702,700
Less capital costs, excluding building	790,700
	£1,912,000

From the £1,912,000 an amount must be deducted for professional fees and general site works

	£	£
Less Professional fees 12½ per cent of building costs, i.e.		1,912,000
$\frac{1,912,000}{112\cdot5} \times 12\cdot5 = $ say	212,000	
Site works estimated cost	60,000	272,000
Amount available for building construction		£1,640,000

If the development is to be profitable, it will be necessary to provide a building of 5,000 m² having 4,200 m² of lettable accommodation within a total cost of £1,640,000. The cost of the building per square metre gross floor area will, therefore, have to be

$$\frac{£1,640,000}{5,000 \text{ m}^2} = £328 \text{ per m}^2$$

The professional team would need to consider the feasibility of working to a figure of £328 per m².

If the brief is accepted, then it is essential that the professional team produce a building that satisfactorily fulfils the major requirements of the brief – of 4,200 m² of lettable area costing no more than £1,640,000 and of a standard that will command a rent of £45 per m² per annum.

Discounted Cash Flow

It will be noted that in this chapter future cash flows in the form of rent income have been discounted to convert them to present-day equivalent values, using the technique explained in Chapter 8 dealing with 'Costs in Use'.

Money paid out during development, and on future

maintenance and repairs, etc. is associated on a time basis and needs to be expressed in present-day values if the true worth of a project is to be assessed. The technique involving the use of present value is similar to the accountancy method of estimating the return of funds over a period of time usually referred to as the D.C.F. (yield) method, D.C.F. meaning Discounted Cash Flow.

Visual Presentation

In some circumstances it is useful to have a method of presenting the developer's equation in pictorial form. Where, for example, there is repetition of a particular type of development, it is convenient to reduce the various parameters to those which carry the most significance and prepare a 'calculator'.

Figure 13.1 shows a calculator devised for use with student residential accommodation, which in recent years has been financed by private borrowing. The calculator relates the four factors of income, expenditure, interest rate, and term of years to capital sum, which could be supported by a loan.

The use of this device is quite straightforward. In the lower left-hand quadrant a vertical line taken from the junction of a horizontal line on the income scale and a diagonal line on the expenditure scale indicate the amount available for loan charges. A horizontal line taken from the

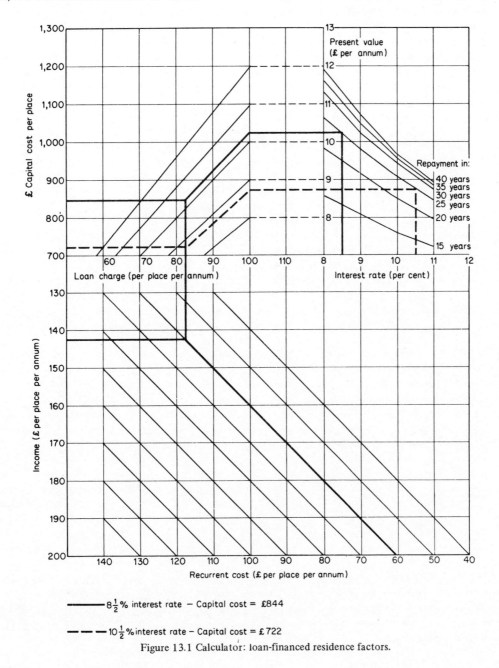

Figure 13.1 Calculator: loan-financed residence factors.

85

junction of a vertical drawn from the scale indicating the rate of interest and the curved line indicating the term of years will give the present value per annum. Finally, a horizontal line from the junction of the diagonal drawn from the present value scale and the vertical indicating the loan charge or net income give the capital cost, or the loan.

Drawing a graph such as this is mainly a matter of reference to valuation tables and simple arithmetic. Once the correct scale is determined, it presents no difficulties in construction. This example has been based on the cost per place (per student in residence), but it could equally have been in terms of a cost per flat for a housing development, or income per annum per square metre and capital cost per square metre for offices.

14
Cost Limits

The financial environment in which public expenditure on new building is managed is described in Chapter 3 and attention is drawn to the fact that various methods of expenditure limit control have been employed.

The particular procedures followed for different types of building were developed to meet a wide range of circumstances and even for a particular category of buildings the methods have been adapted during the period. The fundamental question has been how far the control is designed to determine how the building should be used or simply to control the standards of finish and area of the accommodation to be provided. This chapter describes the basic theory underlying expenditure limit control and the observed facts of its application on the costs of educational buildings.

It is truism that all expenditure limit control must be related to the functional requirements of the particular building type, but it is perhaps less obvious that functional cost limits may be expressed in a variety of units. The factors that determine the brief and the costs of a project may be summarized as follows:

1. The number of occupants.
2. The activities in which the occupants will be engaged.
3. The space required for these activities.
4. The timetable of the activities.
5. The division of the space into rooms and zones for circulation or servicing.
6. The environmental conditions required for the activities.
7. The cost of providing the structure and the services that will enclose the space.

If we now wish to devise a theoretical expenditure limit that will satisfy the brief at minimum cost, it can be argued that rooms should only be provided to the extent that they are needed within the framework of a properly constructed timetable. Suppose it were necessary to provide a particular course for thirty students which included two hours of laboratory work each week. The choice might be a laboratory sized for thirty used for two hours, a room for ten used for six hours, or an even smaller room used for longer periods. Any of these solutions might be possible, but each would produce different loads on the teaching and other staff. The most efficient solution will often be a compromise between providing rooms that are under-used for most of the week or heavy and repetitive teaching loads. If it were decided

that teaching three groups of ten was acceptable in these practical spaces, the area requirements would be calculated from the following formula:

$$\text{student numbers} \times \frac{\text{course hours}}{\text{teaching week}} \times \frac{\text{teaching week}}{\text{room hours}} \times \frac{\text{room size}}{\text{group size}}$$

$$\times \text{ gross area per working place}$$

If the working week were 35 hours, the mathematical expression of the formula would be:

$$30 \times \frac{2}{35} \times \frac{35}{6} \times \frac{10}{10} \times \text{area per laboratory place}$$

= 10 places at the appropriate area per place.

In practice, for a complex building, with students following a range of courses needing specialist rooms, it will be impossible to ensure that the group size matches the room size or that a room will be available for each hour of the teaching week. The product of the two factors of room size and room hours is known as the room utilization factor, which will differ for various types of room and student group size, rarely, in practice, exceeding a value of some 60 per cent.

The total cost of a building can, therefore, be set out as follows:

$$\text{number of occupants} \times \frac{\text{activity hours}}{\text{teaching week}} \times \text{utilization factor}$$

$$\times \text{ gross area per working place} \times \text{cost per unit area}$$

In schools, although there is no direct central control of the curriculum, there is sufficient common agreement on the range of subjects and the amount of schooling that is practical within the week for the three centre factors in this formula to be considered as constant. If it is considered that the cost per unit area can also be standardized, the cost limit can be expressed as:

$$\text{student occupants} \times \text{cost per unit place}$$

Buildings for higher education often include a wide variety of spaces for teaching and research, and are designed to accommodate students with varying timetables and specialist requirements. In this case it is impossible to expect standardization, and it is usually necessary to produce a schedule of accommodation. In effect this means combining the first four factors in the formula, which may then be multiplied by a standard cost per unit area.

There will also be buildings, such as hospitals, where the actual numbers for which the building is needed will vary from week to week. The solution is to relate the accommodation to the size of the population to be served, and, therefore, the potential number of occupants. In this instance all the items in the formula are combined to give the total cost of a department, related to a standard number of beds.

In the formula for calculating the cost of a function described above the intention is to provide a total limit of expenditure. Providing that the building design satisfies the functional criteria specified, the precise architectural form and the choice of materials should be left to the designers, by which means it is possible to develop and incorporate advances in building and operational techniques in a way that would be impossible if control is based on standard designs or specifications. In most control procedures the limit on the expenditure is coupled to a requirement that the building will provide some specified minimum area, to ensure that the building will contain sufficient accommodation to meet its brief.

Where control is based on schedules of accommodation, these schedules are usually expressed in terms of the net areas of the usable or scheduled rooms. Since the expenditure limit relates to the total cost of the project, some allowance must be made for the circulation spaces, and the lavatories, plant rooms, internal ducts, and boiler houses.

These are sometimes known as the balance areas. The ratio between the balance areas and the usable areas is usually expressed as a percentage, varying from about 30 per cent in buildings such as libraries, where much of the circulation space is common to the usable areas, to 55–60 per cent in complex and heavily serviced scientific buildings.

The cost per unit area used in the formula for calculating the expenditure limit must be adjusted to allow for certain variations in the functional requirements, especially in the provision of services. The standard cost allows for the provision of heating, lighting, hot and cold water supplies, and sanitation, but for laboratories, for instance, a much wider range of services must be provided, and it is usually necessary to install artificial ventilation or air-conditioning in specialist areas such as lecture theatres, darkrooms, or kitchens. These extra costs may be covered by direct allowances for specific services, or by the application of a formula that adjusts the expenditure limit in relation to the ratio of heavily to lightly serviced areas.

Apart from abnormal site conditions it is unusual to make any specific allowances for the particular design of the building, but in local authority housing the cost allowances are graded in relation to the number of occupants and to the density of the development. This adjustment is necessary because the size of the dwelling is not directly proportional to the number of occupants, and because of the considerable difference in construction and servicing costs between low-rise housing and high-rise flats. However,

this factor makes the computation of the limit more complex, since it increases the number of variables. As has been explained above, limits are normally constant in relation to a particular functional requirement. The expenditure limit is not directly related to a particular design but to a level of cost that will allow for a variety of design solutions. It is, therefore, unusual for a reasonable design solution to be impossible within the limit, but this would not be true for housing if the cost limit was fixed on a cost per person basis regardless of dwelling size or density. Once the limit has been set for a particular mix of dwelling size and density then it is possible to balance the proportion of housing of various types and costs to arrive at a scheme most likely to meet the limit with the highest specification and amenity value. This principle lay behind the Housing Cost yardstick which was used for many years to determine whether local authority schemes were eligible for government subsidy.

When it is necessary to establish a cost control procedure, all the functions in the formula must be carefully considered. The three most important issues are the area per place, the circulation or balance area, and cost per unit area. The areas required for the various functions can be determined by measurement of the operations to be carried out. The determination of the allowances for balance areas will normally come from a statistical examination of the plan analysis of a variety of schemes.

The decisions on specifications and environmental standards are almost entirely subjective and can only be made by examining completed buildings. It is then necessary to collate the results of the examination and the cost analysis. The most effective procedure is to find both the range of costs for individual element and the variation in quantity factors. It is then possible to build up an estimate of a model building with the elemental costs related to the median values of the quantity factors and unit costs. The costs produced by this method can be checked against the range of total costs that have been found satisfactory in earlier schemes.

Once a cost control procedure has been introduced it is necessary to check the standard of design and specification that follow. This is specially important in situations where building costs are increasing. It may seem reasonable to expect that expenditure limits should be directly related to an index of building costs, but the level of the expenditure limit is only one factor in a system of governmental control. A decision to change the level of a cost limit is as much a political judgement as it is technical. The immediate effect of holding an expenditure limit constant in an inflationary situation may be to produce reductions in area or lower expenditure on finishes. The long-term effect is a reappraisal of the technology of the structure and services, and the requirements of the brief. This search for more efficient solutions extends into the field of professional agreements and contracts. For example, the grouping of

local authorities into consortia has reduced costs by the advantages inherent in standardization, bulk buying and serial contracting.

Application of Expenditure Limits

In 1949 the average cost of secondary school buildings was about £320 per place, but some local authorities were building at about two-thirds of this figure. This range of cost did not only result from differences in specification or architectural form: it was also affected by the amount of space provided. The average area related to the figure of £320 per place was 110 sq. ft per place, but some authorities were providing the same amount of teaching space within an area of 76 sq. ft per place. The expenditure limit was calculated to allow buildings with areas approximating to the lower figure, but refinements in design have reduced the area to an average of approximately 70 sq. ft. per place.

A similar situation existed in the provision of residental accommodation in the Universities. Although the general requirements of the students were broadly the same in all institutions there was a wide range in the total area provided

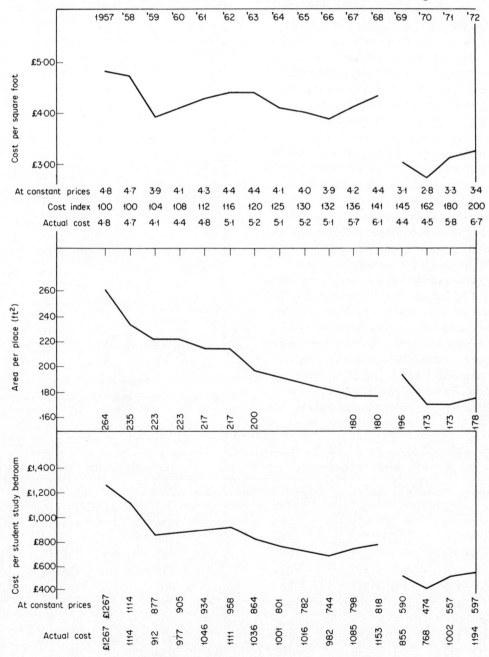

Figure 14.1 University residential buildings: areas and tender costs at constant prices

for each student with a consequent effect on the rate of expenditure. This can be most simply illustrated by Table 14.1.

Cost control for residential buildings was introduced in 1959 and affected costs and designs from 1960 onwards Previously the costs were controlled by an arbitrary limitation on the amount of capital available for individual buildings, giving a sum not necessarily related to the number of occupants or the scale of provision. Therefore whilst it would not be true to describe the situation as uncontrolled, Table 14.1 shows there was a reduction in both cost per square foot and area per place; the further changes in the average area and costs are an indication of the effect of the cost control procedures when they were introduced. Table 14.1 also shows average figures for the most recent schemes. These buildings have been financed by the universities with money borrowed from building societies, banks, and the other financial sources open to the private borrower; there is also some subsidy from Treasury sources and assistance is given towards certain running costs. However, effectively the constraints on the designs and costs rest on the relationship between the income from student rents and the loan charges and recurrent expenditure. The table shows that this concept has produced a further reduction in the scale of provision.

Figure 14.1 shows average costs of university residential building plotted against a building index derived from a comparison of tender prices to a standard schedule of rates. Although using a cost index extended over a period of sixteen years may introduce its own inaccuracies the general impression that can be deduced from this study is that the rate of expenditure has remained fairly constant until the system of loan financed residence was introduced. The combined effect of the constant rate of expenditure and reduced areas produces a steady reduction in the total cost of the provision measured as a cost per student.

Figure 14.2 shows the average cost of structure services and total costs for teaching buildings compared to the basic

expenditure limits. Figure 14.3 shows these total costs expressed as a time series plotted against the same cost index used in Figure 14.1. In this instance the cost control procedures affected buildings from 1961 onwards. This graph shows a more or less constant rate of expenditure for five or six years followed by a period where the average tender costs rose at more or less the same rate as the cost index. In presentation of cost information it is more instructive to illustrate situations such as this in terms of constant

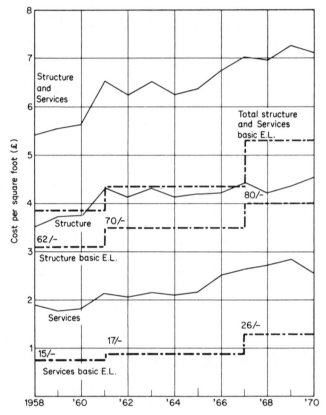

E.L. = Amount included in expenditure limit

Figure 14.2 University teaching buildings: structure and service tenders.

Table 14.1

	Area per Student			Cost per Student (at constant prices)		
Year	Lowest Provision	Average	Highest Provision	Lowest Provision	Average	Highest Provision
1957	221	264	337	1,073	1,267	1,723
1958	186	235	292	934	1,114	1,336
1959	188	223	264	768	877	953
1960	192	223	252	751	905	1,005
1961	200	217	239	828	934	1,095
1962	190	217	247	800	958	1,127
1963	187	200	224	786	864	934
1970	158	173	191	471	474	636
1971	152	173	201	442	557	785
1972	143	178	199	509	597	794

prices, therefore Figure 14.4 plots the actual average costs divided by the cost index. In this form it is apparent that cost control over the period has produced an overall reduction in the rate of expenditure of about 20 per cent. This

may not be as self-evident as is often assumed. Working within tight budgets may reduce standards in this sense, but results can be properly criticized only in relation to the levels of specification and design that are achieved in other sectors of public or private expenditure.

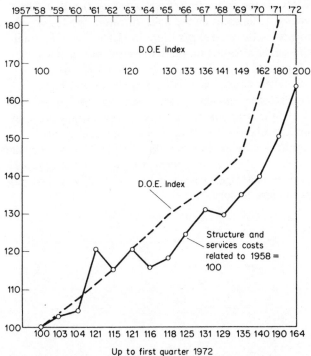

Figure 14.3 University teaching buildings: structure and service tenders related to 1957 costs.

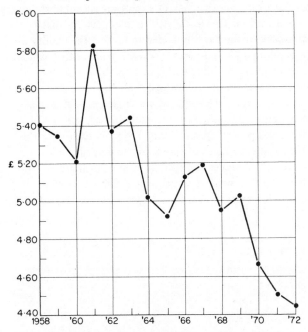

Figure 14.4 University teaching buildings: cost per square foot of structure and services at constant prices.

analysis has only measured the changes in the rate of expenditure in terms of cost per square foot; the limit was set as a total for the project and therefore the architect had freedom to make savings on the amount of circulation space. This also produced reductions in the size of buildings and therefore produced additional economies in the total expenditure. This result can only be achieved by seeking cheaper solutions to constructional problems and choosing cheaper specifications for the building and the services.

It is, of course, impossible to design buildings within expenditure limits, or to set the level of such limits, without being concerned about building standards. The word 'standard' in this context, however, is open to several definitions — for example, the word may be used simply as a synonym for quality, or to suggest an acceptable choice of specifications or area of accommodation, or to indicate specific measurements of the physical properties of the building.

The use of the term in relation to the quality of the building is usually a statement of the obvious. Lower standards of specification in terms of cheaper bricks, thinner partitions, lighter scantling of timber, omission of cover moulds, etc, clearly save money and reduce the standard of quality; but whether these reductions are critical to the functional use of the building or its relation to its neighbours

Defining standards in terms of acceptable levels of specification or design may seem more useful and more accurate, yet even here there are difficulties. The specification is only one of the factors determining the total cost of a building. There will always be a range of acceptable specifications for particular functions, each, inevitably, at different cost levels. The wish to use more expensive specifications can only be balanced by a reduction in the total area of the building, or, alternatively, more generous area standards must be balanced by lower standards of construction and finish. So freedom of choice, within expenditure limit control, entails striking balances, but to some degree this is only possible by working to lower standards of either area or the specifications. In practice there is every possibility that defined standards will become not simply the minimum requirements but the maximum that are attempted.

The alternative of defining standards in terms of physical qualities is quite practical, although the majority of the really important qualities are already controlled by the empirical requirements of the building regulations or by-laws. If minimum levels of performances are set in terms of physical measurement, then it must be assumed that the designers will show that the building, when constructed, will comply to the standards. Yet although, for example, a particular partition may be expected to have a certain sound reduction, its actual performance will depend on the

standards of workmanship, any penetration by pipes, or on sound paths through floors, ceilings, or windows. This difficulty can be eased by assuming standards of construction and specification that are 'deemed to satisfy' the physical requirements. Put in these terms physical standards are, therefore, only another way of expressing accepted standards of specification. This leads back to the difficulty that a framework of standards intended to protect the quality of the building is likely to lead to a rigidity of control over all elements of the building that is incompatible with the normal operation of professional skills.

It is important to discuss why a single rate can be made for buildings that may vary so widely in size, number of storeys and general specification. The main reason for this is the architect's range of choice in deciding his basic structural techniques and specifications. But there are also other factors at work as was shown in Table 5.1. As a building increases in size, the rate per unit area tends to fall, but since a large building will almost inevitably have a higher density of internal partitions, the extra expenditure on this will bring the costs back to a norm. Similarly with a constant rate applied to a building such as a sports hall; as the size increases, the wall perimeter will increase at a linear rate while the area increases as a quadratic function. The amount to be spent on the walls, therefore, is a lower proportion of the total expenditure. A higher rate of expenditure can be afforded for the frame element which will compensate for the increased spans. Similarly the proportionately lower expenditure on foundations for high buildings compensates to some degree for the increased cost of the structural frame. It is, in fact, a happy accident that the relative costs of the constructional elements compensate for each other in this way. If there was a greater diversity in the cost of elements and the effect of changes in quantity factors, estimating and cost control would be very much more complicated.

15
Cost Indices

Cost information is necessarily historical in nature, being collected over a period of years. With the passing of time price levels and market conditions change. Collected information, to be of any use in the cost planning of future projects, must be brought up to date and, in some instances, projected into the future to coincide with the planned tender date for a particular project.

To adjust analysed costs to take account of the passing of time, use can be made of a building cost index, of which several are published from time to time in the technical press. The indices most commonly met with are those devised by the Department of the Environment and the Royal Institution of Chartered Surveyors, Building Cost Information Service.

Index numbers are statistics and, as such, are often discredited on the grounds that 'statistics can be made to prove anything'. Credence given to such a statement may be attributable to the fact that statistical information is commonly used for purposes for which it was never intended, and this is certainly all too often true in the case of index numbers.

The movement in building costs indicated by published indices varies widely, and great reliance must be placed on personal judgement when deciding on the adjustment to be made on analysed cost figures.

Professor Schlaifer has written in his book *Introduction to Statistics for Business Decisions* (McGraw Hill, 1961) that 'there is no substitute for common sense and business judgement'. Statistical theory like many other techniques is meant to complement and enhance good sense and sound judgement.

To appreciate the reason for the variance between index numbers, it is necessary to have a clear understanding and appreciation of the techniques available and of the technique utilized by any particular index measuring the movement of building cost.

An index may be calculated using simple statistical methods or by analysing tender prices and each deserves critical examination. Cost indices have many uses in pre-contract estimating, cost planning and post-contract cost control and more recent times have seen the introduction of the N.E.D.O. Price Adjustment Formulae for use on building contracts.

Index Numbers

An index number measures changes from one period to another: for example, if the index for a building material price was 100 in 1975 and is 130 today, this would indicate a rise since 1975 of 30 per cent. The figure of 30 per cent, however, indicates only the rise in one material. This is known as a *price relative index* where the price of a component in one year is related to the price of a similar component in another year. This is expressed as a percentage by employing the formula:

$$\text{Index} = \frac{P_1 \times 100}{P_0}$$ where P_1 is the price in the given year and P_0 is the price in the base year.

It would be wrong to assume that the cost of each and every material had risen by 30 per cent during this period. Some materials will have risen by perhaps as much as 100 per cent while other materials may have risen hardly at all.

A simple price relative index can measure accurately the movement of the price of a single component, but an index measuring the movement of the cost of buildings, made up of many components changing price independently of each other, is necessarily more complex. Investigation to determine the weighting to be given to the constituent components is needed. Weighting is an attempt to give a value to each component according to its true significance within an index.

It is possible to use a technique where different weights are given to the price of each component. This is expressed as a percentage by the formula:

$$\text{Index} = \frac{\Sigma \frac{P_1}{P_0} \times 100 \times \omega}{\Sigma \omega}$$

where P_1 = current price
P_0 = base year price
w = weighting

This is commonly known as a weighted average of price relatives index.

Price relative indices measure price movements which make them too limited for application to building costs where it is necessary to measure the movement in both prices and quantities.

One accepted method is to relate the current price to price and output at base year — the base year being the year to which index numbers for subsequent years are related. This method is the *Laspeyre Price Index* which is expressed as a percentage by employing the formula:

$$\frac{\Sigma P_1 \, q_0}{\Sigma P_0 \, q_0} \times 100$$

where P_1 = current price
P_0 = base year price
q_0 = base year quantity

This is the more frequently used technique because the use of a constant denominator means that the indices for succeeding points in time can be compared directly with each other also base factors can usually be more easily established than current factors.

An alternative method is to relate the current price and quantity to the cost of current quantity at base year price. This method is the *Paasche price index* which is expressed as a percentage by employing the formula:

$$\frac{\Sigma P_1 \, q_1}{\Sigma P_0 \, q_1} \times 100$$

where P_1 = current price
P_0 = base year price
q_1 = current quantity

In this case however as the denominator changes each time the percentage is calculated the indices for different points in time cannot be directly compared with each other.

Examples of these four indexing methods are given.

2. WEIGHTED AVERAGE OF PRICE RELATIVE INDEX

Component A, B, C.

$$\text{Index} = \frac{\Sigma \dfrac{P_1}{P_0} \times 100 \times \omega}{\Sigma \omega}$$

$$= \frac{(\frac{15}{10} \times 100 \times 50) + (\frac{8}{6} \times 100 \times 120) + (\frac{20}{12} \times 100 \times 80)}{50 + 120 + 80}$$

$$= \frac{7,500 + 16,000 + 13,333}{250} = \frac{36,833}{250} = 147\cdot33$$

3. LASPEYRE PRICE INDEX

$$\text{Index} = \frac{\Sigma P_1 \, q_0}{\Sigma P_0 \, q_0} \times 100$$

$$= \frac{3,310}{2,180}$$

$$= 151\cdot83$$

4. PAASCHE PRICE INDEX

$$\text{Index} = \frac{\Sigma P_1 \, q_1}{\Sigma P_0 \, q_1} \times 100$$

$$= \frac{2,990}{2,000}$$

$$= 149\cdot50$$

Component	Price		Quantity		Price x Quantity			
	Base Year P_0	Current P_1	Base Year q_0	Current q_1	$P_0 q_0$	$P_0 q_1$	$P_1 q_0$	$P_1 q_1$
	£	£						
A	10	15	50	50	500	500	750	750
B	6	8	120	130	720	780	960	1,040
C	12	20	80	60	960	720	1,600	1,200
Σ					2,180	2,000	3,310	2,990

1. PRICE RELATIVE INDEX

Component A	Component B	Component C
$\text{Index} = \dfrac{P_1}{P_0} \times 100$		
$= \frac{15}{10} \times 100$	$\frac{8}{6} \times 100$	$\frac{20}{12} \times 100$
$= 150$	$= 133\cdot33$	$= 166\cdot66$

Some statisticians would progress these theories a stage further and suggest that the ideal index number is the geometric average of the Laspeyre and Paasche index numbers. This suggestion is based on the results of time and factor reversal tests which most indices including Laspeyre and Paasche do not satisfy but which is satisfied by the geometric mean of the two indices.

(*See* I. Fisher, *The Making of Index Numbers*, New York: Houghton Mifflin Co, 1927).

In this case the index would be:

$$\text{Index} = \sqrt{L \times P}$$

$$= \sqrt{151 \cdot 83 \times 149 \cdot 50}$$

$$= 150 \cdot 66$$

To determine an index it is necessary to apply collected data to the formulae in a combination considered by the compiler to be most appropriate. It is the introduction of personal judgements and expertise at this stage that produces the major variations between the various published index figures.

Weighting based on an aggregation of the national output of all materials would not be satisfactory for a building cost index, as the building industry does not absorb the whole output of any one material: also buildings will each use materials of various kinds and in different proportions. Published indices attempt to overcome the problems inherent in calculating a building cost index by adopting a standard approach and adapting it according to the compiler's personal judgement. Two standard approaches are given.

WEIGHTING BASED ON STATISTICS

A building or buildings considered typical of the range of buildings to which it is intended the Index shall apply are analysed for example in terms of labour, plant, materials, overheads, and profit and each of these components adjusted by separately calculated indices which are subsequently compounded into a single index for the total building.

Government departments can utilize this form of approach where they have access to the sort of information essential to the success of this particular method. Contractors may also adopt this approach as their pricing for tenders often follows a similar breakdown of costs. It is difficult however for the professional quantity surveyor to obtain information in this form and consequently he is obliged to resort to too many assumptions to make the attempt worthwhile.

The introduction of the N.E.D.O. formulae for fluctuations may improve the performance of indices using this method. In its simplest form the method is to divide building costs into a limited number of composite units to which movement in costs can be applied. For example total labour costs can be analysed out of the total building costs, and a general cost of labour index applied.

If labour accounted for 40 per cent of the cost of a building then if labour is considered to have increased $47 \cdot 8$ per cent since the base date that is all the information necessary to enable the labour element in the overall index

to be adjusted. If similar information is available for the other elements either from personal records or published data then an overall index can be compiled as

Labour

Grade	Weighting (per cent) W_0	Published Labour Index Base l_0	Published Labour Index Current l_1	Weighted Index Base $W_0 l_0$	Weighted Index Current $W_0 l_1$
Skilled	65	121	180	7,865	11,700
Unskilled	35	115	168	4,025	5,880
	100			Σ 11,890	17,580

$$\text{Labour Index} = \frac{\Sigma W_0\, l_1}{\Sigma W_0\, l_0} \times 100$$
(Laspeyre Formula)

$$= \frac{17,580}{11,890} \times 100 = 147 \cdot 8$$

Material
(Department of Trade and Industry Index)

Base Index	140
Current Index	168

$$\text{Movement} \quad \frac{168}{140} \times 100 = 120$$

Overheads and Profit

Say Base Index	100
Current Index	130

$$\text{Movement} \quad \frac{130}{100} \times 100 = 130$$

	Weighting % W_0	Base Index l_0	Current Index l_1	Weighted Indices $W_0 l_0$	Weighted Indices $W_0 l_1$
Labour	40	100	147·8	4,000	5,912
Material	45	100	120	4,500	5,400
Overheads	10	100	130	1,000	1,300
Profit	5	100	130	500	650
				Σ 10,000	13,262

Overall Index (Laspeyre Formula)

$$= \frac{\Sigma W_0 \, 1_1}{\Sigma W_0 \, 1_0} \times 100$$

$$= \frac{13,262}{10,000} \times 100$$

$$= \underline{132 \cdot 6}$$

N.E.D.O. Formula

N.E.D.O. Formula for Fluctuations uses a similar technique. A sample of 50 contracts was analysed and a list of work categories established which can be grouped together into trade categories using tender value weightings for the work categories within each group to provide trade indices for a particular contract.

This formula measures real movements in costs of labour and materials employed in a particular contract to establish the amount to be recovered by a contractor under the fluctuations clause in the building contract. It does not however take any account of factors such as market conditions and is not therefore suitable for application as a tender price index without a number of adjustments being applied.

In the period 1st quarter 1974 to 1st quarter 1975 whereas the formulae would have given an increase in the index figures of approximately 23 per cent tender levels only increased by approximately 2 per cent reflecting an increasingly competitive climate in the building industry. Increases in basic labour rates were not necessarily reflected in higher payments on site as contractors were under less pressure to pay plus rates and increases in material prices were being absorbed at least partially by contractors and builder's merchants.

WEIGHTING BASED ON TENDER PRICES

A Bill of Quantities contains some 2,000 items — each item individually priced by the contractor. This document provides the complete information on prices and quantities at current levels. (P_1 and q_1 in the earlier formulae):

(a) One accepted method is to reprice the document at base year price levels (P_0) to complete the information required to calculate an index number using the Paasche formula.

One leading local authority uses a method similar to this with considerable success. The main reason for this success is that most of the authority's work is similar in type and form of construction and is locally situated which overcomes the weighting and nationwide base problems inherent in most of the published indices.

(b) A development of this approach is the recognition that a relatively small number of items in any bill of quantities represents a high proportion of the financially significant items and that consideration of the financially significant items only can save a great deal of time. Research has shown that generally some 80 per cent of total costs are contained in less than 20 per cent of the items in a Bill of Quantities. The extent to which the number of items considered is reduced when calculating an index is a matter of personal judgement which may be a factor to consider when assessing the suitability or reliability of an index for any particular purpose.

(c) An alternative is to employ a method similar to either of the above two methods but to produce a standard or balanced Bill of Quantities considered by analysis of a number of Bills of Quantities to be typical of buildings on a national scale or of a particular building type priced at base year price levels (P_0 and q_0 provided). The document is then repriced at current price levels (P_1) to complete the information which is then applied to the Laspeyre formula.

The approaches described are all used to a greater or lesser extent and with a varying degree of aggregation or dis-aggregation by the majority of compilers of building cost indices. It will therefore be appreciated that published indices can only be used as indication of general trends in the movement of building costs over measured periods of time.

The R.I.C.S. — B.C.I.S. in June 1975 wrote that their index series 'measures the trend of tender prices for new building work' and that 'the index is compiled by comparing rates from accepted tenders with a base schedule. A random sample of priced bills of quantities for new work in both the public and private sector is collected and analysed.'

They further stated that 80 projects are required for a statistically reliable index if the number in the sample falls below 80 the reliability of the index is reduced.

The following table shows results of the bills analysed from the 1st quarter 1974 (Index Base Date).

Quarter	Index	No in Sample	70 per cent Range
1974 1st	100	88	78 — 122
2nd	100	84	79 — 121
3rd	99	83	83 — 115
4th*	99	64	85 — 113
1975 1st*	102	37	88 — 118

*provisional

The 70 per cent range indicates the scatter of individual projects around the mean. It gives the range of figures which contains 70 per cent of the projects analysed: in rough statistical terms — those that fall approximately within one standard deviation. They also stated 'these figures should be used with caution'.

Given the limitations inherent in published indices the estimator is faced with the task of interpreting available index figures to suit a particular project. Ideally the estimator would like to have an index applicable to the specific building being considered but unless, as in the case of the local authority previously referred to, he has been able to have an index specially produced for his individual use he will usually have to refer to a more general index which he will need to interpret and apply adjustments, he considers from experience, to be appropriate.

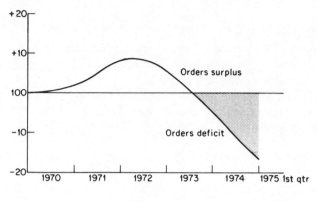

Figure 15.2

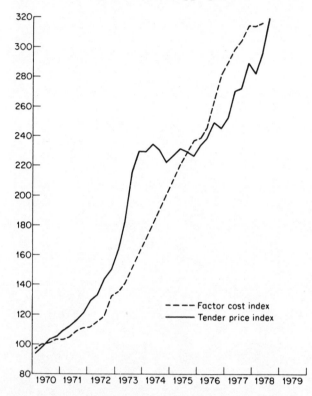

Figure 15.1 Comparison of factor cost and tender price indices (base 1970 = 100)

Market factors such as the competitive state of the industry, productivity, and profitability are the most difficult to measure and to forecast, particularly at the present time. For example faced with Figure 15.1 some understanding can be gained of the reason why tender indices (tender price indices) have sometimes risen out of step with the rate of increase shown on labour and material fluctuations based indices (factor cost indices).

Considering profitability, for example, it is possible given a simple illustration of construction company budgeting to appreciate the effects on tendering attitudes of the orders surplus/orders deficit situation. Companies operate from a financial base of capital employed which is comprised of shares, reserve funds, retained profits and loans. On this capital the company, to justify its activities, will wish to make a profit. For example, a company starting the year with a capital of £1 m may seek to end the year with a

capital of £1·2 m (before payment of tax and distribution to shareholders, etc.).

To produce such an increase in capital the company activities create *income* as value of work done and *expenses* as cost of labour, material, plant and other site costs and overheads (for example, Head Office costs).

A typical company budget may be summarized as:

	£ m	
Capital Employed	1·0	
Value of Work Done	2·0	(Tenders = Payment Received)
Costs on Site (Labour, Material, etc.)	1·6	(Marginal Costs)
Head Office Costs	0·2	(Fixed Costs)
Profit before Tax	0·2	

This ideal situation may be considered to apply at the 100 point on Figure 15.2.

When the market is in an orders surplus situation then the company may consider increasing its profitability and to take the opportunity to obtain finance expansion or improve its liquidity. When the market is in an orders deficit situation the company is in a very different position. The company could consider stopping its activities until the market improves and this would affect the example in the following way:

	£ m	
Capital Employed	1·0	
Value of Work Done	Nil	(Tenders = Payment Received)
Costs on Site (Labour, Material, etc.)	Nil	(Marginal Costs)
Head Office Costs	0·2	(Fixed Costs)
Profit before Tax	Nil	

This decision would have the effect of reducing capital by £0·2 m, i.e. no activity = loss.

The alternative is for the company to consider reducing tenders to a level that will provide sufficient work to at least retain capital at the level of £1 m which would affect the example in the following way:

	£ m	
Capital Employed	1·0	
Value of Work Done	1·8	(Tenders = Payment Received)
Costs on Site (Labour, Material, etc.)	1·6	(Marginal Costs)
Head Office Costs	0·2	(Fixed Costs)
Profit before Tax	Nil	

In the extreme market conditions it may be necessary to consider reducing tenders further so that fixed costs are only partially covered. How long this trend is likely to continue and what the attitude of contractors will be at different points in time calls for a high level of personal judgement on the part of the estimator.

16
Cost Planning—Theory

Cost planning is the term used to describe any system of bringing cost advice to bear upon the design process.

Cost planning demands close cooperation between architect, engineer, and quantity surveyor, and an appreciation of each other's objectives if the ideal voiced by Sir Thomas Bennett at the 1955 R.I.B.A. Conference that 'the client should be able to set out to spend a given sum of money and finish with a building that has cost precisely this sum', is to be achieved.

In earlier chapters it has been shown how the commercial client proceeds and how the probable profitability of his project is assessed by a budget. The public or non-commercial client, whose building is paid for from the public purse, will be required to show that value for money has been obtained — again from a budget.

There are two methods of cost planning most commonly discussed and illustrated in technical journals — elemental cost planning and comparative cost planning. Both systems have their advocates and their advantages, but the majority of offices practising cost planning combine those aspects of each method most suited to a particular project.

All forms of cost planning have three phases.

Phase 1. The estimate, or establishing the target cost.
Phase 2. The cost plan.
Phase 3. The cost checking.

Elemental or Target Cost Planning

PHASE 1 – ESTIMATE

The first of these phases, the establishment of target cost, is common to all methods of cost planning. The figure set must be realistic, i.e. it must amount to a sum of money sufficient for the architect to provide a building that will satisfy all the requirements of the client's brief. The estimate or target cost may be arrived at by any of the methods considered in earlier chapters.

PHASE 2 – COST PLAN

Elemental cost planning enables one to satisfy precisely the ideal expressed by Sir Thomas Bennett, referred to earlier.

It is often described as 'designing to a cost', as the method is based on the proposition that the client is not only able to set a limit to the amount of money that he wishes to spend on the building, but is willing to agree to the expenditure of a fixed amount to provide a certain quantity of building. This point must be emphasized, because the method will allow good buildings to be produced within a limited budget, but is not designed to produce the cheapest possible building; the intention is to produce a building that satisfies all the requirements of the client at an agreed expenditure.

The target is, therefore, the key factor in elemental cost planning.

There will be some circumstances where the target is set by an expenditure limit imposed by a Government department, as would be the case for hospitals, schools, or universities, and here, because the limit is applied to a large number of buildings, there will be plenty of evidence to suggest the standards of specification or the amount of accommodation that is possible within the limit, and there will be sufficient comparative evidence to suggest targets for individual parts of the building.

In other circumstances the limit may be calculated on the basis of the average costs of similar accommodation elsewhere — office buildings, for example. Site difficulties or restrictions, however, may make it necessary for the architect to carry out a considerable amount of preliminary work before arriving at a satisfactory and individual solution to the design problem.

The cost target may be based on an approximate estimate for a design favoured by the client. If the client is satisfied that the estimate accords with his budget for the expected return on rents etc., and is a reasonable comparison with similar buildings elsewhere, the breakdown of the estimate provides a cost plan with targets for the individual elements.

There may also be extreme cases when, for reasons of finance, the limit is so low that none of the standard solutions will apply, or, in the case of development work, new solutions have to be found. In such cases judgements have to be made on what proportion of the total sum can be spent on the functional characteristics of particular elements before targets are set.

Because of the investigation and preparation of the individual targets, the processes of elemental cost planning will automatically show at a very early stage whether the final costs will remain within the budget — a useful assurance to client and design team.

The usual processes of elemental cost planning are as follows:

1. *Client.* He will prepare a brief giving information of the areas required, details of specifications that are, or may be, necessary, and functional information on floor loadings, clear spans, and floor to ceiling heights, etc.
2. *Architect.* He will prepare a sketch plan based on the client's brief, showing general disposition of rooms, form of the elevations, and specification notes.
3. *Quantity Surveyor.* In close liaison with the architect he will prepare a cost plan based on the client's brief, architect's sketch plan and specification notes, and cost analysis of other similar building or buildings.

Preparation of Elemental Cost Plan

The yardstick by which costs are expressed in the cost plan is the rate per square metre of floor area, as experience has shown this to be the most convenient unit of measurement.

The first step is to take the total sum available and to divide it by the gross floor area of the proposed building, measured from the sketch plans, to present the target in terms of cost per square metre — and then to distribute this cost among the various elements of the building.

The second step is to ensure that each allocated cost is realistic, reference being made to the cost analysis information available from earlier buildings of a similar type. In consultation with the architect the analyses most closely reflecting his proposals in relation to the standard of specification and general design are consulted.

Elemental Cost Targets

The proposed building will almost certainly be of a different size and shape than the analysed building, and rather different in specification, making adjustments to the analysis figures necessary in order to produce the cost plan.

All analysed costs comprise three factors: (1) price, (2) quantity, and (3) quality.

Price. Analysed costs reflect the market price level at the date of tender of the building analysed. It is necessary to up-date these costs by the use of an appropriate index.

The changes in market price levels between the date of preparation of the cost plan and the date of tender for the proposed building can only be assessed by projection of current indices, and personal judgement of the likely effect of future labour and material cost increases is necessary. Assessment of the change in price level in this second period is usually allowed for in the cost plan under the elemental heading of 'Price and Design Risk'.

Quantity. The quantity of an element is the amount of that element in the building. The selected analysis should give some measure of the quantity of each element, and the quantity surveyor must take off quantities from the sketch plans of the proposed building in comparable units of measurement.

It was shown in previous chapters that the yardstick of cost per square metre is eminently suited to certain elements — namely those elements in the horizontal plane — but not so suitable for those in the vertical plane, like walls. This is the reason for the introduction of quantity factors, which are an expression of the quantity of a component related to the square metre of floor area.

Quantity may be adjusted in three ways: (a) by proportion, (b) by approximate quantities, and (c) by inspection.

(a) Proportion. This involves the use of quantity factors and is to be preferred, as the analysed cost is comprehensive and a proportional adjustment will ensure that the cost plan will automatically include allowances for all the elements required in the proposed building.

For example, if the cost analysis shows for external walls (*see* Table 16.1) a cost of £17·42 per m² of gross floor area and a quantity factor of 0·52, then, if the proposed building for which the cost plan is being prepared has a measured area of 760 m² of external walls and gross floor area of 1,310 m², i.e. a quantity factor of 760 m²/1,310 m² = 0·58, the cost plan calculated would be:

$$\frac{£17·42}{0·52} \times 0·58 = £19·43$$

N.B. This calculation ignores up-dating price level.

To emphasize its simplicity, the full details are set out below:

Analysis:

$$\frac{£17·42 \times 1,200 \text{ m}^2 \text{ (floor area)}}{624 \text{ m}^2 \text{ (wall area)}}$$

$$\times \frac{760 \text{ m}^2 \text{ (proposed wall area)}}{1,310 \text{ m}^2 \text{ (proposed floor area)}}$$

= £19·43 cost plan rate per m² of floor area.

Taking this step by step:
1. From analysis

£17·42 × 1,200 m² floor area = £20,900, which is the total cost of wall in analysed building.
2. Dividing this by the wall area of 624 m² gives the unit rate of the wall construction per m² of actual wall.

$$£20,900 \div 624 \text{ m}^2 = £33·50 \text{ per m}^2$$

N.B. Usually this figure may be taken directly from the cost analysis, if that is in the form suggested by the R.I.C.S. — B.C.I.S.

Element and design criteria	Total cost of element £	Cost of element per m² of gross floor area £	Element unit quantity	Element unit rate £	Specification
2.E EXTERNAL WALLS					
$\dfrac{\text{External walls}}{\text{Gross floor area}} = \dfrac{624 \text{ m}^2}{1200 \text{ m}^2}$ $= 0.52$	20,900	17·42	624 .... m² Area of external walls.	33·50	Cavity wall in facing bricks PC £140 per thousand one side, fair faced other side
$\dfrac{\text{Basement walls}}{\text{Gross floor area}} = \dfrac{- \text{ m}^2}{- \text{ m}^2}$ $= -$					
The approximate value of thermal conductivity .... 1·00 W/m°C.					
Preliminaries .... % of remainder of contract sum.					

External walls	£	Area m²	All-in unit rate £
280 mm wall faced one side, fair faced other side	20,900	624	33·50

Table 16.1

3. Now if the £33·50 per m² is multiplied by the actual wall area of the proposed building, the total target cost for the wall element is obtained.

£33·50 x 760 m² = £25,460, which is the total target cost for the proposed building.

4. In order to enter this in the cost plan, it is necessary to express the cost in terms of cost per m² of the gross floor area of the proposed building, i.e. divided by 1,310 m².

£25,460 ÷ 1,310 m² = £19·43 per m², which is the cost plan rate per m² of gross floor area.

In addition to reducing the length of calculations necessary when building up cost plan rates, quantity factors provide a more easily assimilated visual check on the economics of particular designs and correctness of calculations: for example, it is easier to appreciate the relative economics given the ratio A = 0·52: B = 0·58 than to make a similar judgment given only the comparison of

$$A = \frac{624 \text{ m}^2}{1,200 \text{ m}^2} \quad : \quad B = \frac{760 \text{ m}^2}{1,310 \text{ m}^2}$$

(b) *Approximate Quantities.* These involve taking off dimensions, and, since the cost plan is prepared at an early stage in the design process with only sketch plans and brief specification notes available, it follows that it will be easy for essential details to be overlooked. Although this way of arriving at elemental cost targets should be avoided wherever possible, it is sometimes necessary to resort to approximate quantities when there are new requirements that cannot be assessed by proportionate calculations from cost analysis.

(c) *Inspection.* Is used to assess the elemental cost target when the element is one to which it is difficult to attach an appropriate quantity factor, e.g. external works. To improve the accuracy of the cost target, it is usual to examine a number of analyses of similar building projects to obtain a range of costs, and then to exercise personal judgement of the figure to include in the cost plan.

Quality may also be adjusted in the three ways outlined for quantity – by proportion, approximate quantities, or by inspection – but as the detailed specification is not available at the stage when the cost plan is drawn up, it is usual to make the quality adjustment by coupling inspection with simple calculation.

For example we may use the previous cost analysis, showing external walls at a cost of £17·42 per m² of gross

floor area as the basis of the assessment of the appropriate elemental cost target and assuming the only adjustment necessary is a quality change from facing bricks PC £140 per thousand to facing bricks PC £168 per thousand. Ignoring up-dating price level and quantity changes, the simple calculation may be taken to be a percentage adjustment of plus 20 per cent, i.e. 100(168 − 140)/25 per cent, though this incorrectly assumes that all the constituent parts of the element of walls will be equally affected by the change in the PC rate for the facing bricks. It would be more correct and produce a more accurate figure if the unit rate (N.B. not the all-in unit rate of £33·50 per m²) of cavity brickwork in facing bricks PC £140 per thousand one side were compared to cavity brickwork in facing bricks PC £168 per thousand one side. Reference to bills of quantities or a standard pricing book would provide a quick and ready answer.

Assuming comparable unit rates are £28·00 and £30·80 respectively, then the calculation would be

$$\frac{£30·80}{£28·00} \times 100 = 110, \text{ i.e. a 10 per cent increase}$$

and the £17·42 in the analysis would be increased by 10 per cent to take into account the change in the quality of the brickwork in the element of external walls.

Let us summarize the element of external walls detailed in this example, assuming a price adjustment of say 8 per cent.

The analysis gives external walls at a cost of £17·42 per m² of gross floor area, and it is required to transpose this figure to the cost plan with adjustments for price, quantity, and quality.

Analysis: £17·42 per m²

Adjust for price: plus 8 per cent

quantity: analysis quantity factor 0·52
new quantity factor   0·58

quality: plus 10 per cent

∴ Elemental cost target for cost plan is

$$\frac{£17·42 \times 1·08 \times 0·58 \times 1·10}{0·52} = £23·08$$

Each element is dealt with in turn and, when completed, the amount against the individual elements is totalled and checked against the amount available, i.e. the estimate, target cost, or cost limit.

If the first totalling produces a figure that is too high or too low, the cost plan can be adjusted by raising or lowering the specification of some or all of the elements until the sum of the elements equals the total target.

At this point the cost plan is finalized and the architect is equipped with an additional tool to guide him through the process of design.

To assist the architect where necessary the cost plan may include any items of useful information that have been revealed in the calculations leading up to its completion, and the cost plan may be presented in a form similar to the cost analysis, with a similar range of detailed information. For an example, see Table 16.2.

PHASE 3 – COST CHECKING

After a satisfactory cost plan has been agreed between all the parties involved in the project, the more detailed design of the elements is prepared and cost checking commences.

As each element is designed, the draft drawing and specification notes are passed to the quantity surveyor to check, by estimates based on approximate quantities, that the cost of each element does not exceed its target cost set out in the agreed cost plan. If it proves impossible to keep within the target set for the element under consideration, it is necessary to adjust the costs of other elements to make a balance, or perhaps draw some money from the reserve set aside in the cost plan. If the design solution for an element shows a saving, the surplus money can be fed into the reserve or spent to improve the remaining elements.

The object is to check each element as soon as possible during the development of the design, and adjust as frequently as necessary. In this way the difficulties that so often arose before the development of more sophisticated cost-planning procedures can be avoided, when no checks were made or estimates prepared until the detail design stage was completed, any pruning necessary to keep costs within the client's budget figure tended to be made on those items that would not involve redesign, like finishings and fittings. Such pruning was often unsatisfactory if not disastrous, and obvious to all the users of the building.

With this stage completed, the architect will be able to go to tender with a reasonable assurance that the client's budget figure or estimate has not been exceeded, and that the frustrations of changing working drawings and reducing bills will not come his way.

Comparative Cost Planning

PHASE 1 – ESTIMATE

This phase, the establishment of the estimate, is common to all methods of cost planning. The essential factor is that the figure set must be realistic – it must suffice to produce a building that will satisfy all the requirements of the client's brief. The estimate may be arrived at by any of the methods considered in earlier chapters.

PHASE 2 – COST PLAN

The object of comparative cost planning is to obtain economy through investigating sections of the design and presenting a range of alternatives for various elements, all of which satisfy the requirements of the client's brief in terms of function, construction and specification. The architect chooses the optimum solution, weighing economy in terms of cost against design.

Comparative cost planning starts from the premises that the client should set out with a particular standard of building in terms of amenity and finish, and the architect should expect to provide a building to satisfy these standards at a cost consistent with good design. The client, although giving a cost limit, will expect this to be treated as an upper limit, not necessarily to be spent in full. This is the point of major difference between the two methods of cost planning discussed in this chapter.

Comparative cost planning is often described as 'costing a design'.

The architect has to take his scheme to an advanced stage of sketch design, and to prepare a number of drawings for alternative solutions that will never be utilised. The quantity surveyor prepares estimates for the alternatives based on approximate quantities.

The comparative cost plan is a statement of the estimated cost consequences of decisions the architect may take. It thus acts as a guide towards an economic design. On being presented with the cost plan in this form, the architect can consider the information and select the solution for each part of the building which he considers to be most suitable, either on grounds of cost or of desirability having regard to cost.

The selections made are totalled up and the total cost computed. Provided the total does not exceed the original upper estimate figure, the architect can proceed to prepare working drawings.

It is clear that until the whole scheme has been costed there can be no guarantee that the aggregate cost will come within the limit, and it may be that fundamental decisions taken on elements early in the design stages will have to be altered later.

Referring to the example of external wall set out when considering elemental or target cost planning (p. 96) this element may appear in a comparative cost plan as two alternatives – (1) with facing bricks PC £140 per thousand and (2) with facing bricks PC £168 per thousand. As the drawings are at an advanced sketch design stage, enabling approximate quantities to be taken off, there will be no need to refer to cost analysis quantity factors or to up-date

Table 16.2
Example Presentation of Cost Plan

Job 31/71
   Floor Area   *2,700 m²*
   No. of Storeys *3*
   Cost Target   *£735,000*

Cost Plan Number: 1
Prepared: June 1979
Price Level: March 1980

Ref. No.	Element	Specification	Element Unit Rate	Element Quantity Factor	Costs £/m²	Costs Total £
1	SUBSTRUCTURE	Concrete strip foundation 150 mm hardcore bed and 125 mm concrete bed — soil sandy gravel with some clay 14,000 kg/m² bearing capacity	—	—	19·00	51,300
2	SUPERSTRUCTURE					
	A Frame	—			—	—
	B Upper floors	130 mm RC slab-loading 200 kg/m², max span 5 m	£26·50 m²	0·67	17·75	47,925
	C Roof	130 mm RC slab with 25 mm screed and 19 mm asphalt	£40·00 m²	0·36	14·40	38,880
	D Stairs	900 mm wide RC construction with ms balustrading	£500 per m rise	5·6 m rise	1·04	2,808
	E External walls	280 mm brick cavity wall, facings PC £168 per thousand	£39·79 m²	0·58	23·08	62,316
	F Windows and external doors	Standard unit softwood casements and doors	£52·00 m²	0·30	15·60	42,120
	G Internal walls and partitions	76 mm block partitions generally	£10·50 m²	0·92	9·66	26,082
	H Internal doors	35 mm flush doors BS 459 Pt2 — 90%: fire check—10%	£100 per door	0·043	4·30	11,610
3	INTERNAL FINISHES					
	A Wall finishes	Plaster and 2 coats emulsion generally	£5·20 m²	2·42	12·58	33,966
	B Floor finishes	3·2 mm linoleum tiles—90%: 25 mm wood block—10%	£14·75 m²	—	14·75	39,825
	C Ceiling finishes	Plaster and 2 coats emulsion generally	£5·30	—	5·30	14,310
4	FITTINGS AND FURNISHINGS	Nominal allowance	—	—	20·00	54,000
5	SERVICES	Total agreed to be allocated in discussion with Engineer	—	—	60·00	162,000
6	EXTERNAL WORKS A Site works B Drainage C External services D Minor building works	As detailed on drawing (reference 7/1018/C)	—	—	23·26	62,802
					240·72	649,944
		Preliminaries	8%	—	19·26	51,996
		Contingencies	2%	—	4·82	13,000
					264·80	714,940
		Price and design reserve	say 2·80%	—	7·42	20,060
					272·22	735,000

by use of cost indices. The elemental cost plan would, therefore, appear as shown in Table 16.3.

PHASE 3 – COST CHECKING

This phase differs again in a fundamental way from the cost checking phase of elemental cost planning. The architect in his cost plan has already decided the main lines of his design. If he follows this closely, the cost should not stray from the estimated cost computed in the cost plan. During this stage the quantity surveyor will need to check that the architect and his assistants are keeping to the specification decided upon in the cost plan. The architect may want further comparative cost studies to be carried out against the decision made in the cost plan.

natives, knowing that he is being reasonably economical, but with no certainty that a target will be achieved.

Similar considerations apply to the client. Elemental cost planning implies that a certain sum will be set as the target and spent, irrespective of whether cheaper alternatives exist or not. Some clients will accept this and claim that it is their responsibility to agree the budget, and the job of the architect and quantity surveyor to provide maximum value for money within the figure. Other clients might insist that they want the cheapest scheme that will provide certain standards of specification and maintenance for all elements. In the latter circumstances, the comparative method of costing a design will demonstrate the economy of the scheme more clearly. It must be remembered that if absolute economy is required there is nothing to prevent the preparation of a cost plan with a target cost lower than the client's

Table 16.3

Ref No.	ELEMENT	ALTERNATIVE	SPECIFICATION	SOLUTION COSTS		SELECTED SOLUTION COST PLAN	
				£/m²	Total £	£/m²	Total £
			Brought forward			52·19	140,913
2E	External walls	A	280 mm brick cavity wall facings PC £140 per thousand	21·00	56,660		
		B	280 mm brick cavity wall facings PC £168 per thousand	23·08	62,316	23·08	62,316

Conclusion

The advantages and disadvantages of the two systems described in this chapter depend on the type of scheme to which they are applied and the personalities of the individuals concerned with the design and costing. It is sometimes argued that cost planning by elemental cost targets, or designing to a cost, is a considerable and intolerable restriction on the architect, adversely affecting all the basic tenets of his profession. Possibly this may be true for some architects, but, whether true or false, it is irrelevant in the situation where the architect must design within a cost limit, because, unless the limit is so generous that it would cover any possible design or specification, the architect's freedom of action and choice must be limited. From this it follows that it will depend largely on the temperament of the architect whether he wishes to be reminded of these limits and have specific targets at which to aim for every part of the building, or whether he prefers to make choices from a range of alter-

permitted expenditure limit; as a converse to this, if the client wishes for 'prestige' building or the Architect is unwilling to accept any restriction on his design, then elemental cost planning would be a needless irritation, but the comparative method might be used to show the advantages of the particular specification and design of elements or parts of the building from the point of view of cost.

From this follows the difference between estimating and cost planning. Cost planning implies that the design of the building will be determined in some degree by the amount of money available, and the term cost planning is a description of the methods of job management employed jointly by architect and quantity surveyor to achieve this end. Estimating, on the other hand, is the process of determining the likely cost of a design decision. The cost of a scheme designed without reference to an expenditure limit may at some stage be estimated approximately, to allow evaluation of the tender and to predict the client's liabilities. If the client is unable to afford the scheme, then adjustments will

have to be made to meet his limit. In this sense estimating might appear to give the same end result as cost planning, but the point that must be emphasized is that cost planning means that the scheme is designed to a cost, whether to targets or to comparative specifications from its initial conception. Estimating plays a crucial role in the processes of cost planning; but cost planning is not always implied by the preparation of estimates.

17
Cost Planning—Application

The examples illustrated in this chapter have been based on examination questions set during the period when one of the authors was an examiner in the subject of Building Economics and Cost Planning for the Royal Institution of Chartered Surveyors. The examples have been converted to metric where necessary, and adapted to broaden their scope and interest to the reader.

Example 1

It is possible to apply cost planning techniques to pro-

jects when the very minimum of design and cost analysis information is available.

For example, the client requires a budget estimate for a residential hostel block he proposes to submit to tender in April 1981. Information available comprises a schematic layout of the proposed scheme, together with a brief cost analysis and schematic layout of a previous building constructed in a similar fashion.

Note: 1. Heating to be provided from an existing boiler house on the site.

2. Proposed block four storeys – previous block analysed three storeys.

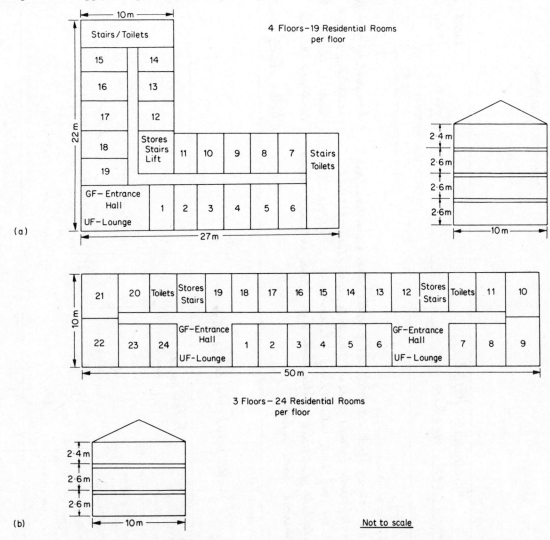

Figure 17.1 Sketch plans of (*a*) proposed residential hostel block; (*b*) analysed residential hostel block.

Table 17.1

BRIEF COST ANALYSIS

CI/SfB	**98**
	Residential Block
BCIS Code	**C - 3 - ????**

Job title:	*Residential Hostel*
Location:	*East Berkshire*

Client:	*Local Authority*
Tender date:	*November 1979*

INFORMATION ON TOTAL PROJECT

Project and contract information

Project details and site conditions:

Three-storey block with brick cavity walls, aluminium windows in softwood frames, precast concrete beam floors, pitched timber roof with interlocking tile covering. "Thermalite" internal partitions. Standard size flush internal doors veneered both sides.

Contract: (To be completed by BCIS from the Contract particulars given below)

Competitive firm price tenders, six tenders received, lowest accepted, second lowest ½% above accepted tender. All tenders within 6% of accepted tender. Stipulated contract period 15 months.

Note: Boots exclude the boilerhouse.

Market conditions:

Stable market — competitive.

Contract particulars:

Type of contract:	*Fixed price*	
Basis of tender*:		
Bill of quantities	✓	Open/Selected competition ✓
Bill of approximate quantities		Negotiated
Schedule of rates		Serial
		Continuation
Contract period stipulated by client	*15*	months
Contract period offered by builder	*15*	months
Number of tenders issued	*7*	
Number of tenders received	*6*	
* Tick as appropriate		

Cost fluctuation*	YES ☐	NO ✓
	LABOUR	
Adjustments based on formula*	MATERIALS	
	YES ☐	NO ✓
Provisional sums	£ *4,500*	
Prime Cost sums	£ *9,000*	
Preliminaries	£ *24,075*	
Contingencies	£ *9,000*	
Contract sum	£ *305,100*	
* Tick as appropriate		

Competitive tender list	
£	N/L
305,100	L
306,460	L
309,307	L
315,998	L
320,206	L
323,203	L

ANALYSIS OF SINGLE BUILDING

Design shape information

Accommodation and design features:

Three-storey residential hostel block 50m x 10m x 7.6m high to eaves divided by crosswalls into sixteen bays with central corridor 1.2m wide.

The building contains seventy-eight residential rooms and two entrance lobbies.

Areas		
Basement floors	—	m²
Ground floor	465	m²
Upper floors	930	m²
Gross floor area	1395	m²
Usable area		m²
Circulation area		m²
Ancillary area		m²
Internal division		m²
Gross floor area		m²
Floor spaces not enclosed	—	m²
Roof area	500	m²

Functional unit 72 Residential rooms

$$\frac{\text{External wall area}}{\text{Gross floor area}} = \frac{685}{1395} = 0.49$$

Internal cube = 10600 .... m³

Storey heights

Average below ground floor .... —

at ground floor .... 2.60 m

above ground floor .... 2.50 m

Design/Shape

Percentage of gross floor area:-

a) below ground floor .... %

b) Single-storey construction .... %

c) Two storey construction .... %

d) 3 * storey construction .... 100 %

e) * storey construction .... %

* Insert number of storeys.

Brief Cost Information

* Contract sum £ 305,100
* Provisional sums £ 4,500
* Prime Cost sums £ 9,000
* Preliminaries £ 27,075 being 8.85 % } of remainder of
* Contingencies £ 9,000 being 3.31 % } contract sum
* Contract sum less contingencies £ 296,100

Functional unit cost }
excluding external works } Tender £ 4,095 per room
Base date £ —

* Amounts for single building analysed.

109

Table 17.1 — *continued*

SUMMARY OF ELEMENT COSTS

Gross internal floor area: 1395 m²

Tender date: November 1979

Element	Preliminaries shown separately — Total cost of element £	Cost per m² gross floor area £	Element unit quantity	Element unit rate £	Preliminaries apportioned amongst elements — Total cost of element £	Cost per m² gross floor area £	Cost per m² gross floor area (base date) £
1 Substructure	£ - 15,367	£ - 11·02	-	-	£ - 16,726	£ - 11·99	£ -
2 Superstructure							
2.A Frame	11,745	8·42			12,785	9·16	
2.B Upper floors	11,880	8·52			12,933	9·27	
2.C Roof	4,432	3·18			4,824	3·46	
2.D Stairs	23,625	16·94			25,718	18·44	
2.E External walls	17,620	12·77			19,395	13·90	
2.F Windows and external doors	15,300	10·97			16,654	11·94	
2.G Internal walls and partitions	18,135	13·00			19,742	14·15	
2.H Internal doors							
Group element total	£ 102,937	£ 73·80	-	-	£ 112,051	£ 80·32	£
3 Internal finishes							
3.A Wall finishes	28,552	20·47			31,082	22·28	
3.B Floor finishes	12,960	9·28			14,107	10·12	
3.C Ceiling finishes	6,620	4·75			7,204	5·16	
Group element total	£ 48,132	£ 34·50			£ 52,393	£ 37·56	£
4 Fittings and furnishings	£ - 17,029	£ - 12·21			£ - 18,535	£ 13·29	£

	£	£	£	£
5 **Services**				
5.A Sanitary appliances	4·18	5,832	4·55	6,350
5.B Services equipment				
5.C Disposal installations				
5.D Water installations	33·92	47,313	36·92	51,502
5.E Heat source				
5.F Space heating and air treatment				
5.G Ventilating system	12·55	17,565	13·66	19,053
5.H Electrical installations	—	—		
5.I Gas installations	—	—		
5.J Lift and conveyor installations	—	—		
5.K Protective installations				
5.L Communication installations				
5.M Special installations	3·06	4,275	3·34	4,653
5.N Builder's work in connection with services	2·35	3,285	2·56	3,573
5.O Builder's profit and attendance on services				
Group element total	£ 56·06	£ 78,210	£ 61·03	£ 85,131
Sub-total excluding External works, Preliminaries and Contingencies	£	£	£	£
6 **External works**				
6.A Site work	3·97	5,535	4·32	6,025
6.B Drainage	3·45	4,815	3·75	5,238
6.C External services	—	—	—	—
6.D Minor building works	—	—	—	—
Group element total	£ 7·42	£ 10,350	£ 8·07	£ 11,264
Preliminaries	£ 17·25	£ 24,075	—	—
TOTALS (less Contingencies)	£ 212·26	£ 296,100	£ 212·26	£ 296,100

Table 17.1 – *continued*

SPECIFICATION AND DESIGN NOTES

Check List	PLEASE INCLUDE BRIEF SPECIFICATION AND DESIGN NOTES TO DESCRIBE ADEQUATELY THE FORM OF CONSTRUCTION AND QUALITY OF MATERIAL SUFFICIENTLY TO EXPLAIN THE PRICES IN THE ANALYSIS.
1 SUBSTRUCTURE	Strip foundations. 100 mm concrete ground floor slab.

2   SUPERSTRUCTURE
2.A   Frame
2.B   Upper floors
2.C   Roof
  2.C.1   Roof structure
  2.C.2   Roof coverings
  2.C.3   Roof drainage
  2.C.4   Roof lights
2.D   Stairs
  2.D.1   Stair structure
  2.D.2   Stair finishes
  2.D.3   Stair balustrades and handrails
2.E   External walls
2.F   Windows and external doors
  2.F.1   Windows
  2.F.2   External doors
2.G   Internal walls and partitions
2.H   Internal doors
	150 mm precast concrete flooring units
	
	30° pitch timber roof carried on purlins bearing on crosswalls
	interlocking concrete tiles
	P.V.C. rainwater installation
	
	in-situ concrete
	grano-lithic
	mild steel balustrade and wall handrailing
	
	cavity walls of brick facing, cavity and "thermalite" inner skin
	
	aluminium sliding sash in softwood frames
	Iroko framed doors glazed to entrances
	One brick structural crosswalls and 102 mm "thermalite" partitioning
	standard size flush doors veneered both sides

3   INTERNAL FINISHES
3.A   Wall finishes
3.B   Floor finishes
3.C   Ceiling finishes
  3.C.1   Finishes to ceilings
  3.C.2   Suspended ceilings
	emulsion paint on plaster or block partitioning
	vinyl tiles generally, granolithic to stores and clay tiles to toilet areas
	emulsion paint on plaster

4   FITTINGS AND FURNISHINGS
4.A   Fittings and furnishings
  4.A.1   Fittings, fixtures and furniture
  4.A.2   Soft furnishings
  4.A.3   Works of art
  4.A.4   Equipment
	built-in bedroom and kitchen units

5 SERVICES

5.A Sanitary appliances
5.B Services equipment
5.C Disposal installations
5.C.1 Internal drainage
5.C.2 Refuse disposal
5.D Water installations
5.D.1 Mains supply
5.D.2 Cold water service
5.D.3 Hot water service
5.D.4 Steam and condensate
5.E Heat source
5.F Space heating and air treatment
5.F.1 Water and/or steam (heating only)
5.F.2 Ducted warm air (heating only)
5.F.3 Electricity (heating only)
5.F.4 Local heating
5.F.5 Other heating systems
5.F.6 Heating with ventilation (air heated locally)
5.F.7 Heating with ventilation (air heated centrally)
5.F.8 Heating with cooling (air heated locally)
5.F.9 Heating with cooling (air heated centrally)
5.G Ventilating systems
5.H Electrical installations
5.H.1 Electric source and mains
5.H.2 Electric power supplies
5.H.3 Electric lighting
5.H.4 Electric lighting fittings
5.I Gas installation
5.J Lift and conveyor installations
5.J.1 Lifts and hoists
5.J.2 Escalators
5.J.3 Conveyors
5.K Protective installations
5.K.1 Sprinkler installations
5.K.2 Fire-fighting installations
5.K.3 Lightning protection
5.L Communication installations
5.M Special installations
5.N Builder's work in connection with services
5.O Builder's profit and attendance on services

white vitreous china sanitary ware generally, cast-iron baths, stainless steel sinks, copper waste and service pipes and fittings

Heating supplied from central boiler house – not included in this analysis

6 EXTERNAL WORKS

6.A Site works
6.A.1 Site preparation
6.A.2 Surface treatment
6.A.3 Site enclosure and division
6.A.4 Fittings and furniture
6.B Drainage
6.C External services
6.C.1 Water mains
6.C.2 Fire mains
6.C.3 Heating mains
6.C.4 Gas mains
6.C.5 Electric mains
6.C.6 Site lighting
6.C.7 Other mains and services
6.C.8 Builder's work in connection with external services
6.C.9 Builder's profit and attendance on external services
6.D Minor building work
6.D.1 Ancillary buildings
6.D.2 Alterations to existing buildings

precast concrete flag pavings and concrete steps

stoneware drainage, brick inspection chambers

copper water mains

PRELIMINARIES

Drawings: Drawings or a thumbnail sketch should accompany the Brief Cost Analysis

BUDGET ESTIMATE FOR PROPOSED RESIDENTIAL HOSTEL BLOCK

Base information:		
	Cost analysis	Table 17.1
	Reference	BCIS C–3–????
	Index	193
	Gross internal floor area	1,395 m²
	Number of storeys	3
	Type of tender	fixed price
	Cost excluding contingencies	£212·26 m²

Proposed building:		
	Price level	tender date April 1981
	Index	projected 216
	Gross internal floor are	1,420 m²
	Number of storeys	4
	Type of tender	fixed price

Budget Estimate:

Cost as analysis   £/m²: 212·26

Adjustments:

1. SUBSTRUCTURE

Analysis – (£2·45 m²) ground area covered 50 m x 10 m   500 m²

Proposed –
ground area covered

27 m x 10 m   270

10 m x 12 m   120

390 m²

Budget Cost –

$$\frac{£15,367}{500 \text{ m}^2} \times \frac{390 \text{ m}^2}{1,420 \text{ m}^2} = £8·45$$

Add say 12% for increased number of storeys   £1·01

£9·46

Difference   −1·56

Note: Reference to foundation costs in Table 10.4 shows similar figure for adjustment but calculated in a different manner.

2. SUPERSTRUCTURE

B Upper floors

Analysis   QF = $\frac{2}{3}$ = 0·66

Proposed   QF = $\frac{3}{4}$ = 0·75

Budget cost –

$$\frac{£8·42}{0·66} \times 0·75 \quad = \quad £9·56$$

Difference   + 1·14

C Roof

Analysis   QF = $\frac{500}{1,395}$ =   0·36

Proposed   QF = $\frac{390}{1,420}$ =   0·27

Budget cost –

$$\frac{£8·52}{0·36} \times 0·27 \quad = \quad £6·39$$

Difference   − 2·13

Carried forward   209·71

	£/m²
Brought forward	209·71

D Stairs
   Analysis 4 flights – £4,432 – £3·18 m²
   Proposed 9 flights

Budget cost –

$$\frac{£4,432}{4} \times \frac{9}{1,420} = £7·02$$

Difference	+ 3·84

E External walls
   Analysis   QF 0·49
   Proposed   QF

   Calculation – external cladding area

   2/27 m   = 54 m
   2/22 m   = 44 m

   98 m x 10·2 m high
   = 999·6 m²
   Wall 75% = 749·7 m²

   ∴ QF $= \dfrac{749·7 \text{ m}^2}{1,420 \text{ m}^2} = 0·53$

Budget cost –

$$\frac{£16·94}{0·49} \times 0·53 = £18·32$$

Difference	+ 1·38

F Windows and external doors
   Analysis   QF 0·16
   Proposed   QF

   Calculation: *see* External walls

   External cladding area 999·6 m²
   Window 25% = 249·9 m²

   ∴ QF $= \dfrac{249·9 \text{ m}^2}{1,420 \text{ m}^2} = 0·18$

Budget cost –

$$\frac{£12·77}{0·16} \times 0·18 = £14·37$$

Difference	+ 1·60

G Internal walls and partitions
   Quantity factors can only be approximated from the schematic
   layouts as a check against major differences.

   Analysis QF say
   2/10 m + 24/4·4 m + 2/3 m + 44 m + 32 m = 207·6 m
   = length of partitioning per floor
   ∴ Area = 3/207·6 m x 2·4 m = 1,495 m²

   ∴ QF $= \dfrac{1,495 \text{ m}^2}{1,395 \text{ m}^2} = 1·07$

   Proposed QF say
   1/10 m + 19/4·4 m + 14·6 m + 13·4 m + 19·6 m + 18·4 m = 169·6 m
   = length of partitioning per floor
   ∴ Area = 4/169·6 m x 2·4 m = 1,628 m²

   ∴ QF $= \dfrac{1,628 \text{ m}^2}{1,420 \text{ m}^2} = 1·15$

Carried forward	216·53

115

£/m²

Brought forward | 216·53

Budget cost —

$$\frac{£10·97}{1·07} \times 1·15 = £11·79$$

Difference | + 0·82

Note. Internal door adjustment ignored as similar in each scheme but adjustment could be made by deducting number of rooms x 1·5 m² for approximate total area of doors.

H Internal doors
   Similar number of rooms, therefore no adjustment proposed

3. INTERNAL FINISHES
   A Wall finishes
      QF take external walls x 1
                 internal walls x 2

   Analysis QF
   external walls 0·49 x 1 = 0·49
   internal walls 1·07 x 2 = 2·14

                              2·63

   Proposed QF
   external walls 0·53 x 1 = 0·53
   internal walls 1·15 x 2 = 2·30

                              2·83

Budget cost —

$$\frac{£20·47}{2·63} \times 2·38 = £22·03$$

Difference | + 1·56

Note. Areas could have been used, instead of the relative quantity factors, with similar result. e.g. Proposed QF
   external walls area   749·7 m² x 1 =   749·7 m²
   internal walls area   1,628 m² x 2 = 3,256·0 m²

                                          4,005·7 m²

$$\therefore \quad QF \quad = \frac{4,005·7 \text{ m}^2}{1,420 \text{ m}^2} = 2·83$$

This is one demonstration of the simplification of future calculations that can be effected by setting down the calculated quantity factor in the cost analysis.

B Floor finished }
C Ceiling finishes } no adjustments

Note. No adjustments are considered necessary as the QF in both instances will always be 1·00, and in the absence of any detailed information of the proposed building it can only be assumed that the mix of different types of finishes will remain similar between the analysed and proposed building.

4. FITTINGS AND FURNISHINGS — no adjustment
   Note. As by inspection the buildings are so similar no adjustment is considered necessary

Carried forward | 218·91

	£/m²
Brought forward	218·91

5. SERVICES – no adjustments proposed to the general services.

   J Lift installation
      One lift proposed serving four floors, say total
      cost £25,000 = £17·61 m²

	£/m²
Difference	+ 17·61

6. EXTERNAL WORKS
    No details available, therefore assume similar cost

	£/m²
Sub-total	236·52

Preliminaries
   Analysis – £17·25 m²
   Budget cost –
$$\frac{£17·25}{£212·26 \text{ m}^2} \times £236·52 \text{ m}^2 = £19·22$$

	£/m²
Difference	+ 1·97
	238·49

Price levelling factor
   Analysis index   193
   Proposed index 216 = + 11·92%

	£/m²
	+ 28·43
	£266·92

∴ Total budget cost excluding contingencies
    £266·92 m² x 1,420 m² = £379,026 say
                            Contingency

                 Total budget cost

380,000
12,000
392,000

The total of £392,000 would be reported to the client as the budget estimate.

The method employed to calculate the budget estimate should enable the architect and quantity surveyor to proceed with planning confident that, provided normal checking procedures are followed, the eventual tender will match the estimate.

Note. If the analysis figure had been taken without plan adjustments the result would have been

	£/m²
Analysis	212·26
Price levelling	
factor + 11·92%	25·30
	237·56

	£
£237·56 x 1,420 m² = £337,335 = say	338,000
Contingency	10,000
Total budget cost	£348,000

This approach could have introduced a budgeting error of as much as 12½ per cent, which could prove serious to the client's financial appraisal of the project.

Example 2

Assuming that the budget cost in Example 1 is acceptable, the architect develops the design a stage further, and the quantity surveyor prepares the cost plan, based on more detailed information – by considering each element in the way external walls were dealt with in Chapter 16. The cost plan figure for external walls there was calculated by measurement of areas converted to a quantity factor related to floor area, and this approach will be applicable to the majority of elements.

Some elements, however, are better related to number form, and the following calculations are for sanitary appliances, using the buildings considered in Example 1.

The cost analysis 5A sanitary appliances (Table 17.2) is obtained from the B.C.I.S. Amplified Cost Analysis version of the previous brief cost analysis and provides more detailed information than was previously available.

Quantities required for proposed residential hostel obtained from detailed sketch plans are as follows.

Table 17.2

Element and design criteria	Total cost of element £	Cost of element per m² of gross floor area £	Element unit quantity	Element unit rate £	Specification
5.A SANITARY APPLIANCES	5,832	4.18	—	—	White vitreous china generally, cast-iron baths, stainless steel sinks supplied and fixed by contractor

Sanitary appliances type and quality	Number	Cost of unit £	Total £
W.C. suites	10	81	810
urinals	10	180	1,800
wash hand basins	33	63	2,079
cleaners sinks	3	135	405
soap dispensers	33	18	594
towel rails	6	9	54
toilet roll holders	10	9	90
	105		5,832

Preliminaries ....8.85........ % of remainder of contract sum.

118

	Number
W.C. suites	16
Wash hand basins	32
Cleaners' sinks	4
Soap dispensers	32
Towel rails	8
Toilet-roll holders	16
Total	108

In the absence of detailed information the analysis figure for total cost of element could be used against the quantity factor of the number of fittings, i.e.

$$£5,832 \times \frac{1,395}{105} \times \frac{108}{1,420} = £5,893 = \text{total cost to cost plan}$$

then £5,893 ÷ 1,420 m² = £4·15 m² to cost plan.

However, the amplified cost analysis provides the best information in the right-hand columns, which schedule the individual fittings and their unit cost.

Using this information the cost plan calculation becomes:

	Number	Cost of Unit	Total
W.C. suites	16	£ 81	£1,296
Wash hand basins	32	63	2,016
Cleaners sinks	4	135	540
Soap dispensers	32	18	576
Towel rails	8	9	72
Toilet-roll holders	16	9	144
	108		£4,644

The element would then appear in the cost plan as follows:

	Total cost of element	Cost of element per m² of gross floor area	Specification
	£	£	
5A Sanitary appliances	4,644	3·27	White vitreous china generally, cast-iron baths, stainless steel sinks

	Number
W.C. suits	16
Wash hand basins	32
Cleaners' sinks	4
Soap dispensers	32
Towel rails	8
Toilet-roll holders	16
	108

In this way the variation to the range of fittings has been catered for, and it is a simple matter to discount fittings that may appear in the analysis but are not required in the proposed building, i.e. fittings are given their correct cost weighting.

Cost checking becomes a simple matter against the cost plan allowance.

Example 3

A more complex example may be a requirement to examine proposals for two alternative office buildings (Figure 17.2) taking account of capital costs, running costs, planning efficiency in terms of lettable and balance areas, and the effect on the developer's budget calculations.

Scheme A: a shallow planned building relying on natural ventilation through windows in the external walls and from the light wells.

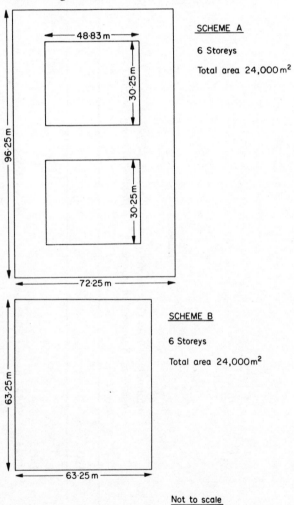

Figure 17.2 Proposed office building: alternative proposals.

Scheme B: a deep planned building requiring mechanical ventilation and permanent artificial lighting to a large area.

It is anticipated that the Scheme A offices can be let for an annual rent of £155 per m² of lettable area, inclusive of running costs and Scheme B offices can be let for an annual rent of £175 per m² of lettable area, inclusive of running costs. A return of 13 per cent on capital is required.

Table 17.3

	Cost Index	Information from Cost Analysis 16,000 m² 8 floors 4 m storey height	Scheme A 24,000 m² 6 floors 4 m storey height	Scheme B 24,000 m² 6 floors 4 m storey height
	120		150	150
	£			
Preliminaries & Contingencies	25·85			
Work below ground level	13·45	50 No. bases £2,000 each; 350 m perimeter beam £60 m; Concrete site slab £43 m²	86 No. bases; 654 m perimeter beams	66 No. bases; 253 m perimeter beams
Frame	32·75	Concrete frame bay size 6 m x 6 m	General specification as analysis; Estimate £900,000	General specification as analysis; Estimate £750,000
Upper floors	18·85	Precast concrete beams 6 m span	Precast concrete beams 6 m span	Precast concrete beams 6 m span
Roof	5·40	Concrete roof slab, etc., £32·5 m²; 350 m Parapet £60 m	654 m parapet; General specification as analysis	253 m parapet; General specification as analysis
Stairs	1·90	Per flight £1,000	12 No. Stair wells	8 No. Stair wells
External walls	13·45	Wall to floor ratio 0·32		
Windows	33·65	Window to floor ratio 0·32; Single glazed metal windows	Windows comprise 50 per cent of the external cladding and shall be single glazed	Windows comprise 25 per cent of the external cladding and shall be double glazed
Internal walls & partitions	4·30		Taken as analysis	Taken as analysis
Internal doors	1·50		Taken as analysis	Taken as analysis
Floor finishes	10·75		Taken as analysis	Taken as analysis
Decoration & wall finishes	2·15		Estimate £72,500	Estimate £35,000

Item		Option 1	Option 2	Option 3
Ceiling finishes	1·35	Self finished soffites	Suspended ceiling required	Included in estimate for ventialation ventilation services
Heating and ventilating	21·55		Estimate £600,000 Running costs £240,000	Estimate £1,800,000 Running costs £360,000
Electrics	13·45		Estimate £400,000 Running costs £72,000 PA	Estimate £350,000 Running costs £96,000 PA
Sanitary fittings	2·70	100 W.C.'s 100 L.B.'s 60 urinals 15 No. sinks Centrally	144 No. W.C.'s 144 No. L.B.'s 90 No. urinals 22 No. sinks Dispersed	144 No. W.C.'s 144 No. L.B.'s 90 No. urinals 22 No. Sinks Centrally
Hot & cold internal plumbing & wastes	8·75	Includes fire mains and dry risers		
Lifts	10·75		Estimate £600,000 Running costs £36,000 PA Estimate 6 per cent	Estimate £350,000 Running costs £36,000 PA Estimate 4 per cent
External works	11·20			
Total	£233·75			
Cost of site			£2,400,000 (freehold exclusive of fees and charges)	£2,400,000 (freehold exclusive of fees and charges)
Planning efficiency			Ratio of lettable space to circulation areas, etc. 100:40	Ratio of lettable space to circulation areas, etc. 100:25
Annual cost of operating Heating and Ventilation plant and all repairs and maintenance			£180,000	£300,000
Annual costs of office services, caretakers, and portering			£240,000	£240,000

STAGE 1 – ELEMENTAL ESTIMATE

	Scheme A			Scheme B		
Price levelling factor— Analysis index Scheme index	$\dfrac{120}{150}$ = +25%			$\dfrac{120}{150}$ = +25%		
1. SUBSTRUCTURE	86 No. bases @ £2,000 654 m beams @ £ 60 4,000 m² slab @ £ 43	172,000 39,240 172,000 383,240 95,810		66 No. bases @ £2,000 253 m beams @ £ 60 4,000 m² slab @ £ 43	132,000 15,180 172,000 319,180 79,795	
	PLF + 25%		479,050	PLF + 25%		398,975
2. SUPERSTRUCTURE A frame	as estimate		900,000	as estimate as Scheme A		750,000
B upper floors	Analysis: QF = $\frac{7}{8}$ = 0·88 Proposed: QF = $\frac{5}{6}$ = 0·83 Estimate: $\dfrac{£18·85}{0·88}$ × 0·83 = £17·78 £17·78 × 24,000 m² = PLF + 25%	426,720 106,680	533,400			533,400
C roof	654 m parapet @ £60 4,000 m² slab @ £32·50 PLF + 25%	39,240 130,000 169,240 42,310	211,550	253 m parapet @ £60 4,000 m² slab @ £32·50	15,180 130,000 145,180 36,295	181,475
D stairs	12 No. stair wells 5 No. flights = 60 No. flights @ £1,000 PLF + 25%	60,000 15,000	75,000	8 No. stair wells 5 No. flights = 40 No. flights @ £1,000	40,000 10,000	50,000
E external walls	Analysis QF 0·32 Proposed QF calculation: cladding 654 m × 24 m high = 15,696 m² less windows 50% = 7,848			cladding 253 m × 24 m high = 6,072 m² less windows 25% = 1,518		

Item							
F windows and external doors	$QF = \dfrac{7,848 \text{ m}^2}{24,000 \text{ m}^2} = 0.33$ Estimate: $\dfrac{£13.45}{0.32} \times 0.33 = £13.87$ £13.87 × 24,000 m² PLF + 25%	332,880 83,220	416,100	$QF = \dfrac{4,554 \text{ m}^2}{24,000 \text{ m}^2} = 0.19$ $\dfrac{£13.45}{0.32} \times 0.19 = £7.99$ £7.99 × 24,000 m²	191,760 47,900	239,700
	Analysis QF 0.32 Proposed QF calculation – see external walls window 7,848 m² $QF: \dfrac{7,848 \text{ m}^2}{24,000 \text{ m}^2} = 0.33$ Estimate: $\dfrac{£33.65}{0.32} \times 0.33 = £34.70$ £34.70 × 24,000 m² PLF + 25%	832,800 208,200	1,041,000	window 1,518 m² $QF: \dfrac{1,518 \text{ m}^2}{24,000 \text{ m}^2} = 0.06$ $\dfrac{£33.65}{0.32} \times 0.06 = £6.31$ £6.31 × 24,000 m² Add for double glazing say 30%	151,440 37,860 189,300 56,790	246,090
G internal walls and partitions	as analysis £4.30 × 24,000 m² PLF + 25%	103,200 25,800	129,000	as Scheme A		129,000
H internal doors	as analysis £1.50 × 24,000 m² PLF + 25%	36,000 9,000	45,000	as Scheme A		45,000
3. INTERNAL FINISHES						
A wall finishes	as estimate		72,500	as estimate		35,000
B floor finishes	as analysis £10.75 × 24,000 m² PLF + 25%	258,000 64,500	322,500	as Scheme A		322,500
C ceiling finishes	suspended ceiling say £15 per m² Proposed QF: 1.00 £15 × 24,000 m²		360,000	included in estimate for ventilation services		
4. FITTINGS AND FURNISHINGS	nil		—	nil		—
	Carried forward		£4,585,100	Carried forward		£2,931,140

	Scheme A			Scheme B		
		£	£		£	£
			Brought forward 4,585,100			Brought forward £2,931,140
5. SERVICES **A sanitary appliances**	Analysis: QF W.C.s 100 L.B.s 100 Urinals 60 Sinks 15 centrally 275 gross floor area 16,000 m² = 1·72 fittings per 100 m² Proposed: QF No W.C.s 144 L.B.s 144 Urinals 90 Sinks 22 dispersed 400 gross floor area 24,000 m² = 1·66 fittings per 100 m² Estimate: $\frac{£2·70}{1·72} \times 1·66 = £2·61$ £2·61 × 24,000 m² PLF + 25%		62,640 15,660 78,300	Proposed: QF No. W.C.s 144 L.B.s 144 Urinals 90 Sinks 22 centrally 400 as Scheme A		78,300
	Note. This approach considered satisfactory in this instance, as ratio of various types of fittings almost identical between analysis and proposed. Extra cost of dispersed fittings taken into account in 5C – dispersal installations and 5D – water installations					
C and D dispersal and water installations	Analysis QF – as 5A Proposed QF – as 5A Estimate: $\frac{£8·75}{1·72} \times 1·66 = £8·44$ £8·44 × 24,000 m² PLF + 25% Add for dispersal fittings say 20%		202,560 50,640 253,200 50,640	as Scheme A but concentrated provision		

E, F and G heating and ventilating systems	as estimate	600,000	as estimate	1,800,000
H electrical installations	as estimate	400,000	as estimate	350,000
J lift installations	as estimate	600,000	as estimate	350,000
6. EXTERNAL WORKS	6%	6,567,240	4%	5,762,640
Preliminaries and Contingencies		394,034		230,505
		6,961,274		5,993,145

Analysis:

Total cost	233·75
Preliminaries and Contingencies	25·85
	207·90

= 12·43%

Estimate:

12·43% of £6,961,274	865,286	12·43% of £5,993,145	744,947
	£7,826,560		£6,738,092

Note: Scheme B shows a cost advantage over Scheme A of £1,088,468 if capital building costs only are considered.

STAGE 2 – TOTAL CAPITAL COST COMPARISON

	Scheme A	Scheme B
Capital building cost	£7,826,560	£6,738,092
Fees – professional and legal say 15 per cent	1,173,984	1,010,713
Site costs	2,400,000	2,400,000
Finance during construction say 10 per cent of above costs	1,140,054	1,014,880
Total capital cost, including fees, site and finance	£12,540,598	£11,163,685

Scheme B continues to show a cost advantage over Scheme A.

STAGE 3 – TOTAL 'COST IN USE' COMPARISON

	Scheme A	Scheme B
Running Costs –		
Heating and ventilating	£240,000	£360,000
Electrics	72,000	96,000
Lifts	36,000	36,000
Repairs and maintenance	180,000	300,000
Cleaning and portering	240,000	240,000
Total annual running costs	£768,000	£1,032,000

Assuming 13 per cent interest rate = year's purchase in perpetuity = 100/13 = 7,692.

	Scheme A	Scheme B
Total capital costs	£12,540,598	£11,163,685
Running costs capitalized		
Scheme A: £768,000 x 7·692	6,184,560	
Scheme B: £1,032,000 x 7·692		8,215,200
	£18,725,158	£19,378,885

Note: Scheme A now shows a very small advantage over Scheme B.

STAGE 4 – COMPARISON TAKING INTO ACCOUNT PLANNING EFFICIENCY

	Scheme A	Scheme B
Gross floor area	24,000 m²	24,000 m²
Ratio of lettable to circulation areas	100:40	100:25
Lettable area	24,000 m²	24,000 m²
	1·40	1·25
	= 17,143 m²	= 19,200 m²

	Scheme A	Scheme B
Annual rents		
Scheme A 17,143 @ £155	2,657,165	
Scheme B 19,200 @ £175		3,360,000
Less agent's fees and 5 per cent vacant lettings	132,858	168,000
	2,524,307	3,192,000

	Scheme A	Scheme B
Value of rents capitalized at 13 per cent in perpetuity		
Scheme A: 2,524,307 x 7·692	19,417,746	
Scheme B: 3,192,000 x 7·692		24,553,846
Total capital cost and running costs capitalized	18,725,158	19,378,885
Difference expressed as percentage of capital and running costs	3·6%	26·7%

Scheme A therefore shows only a marginal profit to the developer and any change in rental values or extra building costs would make the scheme unprofitable. Scheme B shows a rate of return which should cover most contingencies and indicates an attractive profit to the developer.

This example is intended to demonstrate a number of issues raised in earlier chapters and to emphasize the importance of evaluating all aspects of a project before becoming inescapably committed to any one solution.

Example 4

Evaluate the total costs of the three alternative constructions for the single storey factories described in Figure 17.3.

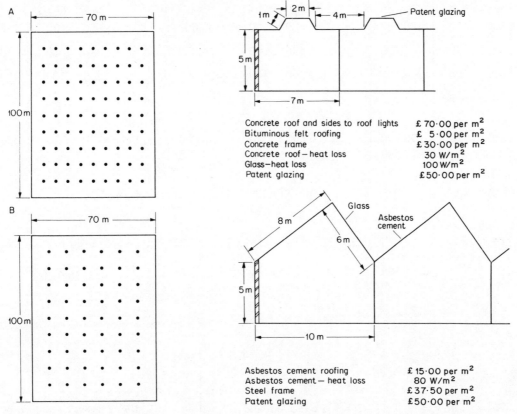

Concrete roof and sides to roof lights £ 70·00 per m²
Bituminous felt roofing   £ 5·00 per m²
Concrete frame   £ 30·00 per m²
Concrete roof – heat loss   30 W/m²
Glass – heat loss   100 W/m²
Patent glazing   £ 50·00 per m²

Asbestos cement roofing   £ 15·00 per m²
Asbestos cement – heat loss   80 W/m²
Steel frame   £ 37·50 per m²
Patent glazing   £ 50·00 per m²

C as B, but with insulated roof, copper covered woodwool £ 40·00 per m² heat loss 30 W/m²

Generally

Capital cost of space heating, 15p per installed W.   Space heating 20 W/m³
Running costs 4·5 p W

Figure 17.3

STRUCTURE

	Capital Costs	*Alternative A*				*Alternative B*				*Alternative C*		
		m²	£	£		m²	£	£		m²	£	£
Roof	2/100				7/100				7/100			
	3	600			8	5,600	15·00	84,000	8	5,600	40·00	224,000
	10/100											
	2	2,000	70·00									
	9/100											
	4	3,600	5·00									
		6,200	75·00	465,000								
Gable	10/2/2·5				2/7/½/8				2/7/½/8			
	1	50	75·00	3,750	6	336	15·00	5,040	6	336	40·00	13,440
Glass	10/100				7/100				7/100			
	2	2,000	50·00	100,000	6	4,200	50·00	210,000	6	4,200	50·00	210,000
Frame	100				100				100			
	70	7,000	30·00	210,000	70	7,000	37·50	262,500	70	7,000	37·50	262,500
				778,750				561,540				709,940

HEATING INSTALLATION

Heat Losses

	Alternative A				Alternative B				Alternative C		
	m²	Watts	Watts		m²	Watts	Watts		m²	Watts	Watts
Roof	6,200	30	186,000		5,600	80	448,000		5,600	30	168,000
Gable	50	30	1,500		336	80	26,880		336	30	10,080
Glass	2,000	100	200,000		4,200	100	420,000		4,200	100	420,000

Volume above wall levels

10/100	m³			7/100	m³			7/100	m³		
2·5	2,500	20	50,000	24	16,800	20	336,000	24	16,800	20	336,000
			437,500				1,230,880				934,080

Running Costs

x 4·5p = £19,687   x 4·5p = £55,389   x 4·5p = £42,033

Capital Costs

437,500 x 15p = £65,625   1,230,880 x 15 p = £184,632   934,080 x 15p = £140,112

Structure and Heating Costs   £844,375   £746,172   £850,052

	£						
Annual Costs	19,687			55,389			42,033
Capital discounted at 9% 60 years							
844,375 x 0·0905	76,416	746,172 x 0·0905	67,528		850,052 x 0·0905		76,929
	96,103		122,917				118,962
Annual Costs	19,687			55,389			42,033
Capital discounted at 9% 15 years							
844,375 x 0·1241	104,786	746,172 x 0·1241	92,599		850,052 x 0·1241		105,491
	124,473		147,988				147,524

Order of Advantages	1	2	3
Capital only	B	A	C
Running costs only	A	C	B
Total over 60 years	A	C	B
Total over 15 years	A	C*	B*

*Difference less than £500

18

Cost in Use and Cost Planning

In the previous chapters we have described cost planning by elements and by comparative estimates. The first divides the total amount available for the project into targets for individual elements and uses these target costs as a guide during the development of the scheme at the working drawing stages. The second method is based on preparing an estimate for a design which has reached a reasonably settled stage and using this estimate, expressed in elemental form, as the cost plan. This method of comparative cost planning, because it is based on a series of estimates, would allow 'cost in use' information to be considered for each alternative choice when deciding the optimum specification. This chapter is concerned with investigating how future costs could be incorporated in a target cost plan by elements, since it is this method that most clearly demonstrates the relation between various parts of the building. An example of such a cost plan is shown in Table 18.1.

In the past preparing a cost plan has been an exercise in allocating capital resources. Most expenditure limit controls are applied to the capital sums to be spent in the immediate present. Maintenance and running costs are not normally taken into account except in the sense that the limits are set with regard to 'normal' buildings, which are expected to produce 'normal' running costs. The analysis shown at Table 18.1 demonstrates that the three forms of cost, capital, maintenance and running costs, can be calculated and displayed for use in the same mode that can be used for initial costs. The advantage of such a presentation as this is that the total cost implications of design decisions are shown and can be related to the quantity factors and the yardstick of area used in elemental cost planning.

Table 18.1 is based on a building that is assumed to have a total floor area of 2,700 m² and a capital cost of £898,750. The first columns show an elemental breakdown of this capital cost and the same figures represented as an annual equivalent cost calculated at an interest rate of 9 per cent. The present value of £1 per annum at this interest rate over a period of 60 years is £11·048. This means that an investment of this sum would produce an income of £1 in each year, or alternatively a loan of this figure would need to be repaid at a rate of £1 in each year.

Table 18.2 shows the present value per annum table for 9 per cent; in addition a table of reciprocals is given which indicates the rate of return for an investment of £1, or the repayment necessary on a loan of £1.

If each elemental total in Table 18.1 is multiplied by the reciprocal of the present value per annum the resulting figure is the annual equivalent. This annual figure relates to the total cost and it is necessary as a second step to relate this cost to the area of the building. To give a reasonable scale to the figures the most suitable unit of measurement for this type of analysis proves to be a unit of 100 square metres. Since the area of the building is 2,700 square metres, the final column gives the annual equivalents divided by 27. Certain elements have been further adjusted to transfer part of the heating costs to other elements, a point of detail that will be explained later.

The annual equivalent cost of the replacement and maintenance items is calculated by finding the amount that would be needed annually to repay a loan equal to the cost of the replacement items during the life of those components. At an interest rate of 9 per cent a component with a life of 10 years would require a repayment of about 15·6p for each £1 borrowed; this figure is the reciprocal of the present value per annum and can be read from Table 18.2.

The form in which this analysis has been prepared requires that the initial and replacement costs should be presented separately. The annual equivalent of the initial capital costs has been taken into account in the first three columns of Table 18.1. Calculating the annual equivalent costs of the replacement items described above assumes that there will be a payment at the start of each period. Clearly this will also include a payment at the start of the building's life, but since this payment has been included with the initial costs, it must be deducted from those that represent the maintenance costs. This problem is solved by calculating the annual equivalent of this particular payment related to the whole life of the building and deducting this sum from the equivalents calculated in relation to the life of the components. Reference to the column of reciprocals in Table 18.2 (cols. 4, 5) shows that the annual repayment related to the whole life of the building is 9p for each £1 borrowed. For a component with a life of 10 years, therefore, the annual equivalent of the replacements alone will be 15·6p minus 9p, or 6·6p for each £1. The replacement costs are also set out in Table 18.1, in which an amount has been assumed for the various elements and the period of the repairs suggested. The calculated annual equivalent has then been divided by 27 to give the costs in relation to the yardstick of 100 square metres. In general the annual equivalent costs

INITIAL CAPITAL COSTS

Element (Area)	Initial Capital £	Ann. Equiv. for 60 years at 9% (note 1) £	Ann. Equiv. (Note 2) £	Value £	Period Years	Multiplier
Foundations (540)	42,500	3,846	142·44 + 12·45 = 154·89			
Frame	105,000	9,503	351·96			
Upper floors (2,160)	90,000	8,145	301·67			
Roof (540)	37,500	3,394	125·70 + 17·35 = 143·05	18,000	20	0·0190
Stairs	20,000	1,810	67·04			
Walls (930)	60,000	5,430	201·11 + 37·45 = 238·56			
Windows (510)	65,000	5,883	$217·89 + \dfrac{54·15}{121·40} = 272·04$	1,500	10	0·0653
Partitions	42,500	3,846	142·44			
Doors	20,000	1,810	67·04	1,200	5	0·1666
Wall finishes	42,500	3,846	142·44	1,500	5	0·1666
Ceiling finishes	42,500	3,846	142·44			
Floor finishes	62,500	5,656	209·48	30,000	15	0·0336
Decorations	20,000	1,810	67·04	15,000	6	0·1324
				9,000	3	0·3046
Sanitary fittings	8,750	792	29·33	300	5	0·1666
Cold water	21,250	1,923	71·22	18,000	30	0·0068
Hot water	17,500	1,584	58·67	18,000	30	0·0068
Heating	83,750	7,579	280·70 − 121·40 = 159·30	84,000	30	0·0068
Electricity	62,500	5,656	209·48	75,000	30	0·0068
Lamps	10,000	905	33·52	10,000	2	0·4780
Drainage	15,000	1,358	50·30	5,000	15	0·0336
Pavings	30,000	2,715	100·55			
	898,750	81,337	3,012·46			

Notes: 1. Obtained by multiplying first column by 0·0905.
2. Floor area 2,700 m², therefore divide by 27.
3. Costs based on formulae:

$$\text{Fuel cost per installed kJ} = \frac{\text{Max. hourly heat loss (kJ)} \times 1{,}800 \times 24}{1{,}000 \times 38 \times 20 \times 0·8} \times £0·15$$

$$= \text{Max. hourly heat loss (kJ)} \times £0·01065$$

where £0·15 cost of fuel per litre
38 mJ per litre = calorific value
0·8 Overall efficiency
20 °C = Temperature difference
1,800 = Degree days
3·6 = Conversion factor to convert transmission coefficient given in seconds to hours divided by 1,000 to give result in kilo joules 3,600/1,000.

18.1

REPLACEMENTS		HEATING COSTS (NOTE 3)			TOTAL EQUIVALENT
Ann. Equiv. for 60 years at 9% £	Ann. Equiv. per 100 m² £	Heat Losses kJ per hour	Fuel Costs Oil £	Annual Equiv. per 100 m² £	Annual Equiv. per 100 m² £
		3·6 x 540 x 20° x 1·14 = 44,323	472·39	17·50	172·39
					351·96
					301·67
342·00	12·67	3·6 x 540 x 20° x 1·59 = 61,819	658·86	24·40	180·12
					67·04
		3·6 x 930 x 20° x 1·99 = 133,250	1,420·16	52·60	291·16
97·95	3·63	3·6 x 510 x 20° x 5·25 = 192,780	2,054·63	76·10	351·77
					142·44
199·92	7·40				74·44
249·90	9·26				151·70
					142·44
1,008·00	37·33				246·81
1,986·00	73·56				
2,741·40	101·53				242·13
49·98	1·85				31·18
122·40	4·53				75·75
122·40	4·53				63·20
571·20	21·16	8,100 m³ x 5 x 20° x 0·7 = 567,000	6,043·03	223·82	404·28
510·00	18·89	999,172	10,649·07		228·37
4,780·00	177·04				210·56
168·00	6·22				56·52
					100·55
12,949·15	479·60			394·42	3,886·48

of the replacements are considerably less than for those of the initial costs, but this does not hold true of materials with a short life. Redecorations are twice as expensive and the replacement of light fittings is five times as expensive as the original expenditure. The key factor is the period of replacement. Table 18.1 shows that a repair that becomes necessary at intervals exceeding 10 to 15 years is discounted at such a high rate that it loses its significance.

The final columns in Table 18.1 show the running costs of the heating system. The heat loss calculation for the building has been split to allocate the losses against the elements where the loss occurs. The calculation of the heat required for warming the air in the building is entered against the element 'Heating installation'. It is possible by following a formula to calculate the amount of fuel that will be necessary to support the heating requirements. Since this figure is already an annual cost, there is no need to use the discount tables, but the costs must be related to the yardstick of area. The proportion of the heat losses to the useful heat can be used to divide the cost of the heating installation between the elements. This is the adjustment made in the third column of the capital cost section. The final column of Table 18.1 shows the total annual equivalent element by element.

Table 18.2

Years	9 per cent Present Value Per Annum	Reciprocal	Less	Multiplier
2	1·759	0·5685	0·0905	0·4780
3	2·531	0·3951	0·0905	0·3046
5	3·890	0·2571	0·0905	0·1666
6	4·486	0·2229	0·0905	0·1324
10	6·418	0·1558	0·0905	0·9653
15	8·061	0·1241	0·0905	0·0336
20	9·129	0·1095	0·0905	0·0190
30	10·274	0·0973	0·0905	0·0068
60	11·048	0·0905	—	—

A cost plan in this form could be used to demonstrate the relation between initial replacement and running costs and to assist in the choice of specifications and design details. The elemental costs can be manipulated by the use of quantity factors in the same way as simple capital costs. For example a change in the outline of the building, or the proportion of windows to walls, will alter the wall to floor or the window to floor ratios. If the changes in these ratios are applied to the total annual equivalent figures, they will automatically adjust for the changes in heat losses and for the cost of redecoration. The figures could also be used to examine the effect of a change in specification. For example the annual running cost of the fuel used to

offset the heat losses through the windows is £2,054. Suppose it were assumed that this cost could be reduced to £750 by introducing a higher standard of insulation. Over the 60-year life of the building a capital cost of £11·05 will have an annual equivalent of £1; the saving in fuel costs of £1,304 would, therefore, have a capital equivalent of £14,409. This extra capital cost must then be related to the area of the windows, 510 square metres. The extra insulation would need to be provided at a maximum of £28 per square metre.

A factor which merits thought is the ratio of the costs shown in Table 18.1 to those of cleaning and portering and of course for staffing the building to carry out its primary function.

For example, if the average area per occupant was 15 square metres. The average staff cost would therefore, be at least £300 per square metre, while the total annual cost of the whole building shown at Table 18.1 is only about £40 per square metre. For a manufacturing plant the cost of production machinery, labour, materials and work in progress is likely to be much higher in relation to the building costs. It is probably this fact that above any others determines the value society places on its buildings and the choices that are made between expenditure on initial capital costs or on the maintenance and running costs.

The study of the relation between building and maintenance costs of individual elements, or for complete building, naturally leads to the question of why cost limits for buildings should deal only with capital costs. In the example above the annual maintenance costs amount to about £480 per 100 m^2. If all these could be offset by increased capital expenditure, at 9 per cent the extra building costs would have to be limited to 11·048 × £480 per 100 m^2. This represents about 16 per cent of the capital costs assumed. Since there are many items of maintenance that cannot be eliminated completely, especially the deterioration of service installation and wearing surfaces such as floor and stair finishes, the amount that could be transferred is much reduced. This means that the degree of freedom is probably limited to around 5–7½ per cent, but even this would be a very considerable addition to the capital cost if it were applied to all buildings in the public sector now controlled by costs limits. In effect this might well lead to a corresponding reduction in the annual building programmes. Savings on expenditure in years far into the future would seem to be a poor alternative, politically, to maintaining the present quantity of public building. The reasons for limiting capital expenditure on buildings are largely political and administrative, and these must be taken into account in discussing the type of control exercised. In the argument developed above, the amount that might be added can only be of the order of 5 per cent. The amount is well within the variation of cost that might be expected by the changes in wall to floor ratios, floor to ceiling heights, solid cladding

to window ratios, or in the choice of heating system or structure.

In short, the extra expenditure to provide higher standards could be found by alternative decisions within the present cost control system. This in turn leads to a number of related problems; if it is indeed proved that extra expenditure really does offset maintenace costs and if it could be managed under existing procedures, there is no reason to change. If design teams under these procedures do not now make sensible choices to reduce maintenance costs, why not include rules to limit the planning and specification choices to those that are acceptable? Would it not also be thought necessary to introduce rules to prevent any extra money invested to offset maintenance costs being used for other purposes? If capital costs have been increased to offset maintenance, would it not in addition be necessary to have rules to prevent any expenditure on these elements at any time in the future? These questions suggest that the apparent simplification of procedure by considering maintenance costs and capital together might produce a more comprehensive, though unwieldy, system of control.

It is often suggested that maintenance costs need not be considered too seriously, since they are found from income and, therefore, reduce the amount of tax to be paid. Capital expenditure is of course found from accrued income on which tax has already been paid. In simple terms the argument runs that if we consider two buildings for investment with alternative designs, one costing £800,000 and the other £750,000, with maintenance costs £100,000 and £150,000 respectively, and assuming the same income in both cases, the amount of tax paid would be less for the scheme with the higher maintenance costs, and in addition there would be the considerable saving on capital costs. Within the framework of the argument there does appear to be an advantage in accepting the higher maintenance costs, but it does not take into account what use was made of the £50,000 saving. If this is used to produce an income, it then becomes subject to taxation and thus the total tax paid may not differ. The exact balance depends on how far capital expenditure is drawn from savings or is raised by loans or share issues. Similarly the rate of tax and the rate of return on the alternative use of the funds saved will be critical. This fact emphasizes that the data used in 'cost in use' calculations must be related to the client's financial situation, and although it is possible to suggest techniques that can be universally applied, there can be no standardization of the data which is used.

If it were necessary to take into account the fact that the return on the investment was expected to be at a rate different from the interest paid on a loan, or if it were necessary to take taxation into account, this could be done by using dual-rate Years Purchase tables. An example of the use of dual-rate tables and the arguments that would be followed is set out below; a worked example may be found in Chapter 9, Example 10.

The choice of interest rates has a very considerable effect on these calculations, Table 18.1 shows the capital cost at £898,750 and the annual cost of heating £10,649. The annual equivalent cost of the capital compared to the heating costs is set out in Table 18.3, at various interest rates over 60 years. The table also shows the comparison between the capital cost and the present value of the heating.

Whichever way this calculation is performed, for any particular interest rate the ratios of future heating costs to capital costs are the same but when interest rates are low future costs carry a much greater significance than when interest rates are high. This fact is of considerable import-

Table 18.3

Per cent	Present Value Per Annum	Annual Equivalent of Capital Cost	Annual Cost of Heating	Ratio of Heating Cost to Capital Cost
5	18·93	47,477	10,649	0·224
7	14·04	64,013	10,649	0·165
9	11·05	81,334	10,649	0·130
11	9·07	99,090	10,649	0·107
13	7·68	117,025	10,649	0·091

Per cent	Capital Cost	Present Value of Heating	Ratio of Heating Cost to Capital Cost
5	898,750	201,585	0·224
7	898,750	149,511	0·165
9	898,750	117,671	0·130
11	898,750	96,586	0·107
13	898,750	81,784	0·091

Table 18.4

Years	5 per cent PVpA	5 per cent Increment	Per cent	7 per cent PVpA	7 per cent Increment	Per cent	9 per cent PVpA	9 per cent Increment	Per cent	11 per cent PVpA	11 per cent Increment	Per cent	13 per cent PVpA	13 per cent Increment	Per cent
5	4·329			4·100			3·890			3·696			3·517		
		3·393	78		2·924	71		2·528	64		2·193	59		1·909	54
10	7·722			7·024			6·418			5·889			5·426		
		2·658	61		2·084	50		1·643	42		1·302	35		1·036	29
15	10·380			9·108			8·061			7·191			6·462		
		2·082	48		1·486	36		1·068	27		0·772	20		0·563	16
20	12·462			10·594			9·129			7·963			7·025		
		1·632	37		1·060	25		0·694	17		0·459	12		0·305	8
25	14·094			11·654			9·823			8·422			7·330		
		1·278	29		0·755	18		0·451	11		0·272	7		0·166	4
30	15·372			12·409			10·274			8·694			7·496		
		1·002	23		0·539	13		0·293	7		0·161	4		0·090	2
35	16·374			12·948			10·567			8·855			7·586		
		0·785	18		0·384	9		0·190	4		0·096	2		0·048	1
40	17·159			13·332			10·757			8·951			7·634		
		0·615	14		0·274	6		0·124	3		0·057	1		0·027	—
45	17·774			13·606			10·881			9·008			7·661		
		0·482	11		0·195	4		0·081	2		0·034	—		0·014	—
50	18·256			13·801			10·962			9·042			7·675		

ance when considering cost in use calculations during a period of high inflation, where interest rates are always at a high level. Furthermore it raises a question as to the validity of decisions based on this form of calculation if future costs or advantages are discounted to such a degree. For this reason it is essential to look at the problem in more detail.

Table 18.4 gives the present values per annum at various interest rates, for five year intervals up to 50 years and the incremental increase in the present value for the 5 year periods and also the increments represented as percentages of the present value at 5 years. The values for the various interest rates for the first 5 years are not dissimilar but after 10 years the value at 5 per cent exceeds the total present value at 50 years for the 13 per cent rate. The percentage values for each 5 year increment, at the 5 per cent interest rate are significant up to 50 years. With an interest rate of 13 per cent the percentage values of increments after about 25 years can be disregarded.

Another way of looking at this problem is to consider the term of years over which benefits will cover the cost of expenditure. The simplistic approach is to assume that if an expenditure of £10 produced a saving of £1 in each year, then the expenditure would be 'paid back' in 10 years. This rule of thumb calculation ignores the fact that a saving of £1 in 10 years time has a different value to a saving of £1 in 5 years time or to the value of £1 saved this year. Inspection of the table of present values per annum for 5 per cent shows that an investment of £10 would produce an income of £1 over about 14 years or, equally, a debt of £10 would need to be paid back at the rate of £1 in each of 14 years. Therefore at a ratio of expenditure to income of 10:1 the pay-back period at 5 per cent is 14 years; at 13 per cent no pay-back period for this ratio is possible since the present value per annum never exceeds 7·69.

Table 18.5 sets out a range of annual savings that might be achieved for a capital expenditure of £10,000. Column 2 sets out the ratio of capital to savings, columns 3 and 4

show to the nearest year the period of years which will produce a present value per annum equivalent to the required ratio at 5 and 13 per cent. It can be seen that for low ratios of capital to saving, i.e. where the benefits are greatest and the pay-back periods are short the interest rate is not significant, but where the ratios are higher i.e. where the pay-back periods are longer, there is a very marked difference in the columns. First, if the ratio of capital to saving exceeds a cut-off point (calculated by dividing 100 by the rate of interest) no positive return on the investment can be expected. Secondly, there is a range of ratios where the pay-back period changes very rapidly. These facts underline the sensitivity of this type of calculation and require that the estimate of savings and the choice of interest rate is made with care. Anyone using these methods must consider whether the procedure is really appropriate to the decision that must be made; for example in the context of these calculations it must be decided whether the objective of the exercise is to save fuel or to indicate a financial advantage.

Table 18.5
Capital Expenditure of £10,000

Annual Saving	Ratio	Years at 5 per cent	Years at 13 per cent
1,000	10:1	14	—
1,200	8·33:1	11	—
1,300	7·69:1	10	—
1,400	7·14:1	9	22
1,500	6·66:1	8	16
1,750	5·71:1	7	11
2,000	5:1	6	9
3,000	3·33:1	4	5
4,000	2·5:1	3	3
5,000	2:1	2	2

APPENDIX A

Standard Form of Cost Analysis

This is published by The Building Cost Information Service of the Royal Institution of Chartered Surveyors. It is copyright by the Institution, by whose kind permission it is here reproduced.

Note

The Standard Form of Cost Analysis was adopted in 1969; a working party set up by the Building Cost Information Service published a consultative document in January 1980 proposing certain changes. These include, amongst others, recommendations that the Brief and Amplified Analysis should be amalgamated and that new main elements 'Decorations, Fire Fighting, Domestic Hot Water, Lightening Protection' should be introduced and that 'Siteworks, Drainage, External Services and Minor Building Works' should be included as 'External Works'. Since there will be delay before consultations are completed and, if agreed, before changes are adopted, the original form and instructions have been reproduced again in this edition. The general principles and methods of analysis appear to be unchanged.

Contents

INTRODUCTION

Section 1: Principles of Analysis

Section 2: Instructions

2.1 GENERALLY
   2.1.1 Definition of terms
   2.1.2 Complex contracts
   2.1.3 Omissions or exclusions

2.2 PROJECT INFORMATION
   2.2.1 Building type
   2.2.2 BCIS code
   2.2.3 Client
   2.2.4 Location
   2.2.5 Tender date
   2.2.6 Brief description of total project
   2.2.7 Site conditions
   2.2.8 Market conditions
   2.2.9 Contract particulars of total project
   2.2.10 Tender list

2.3 DESIGN/SHAPE INFORMATION OF SINGLE BUILDINGS
   2.3.1 Accommodation, design features
   2.3.2 Floor areas
   2.3.3 Number of storeys
   2.3.4 Storey height

2.4 BRIEF COST INFORMATION
   2.4.1 Preliminaries and contingencies
   2.4.2 Functional unit cost

2.5 SUMMARY OF ELEMENT COSTS
   2.5.1 Main elements
   2.5.2 Group elements

2.6 AMPLIFIED COST ANALYSIS
   2.6.1 Elements
   2.6.2 Design criteria and specification
   2.6.3 Preliminaries
   2.6.4 External works
   2.6.5 Total cost of element
   2.6.6 Cost of element per square metre of gross floor area
   2.6.7 Element unit quantity
   2.6.8 Element unit rate
   2.6.9 Further quality breakdown

Section 3: Definitions
3.1 Enclosed spaces
3.2 Basement floors
3.3 Ground floor
3.4 Upper floors
3.5 Gross floor area
3.6 Net floor area
3.7 Net habitable floor area (residential buildings only)
3.8 Roof area
3.9 External wall area
3.10 Wall to floor ratio
3.11 Element ratios
3.12 Storey height
3.13 Internal cube
3.14 Functional unit

Section 4: Forms for Brief and Amplified Analysis and Guidance Notes

Section 5: Permission to Submit Cost Analysis to BCIS

136

STANDARD FORM OF COST ANALYSIS

INTRODUCTION

      The purpose of cost analysis is to provide data which allows comparisons to be made between the cost of achieving various building functions in one project with that of achieving equivalent functions in other projects.   It is the analysis of the cost of a building in terms of its elements.   An element for cost analysis purposes is defined as a component that fulfils a specific function or functions irrespective of its design, specification or construction. The list of elements, however, is a compromise between this definition and what is considered practical.

      The cost analysis allows for varying degrees of detail related to the design process; broad costs are needed during the initial period and progressively more detail is required as the design is developed.   The elemental cost are related to square metre of gross internal floor area and also to a parameter more closely identifiable with the elements function, i.e. the element's unit quantity.   More detailed analysis relates costs to form of construction within the element shown by "All-in" unit rates.

      Supporting information on contract, design/shape and market factors are defined so that the costs analysed can be fully understood.

      The aim has been to produce standardisation of cost analyses and a single format for presentation.

      This document has been prepared jointly by J.D.M. Robertson, F.R.I.C.S., A.M.B.I.M., on behalf of the R.I.C.S. Building Cost Information Service and by R.S. Mitchell, A.R.I.C.S., on behalf of the Ministry of Public Building and Works.   The principles and definitions are based upon the report of a working party under the chairmanship of E.H. Wilson, F.R.I.C.S., and the analysis of services elements has had the assistance of a report by a working party under the chairmanship of A.W. Ovenden, F.R.I.C.S.

      The principles and definitions of cost analysis and this format are supported by:-

    The Quantity Surveyor's Committee of The Royal Institution of
      Chartered Surveyors

    The R.I.C.S. Building Cost Information Service, and

    The Chief Quantity Surveyors of:-

        The Ministry of Public Building and Works.

        The Department of Health and Social Security.

        The Ministry of Housing and Local Government.

        The Department of Education and Science.

        The Home Office.

        The Scottish Development Department.

BUILDING COST CONTROL TECHNIQUES AND ECONOMICS

<u>SECTION 1:   PRINCIPLES OF ANALYSIS</u>

The basic principles for the analysis of the cost of building work are as follows:-

1.1   A building within a project shall be analysed separately.

1.2   Information shall be provided to facilitate the preparation of estimates based on abbreviated measurements.

1.3   Analysis shall be in stages with each stage giving progressively more detail;   the detailed costs at each stage should equal the costs of the relevant group in the preceding stage.   At any stage of analysis any significant cost items that are important to a proper and more useful understanding of the analysis shall be identified.   (Blank forms have been prepared for a Brief and for an Amplified Analysis).

1.4   Preliminaries shall be dealt with as prescribed for the appropriate analyses.

1.5   Lump sum adjustments shall be spread pro-rata amongst all elements of the building(s) and external works based on all work excluding Prime Cost and Provisional Sums contained within the elements.

1.6   Professional fees shall not form part of the cost analysis.

1.7   Contingency sums to cover unforeseen expenditure shall not be included in the analysis of prices, but shown separately.

1.8   The principal cost unit for all elements of the building(s) shall be expressed in £ to two decimal places per square metre of gross internal floor area.

1.9   A functional unit cost shall be given.

1.10   In Amplified Analyses, design criteria shall be given against each element.   Special design and performance problems shall be identified.

1.11   The definitions of terms for cost analysis shall be those given hereafter.

1.12   The elements for cost analysis shall be those given hereafter.

1.13   The contents of each element shall be as given hereafter.

1.14   The principles of further detailed analysis shall be as given hereafter.

STANDARD FORM OF COST ANALYSIS

<u>SECTION 2:   INSTRUCTIONS</u>

2.1   <u>GENERALLY</u>

2.1.1   <u>Definition of terms</u>

Definitions of terms used throughout the analysis follow these instructions.

2.1.2   <u>Complex contracts</u>

A cost analysis must apply to a single building.   In a complex contract (i.e. a contract which contains a requirement for the erection of more than one building) the size of the contract may have an important bearing on price levels obtained.   If this situation occurs, it should be identified in the box "Project details and site conditions" on the first sheet of the analysis.

2.1.3   <u>Omissions or exclusions</u>

Where items of work which are normally provided under the building contract have been excluded or supplied separately, this should be stated where appropriate.

2.2   <u>PROJECT INFORMATION</u>

2.2.1   <u>Building type</u>

CI/SfB classification will be given and restricted to the "Built environment" classification taken from Table O.

A "College of further education" will therefore be classified and shown as:-

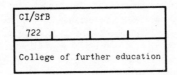

2.2.2   <u>BCIS code</u>

The BCIS reference code classifies buildings by the form of construction, number of storeys and gross internal floor area in square metres.

The different construction classes are:-

  A Steel framed construction

  B Reinforced concrete framed construction

  C Brick construction

  D Light framed steel or reinforced concrete construction.

A single-storey building of 766 square metres of gross internal floor area built in traditional construction would have the following BCIS code:-
C - 1 - 766.

2.2.3   <u>Client</u>

Indication should be given of the type of client, e.g. borough council; chur. authority; owner-occupier; government department; property company; etc.

2.2.4   <u>Location</u>

The location of the project should be given, noting the city or the county borough or alternatively the borough and the county, e.g. Bristol, or Richmond, Surrey.   The location may be reported less precisely if the client so desires.

2.2.5   <u>Tender date</u>

Date of submission of tenders.

2.2.6 <u>Brief description of total project</u>

(a) Brief description of the building being analysed and of the total project of which it forms part.

(b) Any special or unusual features affecting the overall cost not otherwise shown or detailed in the analysis.

2.2.7 <u>Site conditions</u>

(a) Site conditions with regard to access, proximity of other buildings and construction difficulties related to topographical, geological or climatic conditions.

(b) Site conditions prior to building, e.g. woodland, existing building, etc.

2.2.8 <u>Market conditions</u>

Short report on tenders indicating the level of tendering, local conditions with regard to availability of labour and materials, keenness and competition.

2.2.9 <u>Contract particulars of total project</u>

(a) Type of contract, e.g. R.I.B.A. (with or without Quantities), CCC/Wks/1, etc.

(b) Bills of quantities, bills of approximate quantities, schedule of rates.

(c) Open or selected competition, negotiated, serial or continuation contract.

(d) Firm price or, if fluctuating, whether for labour or materials or both.

(e) Number of contractors to which tender documents sent.

(f) Number of tenders received.

(g) Contract periods: (i) stipulated by client;
                   (ii) quoted by builder.

2.2.10 <u>Tender list</u>

(a) List of tenders received in descending value order.

(b) Indicate whether tenders were from local builders (L) or builders acting on a national scale (N).

2.3 <u>DESIGN/SHAPE INFORMATION OF SINGLE BUILDINGS</u>

2.3.1 <u>Accommodation, design features</u>

(a) General description of accommodation.

(b) Where a building incorporates more than one function (e.g. a block of offices with shops or car park deck) the gross floor areas of each should be shown separately.

(c) Where drawings are not provided, a thumbnail sketch shall be given of the building showing overall dimensions and number of storeys in height for each part related to ground floor datum (i.e. ⊕ for ground floor and upper storeys, ⊖ for basement storeys).

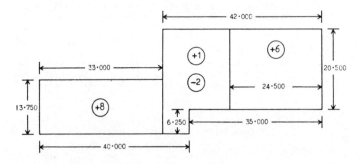

(d) Any particular factors affecting design/cost relationship resulting from user requirements or dictates of the site (user requirement is defined in R.I.B.A. Handbook as the area of accommodation, the activities for which a building is required, and the quality and standards it should achieve as stated by the client).

2.3.2 Floor areas

The measurement of floor areas and the information required on the form is that detailed hereafter under "Definitions".

2.3.3 Number of storeys

(a) Approximate percentage of building (based on gross floor area) having different number of storeys, i.e. 20% single storey, 30% two storey, 50% three storey.

(b) Excludes structures such as lift, plant or tank rooms and the like above main roof slab.

2.3.4 Storey height

Storey heights shall be given and differing heights stated separately. (See Definitions).

2.4 BRIEF COST INFORMATION

2.4.1 Preliminaries and contingencies

The totals for preliminaries and contingencies for the building being analysed should be stated and also each should be expressed as a percentage of the remainder of the contract sum. The analysis of prices does not include Contingencies.

2.4.2 Functional unit cost

The functional unit cost should be calculated by dividing the total of the group elements (including preliminaries but excluding external works) by the total number of functional units. (See Definitions).

2.5 SUMMARY OF ELEMENT COSTS

2.5.1 Elements

The building prices are analysed by the elements.

Preliminaries are shown separately and also apportioned amongst the elements.

Where Preliminaries are shown separately each element is analysed under the following headings:-

(a) Total cost of element.

(b) Cost per square metre of gross floor area £ and decimal parts of a £ (to two decimal places).

(c) Element unit quantity (as later described).

(d) Element unit rate £ and decimal parts of a £ (to two decimal places).

Where Preliminaries have been apportioned each element is analysed under the following headings:-

(a) Total cost of element.

(b) Cost per square metre of gross floor area £ and decimal parts of a £ (to two decimal places).

2.5.2 Group elements

Sub-totals are shown for the group elements:- substructure, superstructure, internal finishes, fittings and furnishings, services and external works.

Costs per square metre of gross floor area expressed in £ and decimal parts of a £ are calculated for the group elements.

Costs per square metre are also shown adjusted to a base date and in the case of analyses submitted to BCIS this will be made by the Service using the BCIS cost indices.

2.6   AMPLIFIED COST ANALYSIS

2.6.1   Elements

The standard list of elements to be used for amplified cost analyses is that described in the following pages.   The cost of each element must conform with the appropriate list of items shown in the specification notes for each element and with the principles of analysis.

2.6.2   Design criteria and specification

Design criteria relate to requirements, purpose and function of the element, and an outline of the design criteria is noted under each element.

The specification notes are considered to reflect architects' solution to the conditions expressed by the design criteria and should indicate the quality of building achieved.

Specification notes provide a check list of the items which should be included with each element.   Notes should adequately describe the form of construction and quality of material sufficiently to explain the costs in the analysis.

The instructions on the specification notes which follow are definitions of principle and where any departure from them seems necessary, a note should be made explaining how these cases have been dealt with.

2.6.3   Preliminaries

In the Amplified Analysis the element costs do not include Preliminaries which are to be analysed separately.   However, under each element is to be included a figure which represents Preliminaries expressed as a percentage of the remainder of the contract sum.

2.6.4   External works

The expression of cost of external works related to gross floor area of the building(s) is not particularly meaningful.   It is used in the "Summary of element costs" so that the totals agree arithmetically, but in the Amplified Analysis there are no detailed costs required by this method.

2.6.5   Total cost of element

This is the cost of each element and the items comprising it should correspond with the notes in the right-hand column headed "Specification".

If no cost is attributed to an element, a dash should be inserted in the cost column and a note made to the effect that this element is not applicable.

Where the costs of more than one element are grouped together, a note should be inserted against each of the affected elements, explaining where the costs have been included.   For example, if windows in curtain walling are included in "External walls" it should be so stated in the element "Windows" and details of the cost included with the element "External walls".

2.6.6   Cost of element per square metre of gross floor area

This is the "Total cost of element" divided by the gross floor area of the building.

2.6.7   Element unit quantity

In an amplified analysis, the cost of the element is expressed in suitable units which relate solely to the quantity of the element itself.

Instructions are given in the appropriate column which show what element unit quantity is to be used for each element, e.g. in the case of "Floor finishes" the element unit quantity is the "Total area of the floor finishes in square metres" and in the case of "Heat source" the element unit quantity is "kilowatts".

(i)   Area for element unit quantities

All areas must be the net area of the element, e.g. external walls should exclude window and door openings, etc.

(ii)   Cubes for element unit quantities

Cubes for air conditioning, etc., shall be measured as the net floor area of that part treated, multiplied by the height from the floor finish to the underside of the ceiling finish (abbreviated to Tm^3).

142

2.6.8 Element unit rate

This is the total cost of the element divided by the element unit quantity. In effect it includes the main items and the labour items of the element expressed in terms of that element's own parameter. For example, in the case of "Floor finishes" it is the total cost of the floor finishes divided by their net areas in square metres; in the case of "Heat source" the elemental unit rate is the total cost of the heat source divided by its own parameter, the number of kilowatts. Elemental unit rates are shown in £ and decimal parts of a £ (to two decimal places).

2.6.9 Further quality breakdown

Where various forms of construction or finish exist within one element the net areas and costs of the various types of construction should be included separately in the specification notes and provision has been made where appropriate.

The area of each form of construction is the net area involved and excludes all openings, etc.

The cost of each form of construction is the total cost of all items pertaining to that construction.

2.6.10 The following is an example of how the amplified analysis form should be completed.

Element and design criteria	Total cost of element £	Cost of element per m² of gross floor area £	Element unit quantity	Element unit rate £	Specification
3.2 Floor finishes	1,664	2.17	694 m²	2.40	19 mm granolithic laid monolithic, no skirting. 3 mm thermoplastic tiles Series 2 on 48 mm cement and sand screed, softwood skirting. 3 mm vinylised tiles on 48 mm cement and sand screed, softwood skirting. 25 mm (1") "West African" sapele wood block floor on 37 mm cement and sand screed, softwood skirting. 16 mm (⅝") red quarries on 34 mm screed, quarry skirting.

Floor finishes	£	Area m²	All-in unit rate £
19 mm granolithic	30	30	1.00
3 mm thermoplastic Series 2	18	13	1.39
3 mm vinylised tiles	616	395	1.56
25 mm (1") sapele blocks	570	161	3.54
16 mm (⅝") quarries	430	95	4.52

Preliminaries 9.73% of remainder of contract sum.

SECTION 3: DEFINITIONS

3.1 Enclosed spaces

    1.   All spaces which have a floor and ceiling and enclosing walls on all sides for the full or partial height.

    2.   Open balustrades, louvres, screens and the like shall be deemed to be enclosing walls.

3.2 Basement floors

All floors below the ground floor.

3.3 Ground floor

The floor which is nearest the level of the outside ground.

3.4 Upper floors

All floors which do not fall into any of the previously defined categories.

3.5 Gross floor area

    1.   Total of all enclosed spaces fulfilling the functional requirements of the building measured to the internal structural face of the enclosing walls.

    2.   Includes area occupied by partitions, columns, chimney breasts, internal structural or party walls, stairwells, lift wells, and the like.

    3.   Includes lift, plant, tank rooms and the like above main roof slab.

    4.   Sloping surfaces such as staircases, galleries, tiered terraces and the like should be measured flat on plan.

        Note: (i)   Excludes any spaces fulfilling the functional requirements of the building which are not enclosed spaces (e.g. open ground floors, open covered ways and the like). These should each be shown separately.

              (ii) Excludes private balconies and private verandahs which should be shown separately.

3.6 Net floor area

Net floor area shall be measured within the structural face of the enclosing walls as "Usable", "Circulation" and "Ancillary" as defined below. Areas occupied by partitions, columns, chimney breast, internal structural or party walls are excluded from these groups, and are shown separately under "Internal divisions".

    1.   Usable

        Total area of all enclosed spaces fulfilling the main functional requirements of the building (e.g. office space, shop space, public house drinking area, etc.).

    2.   Circulation

        Total area of all enclosed spaces forming entrance halls, corridors, staircases, lift wells, connecting links and the like.

    3.   Ancillary

        Total area of all enclosed spaces for lavatories, cloakrooms, kitchens, cleaners' rooms, lift, plant and tank rooms and the like, supplementary to the main function of the building.

    4.   Internal divisions

        The area occupied by partitions, columns, chimney breasts, internal structural or party walls.

        Note: The sum of the areas falling in the categories defined above will equal the gross floor area.

3.7   <u>Net habitable floor area (residential buildings only)</u>

1.   Total area of all enclosed spaces forming the dwelling measured within the structural internal face of the enclosing walls.

2.   Includes areas occupied by partitions, columns, chimney breasts and the like.

3.   Excludes all balconies, public access spaces, communal laundries, drying rooms, lift, plant and tank rooms and the like.

3.8   <u>Roof area</u>

1.   Plan area measured across the eaves overhang or to the inner face of parapet walls.

2.   Includes area covered by rooflights.

3.   Sloping and pitched roofs should be measured on plan area.

3.9   <u>External wall area</u>

The wall area of all the enclosed spaces fulfilling the functional requirements of the building measured on the outer face of external walls and overall windows and doors, etc.

3.10   <u>Wall to floor ratio</u>

Calculated by dividing the external wall area by the gross floor area to three decimal places.

3.11   <u>Element ratios</u>

Calculated by dividing the net area of the element by the gross floor area to three decimal places.

<u>Note</u>:   In the case of buildings, where only a part is treated or served by mechanical or electrical installations, indication of this is given by a ratio as follows:-

$$\frac{t \ m^2}{gross \ floor \ area}$$

where t m^2 is the total net area in square metres of the various compartments treated or served.

3.12   <u>Storey height</u>

1.   Height measured from floor finish to floor finish.

2.   For single-storey buildings and top floor of multi-storied buildings, the height shall be measured from floor finish to underside of ceiling finish.

3.13   <u>Internal cube</u>

1.   To include all enclosed spaces fulfilling the requirements of the building.

2.   The cube should be measured as the gross internal floor area of each floor multiplied by its storey height.

3.   Any spaces fulfilling a requirement of the building, which are not enclosed spaces, such as open ground floors, open covered ways and the like, should be shown separately giving the notional cubic content of each, ascertained by notionally enclosing the open top or sides.

3.14   <u>Functional unit</u>

The functional unit shall be expressed as net usable floor area (offices, factories, public houses, etc.) or as a number of units of accommodation (seats in churches, school places, persons per dwelling, etc.).

SECTION 4:   FORMS OF ANALYSIS AND GUIDANCE NOTES

4.1   Brief and amplified forms of cost analysis

The standard method of cost analysis described here is in stages with each stage giving progressively more detail; the detailed costs at each stage should equal the costs of the relevant group in the preceding stage.   At any stage of analysis any significant cost items that are important to a proper and more useful understanding of the analysis should be identified.

Forms of cost analysis have been prepared in two degrees of detail (Brief and Amplified Analyses), and are identified by different coloured paper as follows:-

            White pages   - Brief and Amplified Analyses Forms

            Yellow pages   - Check list of Specification and Design Notes
                              which should accompany the Brief Analysis

            Grey pages   - Amplified Analysis.

4.2   Tank rooms

Where tank rooms, housings and the like are included in the gross floor area, their component parts shall be analysed in detail under the appropriate elements.   Where this is not the case, their costs should be included as "Builder's work in connection" (5.14).

4.3   Glazing and ironmongery

Glazing and ironmongery should be included in the elements containing the items to which they are fixed.

4.4   Decoration

Decoration, except to fair-faced work, should be included with the surface to which it is applied, allocated to the appropriate element, and the costs shown separately. Painting and decorating to fair-faced work is to be treated as a "Finishing".

4.5   Chimneys

Chimneys and flues which are an integral part of the structure shall be included with the appropriate structural elements.

4.6   Drawings

Drawings, preferably A4 size negatives if these are available, should always accompany Amplified Analyses.   In the case of Brief Analyses drawings would be very welcome, but thumbnail sketches as previously illustrated would be acceptable and should be attached on a separate sheet at the end of the analysis.

BRIEF COST ANALYSIS

CI/SfB

BCIS Code

Job title:

Location:

Client:

Tender date:

INFORMATION ON TOTAL PROJECT

Project and contract information

Contract: (To be completed by BCIS from the Contract particulars given below)

Project details and site conditions:

Market conditions:

Contract particulars:

Type of contract: ....

Basis of tender*:

Open/Selected competition

Bill of quantities []

Negotiated []

Bill of approximate quantities []

Serial []

Schedule of rates []

Continuation []

Contract period stipulated by client .... months

Contract period offered by builder .... months

Number of tenders issued ....

Number of tenders received ....

   * Tick as appropriate

Cost fluctuation *   YES []   NO []

LABOUR

Adjustments based on formula *   MATERIALS

YES []   NO []

Provisional sums   £ ....

Prime Cost sums   £ ....

Preliminaries   £ ....

Contingencies   £ ....

Contract sum   £ ....

   * Tick as appropriate

Competitive tender list

£   N/L

147

TO BE USED WITH THE BRIEF AND AMPLIFIED ANALYSES

ANALYSIS OF SINGLE BUILDING

Design shape information

Accommodation and design features:

Areas

Basement floors	....	m²
Ground floor	....	m²
Upper floors	....	m²
Gross floor area	....	m²
Usable area	....	m²
Circulation area	....	m²
Ancillary area	....	m²
Internal division	....	m²
Gross floor area	....	m²
Floor spaces not enclosed	....	m²
Roof area	m²	

Functional unit ....

$$\frac{\text{External wall area}}{\text{Gross floor area}} = \underline{\hspace{2cm}} = \dots\dots\dots$$

Internal cube = ... m³

Storey heights

Average below ground floor	....
at ground floor	....
above ground floor	....

Design/Shape

Percentage of gross floor area:-

a)	below ground floor	.... %
b)	Single-storey construction	.... %
c)	Two storey construction	.... %
d)	* storey construction	.... %
e)	* storey construction	.... %

* Insert number of storeys.

Brief Cost Information

* Contract sum	£		
* Provisional sums	£		
* Prime Cost sums	£		
* Preliminaries	£	being .... %	of remainder of
* Contingencies	£	being .... %	contract sum
* Contract sum less contingencies	£		

* Amounts for single building analysed.

Functional unit cost   { Tender £ ....

excluding external works   { Base date £ ....

SUMMARY OF ELEMENT COSTS

Gross internal floor area: .... square metres

Tender date ....

Element	Preliminaries shown separately				Preliminaries apportioned amongst elements		
	Total cost of element £	Cost per m² gross floor area £	Element unit quantity *	Element unit rate £	Total cost of element £	Cost per m² gross floor area £	Cost per m² gross floor area (base date) £
1.0 Substructure	£	£	* See Amplified Analysis		£	£	£
2.0 Superstructure							
2.1 Frame							
2.2 Upper floors							
2.3 Roof							
2.4 Stairs							
2.5 External walls							
2.6 Windows and external doors							
2.7 Internal walls and partitions							
2.8 Internal doors							
Group element total	£	£			£	£	£
3.0 Internal finishes							
3.1 Wall finishes							
3.2 Floor finishes							
3.3 Ceiling finishes							
Group element total	£	£			£	£	£
4.0 Fittings and furnishings	£	£			£	£	£

149

TO BE USED WITH THE BRIEF AND AMPLIFIED ANALYSES

5.0 Services

5.1 Sanitary appliances
5.2 Services equipment
5.3 Disposal installations
5.4 Water installations
5.5 Heat source
5.6 Space heating and
     air treatment
5.7 Ventilating system
5.8 Electrical installations
5.9 Gas installations
5.10 Lift and conveyor
     installations
5.11 Protective installations
5.12 Communication installations
5.13 Special installations
5.14 Builder's work in connection
     with services
5.15 Builder's profit and
     attendance on services

          Group element total

Sub-total excluding External works,
Preliminaries and Contingencies

6.0 External works

6.1 Site works
6.2 Drainage
6.3 External services
6.4 Minor building works

          Group element total

Preliminaries

TOTALS (less Contingencies)

Authors' Note

The reader's attention is directed to paragraph 4.1 on page 146 which gives the colour coding for use with Forms of Analysis.

It has not, of course, been considered practical or essential to reproduce the colouring in this book.

TO BE USED WITH THE BRIEF ANALYSIS

SPECIFICATION AND DESIGN NOTES

Please include brief specification and design notes to describe adequately the form of
construction and quality of material sufficiently to explain the prices in the analysis

Check List

Group elements	Elements	Sub-elements
1.0 SUBSTRUCTURE	1.1 Substructure	
2.0 SUPERSTRUCTURE	2.1 Frame	
	2.2 Upper floors	
	2.3 Roof	2.3.1 Roof structure
		2.3.2 Roof coverings
		2.3.3 Roof drainage
		2.3.4 Roof lights
	2.4 Stairs	2.4.1 Stair structure
		2.4.2 Stair finishes
		2.4.3 Stair balustrades and handrails
	2.5 External walls	
	2.6 Windows and external doors	2.6.1 Windows
		2.6.2 External doors
	2.7 Internal walls and partitions	
	2.8 Internal doors	
3.0 INTERNAL FINISHES	3.1 Wall finishes	
	3.2 Floor finishes	
	3.3 Ceiling finishes	3.3.1 Finishes to ceilings
		3.3.2 Suspended ceilings
4.0 FITTINGS AND FURNISHINGS	4.1 Fittings and furnishings	4.1.1 Fittings, fixtures and furniture
		4.1.2 Soft furnishings
		4.1.3 Works of art
		4.1.4 Equipment
5.0 SERVICES	5.1 Sanitary appliances	
	5.2 Services equipment	
	5.3 Disposal installations	5.3.1 Internal drainage
		5.3.2 Refuse disposal
	5.4 Water installations	5.4.1 Mains supply
		5.4.2 Cold water service
		5.4.3 Hot water service
		5.4.4 Steam and condensate
	5.5 Heat source	

5.6	Space heating and air treatment	5.6.1 Water and/or steam (heating only) 5.6.2 Ducted warm air (heating only) 5.6.3 Electricity (heating only) 5.6.4 Local heating 5.6.5 Other heating systems 5.6.6 Heating with ventilation (air heated locally) 5.6.7 Heating with ventilation (air heated centrally) 5.6.8 Heating with cooling (air heated locally) 5.6.9 Heating with cooling (air heated centrally)
5.7	Ventilating systems	
5.8	Electrical installations	5.8.1 Electric source and mains 5.8.2 Electric power supplies 5.8.3 Electric lighting 5.8.4 Electric lighting fittings
5.9	Gas installation	
5.10	Lift and conveyor installations	5.10.1 Lifts and hoists 5.10.2 Escalators 5.10.3 Conveyors
5.11	Protective installations	5.11.1 Sprinkler installations 5.11.2 Fire-fighting installations 5.11.3 Lightning protection
5.12	Communication installations	
5.13	Special installations	
5.14	Builder's work in connection with services	
5.15	Builder's profit and attendance on services	

6.0	**EXTERNAL WORKS**	
6.1	Site works	6.1.1 Site preparation 6.1.2 Surface treatment 6.1.3 Site enclosure and division 6.1.4 Fittings and furniture
6.2	Drainage	
6.3	External services	6.3.1 Water mains 6.3.2 Fire mains 6.3.3 Heating mains 6.3.4 Gas mains 6.3.5 Electric mains 6.3.6 Site lighting 6.3.7 Other mains and services 6.3.8 Builder's work in connection with external services 6.3.9 Builder's profit and attendance on external services
6.4	Minor building work	6.4.1 Ancillary buildings 6.4.2 Alterations to existing buildings

PRELIMINARIES

Drawings: Drawings or a thumbnail sketch should accompany the Brief Cost Analysis

153

Element and design criteria	Total cost of element £	Cost of element per m² of gross floor area £	Element unit quantity	Element unit rate £	Specification
1.1 SUBSTRUCTURE Permissible soil loading .... kN/m² (kilonewtons per square metre) Nature of soil .... Bearing strata depth .... m (metres) Site levels .... (to be given as gradient) Water table depth .... m (metres) Average pile loading .... kN (kilonewtons)			Area of lowest floor measured as for gross internal floor area, (m²).		All work below underside of screed or where no screed exists to underside of lowest floor finish including damp-proof membrane, together with relevant excavations and foundations. **NOTES:** 1. Where lowest floor construction does not otherwise provide a platform, the flooring surface shall be included with this element (e.g. if joisted floor, floor boarding would be included here). 2. Stanchions and columns (with relevant casings) shall be included with "Frame" (2.1). 3. Cost of piling and driving shall be shown separately stating system, number and average length of pile. 4. The cost of external enclosing walls to basements shall be included with "External walls" (2.5) and stated separately for each form of construction.
Preliminaries ...... % of remainder of contract sum.					

Element and design criteria	Total cost of element £	Cost of element per m2 of gross floor area £	Element unit quantity	Element unit rate £	Specification
2.1 FRAME Grid pattern should be stated, giving centres of main columns in both directions.			Area of floors relating to frame, measured as for gross internal floor area, (m²).		Loadbearing framework of concrete, steel or timber. Main floor and roof beams, ties and roof trusses of framed buildings. Casing to stanchions and beams for structural or protective purposes. NOTES: 1. Structural walls which form an integral part of the load-bearing framework shall be included either with "External walls" (2.5) or "Internal walls and partitions" (2.7) as appropriate. 2. Beams which form an integral part of a floor or roof which cannot be segregated therefrom shall be included in the appropriate element. 3. In unframed buildings roof and floor beams shall be included with "Upper floors" (2.2) or "Roof structure" (2.3.1) as appropriate. 4. If the "Stair structure" (2.4.1) has had to be included in this element it should be noted separately.
Preliminaries ...... % of remainder of contract sum.					
2.2 UPPER FLOORS Design loads should be stated in kilo-newtons per square metre (kN/m²) and spans given in metres.			Total area of upper floors, (m²).		Upper floors, continuous access floors, balconies and structural screeds (access and private balconies each stated separately), suspended floors over or in basements stated separately. NOTES: 1. Where floor construction does not otherwise provide a platform the flooring surface shall be included with this element (e.g. if joisted floor, floor boarding would be included here). 2. Beams which form an integral part of a floor slab shall be included with this element. 3. If the "Stair structure" (2.4.1) has had to be included in this element it should be noted separately.
Preliminaries ...... % of remainder of contract sum.					

Upper floors	£	Area m2	All-in unit rate £

2.3 ROOF

Design loads should be stated in kilo-newtons per square metre (kN/m²) and spans given in metres (m).

The angle of pitch of sloping roofs shall be stated.

Area measured overall roof surfaces, (m²).

2.3.1 Roof structure

Construction, including eaves and verges, plates and ceiling joists, gable ends, internal walls and chimneys above plate level, parapet walls and baulstrades.

NOTES:

1. Beams which form an integral part of a roof shall be included with this element.

2. Roof housings (e.g. lift motor and plant rooms) shall be broken down into the appropriate constituent elements.

2.3.2 Roof coverings

Roof screeds and finishings. Battening, felt, slating, tiling and the like.
Flashings and trims.
Insulation.
Eaves and verge treatment.

2.3.3 Roof drainage

Gutters where not integral with roof structure, rainwater heads and roof outlets. (Rainwater downpipes to be included in "Internal drainage" (5.3.1)).

2.3.4 Roof lights

Roof lights, opening gear, frame, kerbs and glazing.
Pavement lights.

Roof	£	Area m2	All-in unit rate £
2.3.1 Roof structure			
2.3.2 Roof coverings			
2.3.3 Roof drainage			
2.3.4 Roof lights			

Preliminaries ..... % of remainder of contract sum.

Element and design criteria	Total cost of element £	Cost of element per m² of gross floor area £	Element unit quantity	Element unit rate £	Specification
2.4 STAIRS The total vertical height of each staircase and its width between stringers should be given in metres (m).			–	–	**2.4.1 Stair structure** Construction of ramps, stairs and landings other than at floor levels. Ladders. Escape staircases. NOTES: 1. The cost of external escape staircases shall be shown separately. 2. If the staircase structure has had to be included in the elements "Frame" (2.1) or "Upper floors" (2.2) this should be stated. **2.4.2 Stair finishes** Finishes to treads, risers, landings (other than at floor levels), ramp surfaces, strings and soffits. **2.4.3 Stair balustrades and handrails** Balustrades and handrails to stairs, landings and stairwells.

Stairs	£	Cost per m² of gross floor area £
2.4.1 Stair structure		
2.4.2 Stair finishes		
2.4.3 Stair balustrades and handrails		

Preliminaries ...... % of remainder of contract sum.

2.5 EXTERNAL WALLS

External enclosing walls including that to basements but excluding items included with "Roof structure" (2.3.1).
Chimneys forming part of external walls up to plate level.
Curtain walling, sheeting rails and cladding.
Vertical tanking.
Insulation.
Applied external finishes.

NOTES:

1. The cost of structural walls which form an integral and important part of the loadbearing framework shall be shown separately.

2. Basement walls shall be shown separately and the quantity and cost given for each form of construction.

3. If walls are self-finished on internal face, this shall be stated.

Area of external walls measured on outer face (excluding openings), (m²).

$\dfrac{\text{External walls}}{\text{Gross floor area}} = \dfrac{\_\_\_\ m^2}{\_\_\_\ m^2}$

$\dfrac{\text{Basement walls}}{\text{Gross floor area}} = \dfrac{\_\_\_\ m^2}{\_\_\_\ m^2}$

The approximate value of thermal conductivity should be given in watt per metre degree Celsius (W/m°C).

If calculated loadbearing brickwork, give indication of structural loading.

Preliminaries ..... % of remainder of contract sum.

External walls	£	Area m²	All-in unit rate £

2.6 WINDOWS AND EXTERNAL DOORS

2.6.1 Windows

Sashes, frames, linings and trims.
Ironmongery and glazing.
Shop fronts.
Lintels, sills, cavity damp-proof courses and work to reveals of openings.

2.6.2 External doors

Doors, fanlights, and sidelights.
Frames, linings and trims.
Ironmongery and glazing.
Lintels, thresholds, cavity damp-proof courses and work to reveals of openings.

Total area of windows & external doors measured over frames, (m²).

$\dfrac{\text{Windows}}{\text{Gross floor area}} = \dfrac{\_\_\_\ m^2}{\_\_\_\ m^2}$

$\dfrac{\text{External doors}}{\text{Gross floor area}} = \dfrac{\_\_\_\ m^2}{\_\_\_\ m^2}$

$\text{Area of opening lights to windows} = \dfrac{\_\_\_\ m^2}{\_\_\_\ m^2}$

Preliminaries ..... % of remainder of contract sum.

Windows and external doors	£	Area m²	All-in unit rate £
2.6.1 Windows			
2.6.2 External doors			

2.7 INTERNAL WALLS AND PARTITIONS

$$\frac{\text{Internal walls and partitions}}{\text{Gross floor area}} = \frac{\quad m^2\quad}{\quad m^2\quad} = $$

Element and design criteria	Total cost of element £	Cost of element per m² of gross floor area £	Element unit quantity	Element unit rate £	Specification
			Total area of internal walls and partitions (excluding openings), (m2).		Internal walls, partitions and insulation. Chimneys forming part of internal walls up to plate level. Screens, borrowed lights and glazing. Moveable space-dividing partitions. Internal balustrades excluding items included with "Stair balustrades and handrails" (2.4.3).

NOTES:

1. The cost of structural walls which form an integral and important part of the loadbearing framework shall be shown separately.

2. The cost of proprietary partitioning shall be shown separately stating if self-finished. Doors, etc., provided therein together with ironmongery, should be included stating the number of units installed.

3. The cost of proprietary W.C. cubicles shall be shown separately stating the number provided.

4. If design is cross-wall construction, the specification shall be stated and the cost shown separately.

	£	Area m2	All-in unit rate £
Internal walls and partitions			

Preliminaries ..... % of remainder of contract sum.

159

2.8 INTERNAL DOORS

	Internal doors	£	Area m2	All-in unit rate £
Doors, fanlights and sidelights. Sliding and folding doors. Hatches. Frames, linings and trims. Ironmongery and glazing. Lintels, thresholds and work to reveals of openings.				
Area of internal doors measured over frames, (m2).				
Preliminaries ..... % of remainder of contract sum.				

Element and design criteria	Total cost of element £	Cost of element per m2 of gross floor area £	Element unit quantity	Element unit rate £	Specification	£	Area m2	All-in unit rate £
3.1 WALL FINISHES			Total area of wall finishes, (m2).		Preparatory work and finishes to surfaces of walls internally. Picture, dado and similar rails. NOTES: 1. Surfaces which are self-finished (e.g. self-finished partitions, fair faced work) shall be included in the appropriate element. 2. Insulation which is a wall finishing shall be included here. 3. The cost of finishes applied to the inside face of external walls shall be shown separately.			
					Wall finishes			
Preliminaries ...... % of remainder of contract sum.								
3.2 FLOOR FINISHES			Total area of floor finishes, (m2).		Preparatory work, screeds, skirtings and finishes to floor surfaces excluding items included with "Stair finishes" (2.4.2), and structural screeds included with "Upper floors" (2.2). NOTE: Where the floor construction does not otherwise provide a platform the flooring surface will be included either in "Substructure" (1.1) or "Upper floors" (2.2) as appropriate.			
					Floor finishes			
Preliminaries ...... % of remainder of contract sum.								

161

3 3 CEILING FINISHES

3.3.1 Finishes to ceilings

Preparatory work and finishes to surfaces of soffits excluding items included with "Stair finishes" (2.4.2) but including sides and soffits of beams not forming part of a wall surface. Cornices, coves.

3.3.2 Suspended ceilings

Construction and finishes of suspended ceilings.

NOTES:

1. Where ceilings principally provide a source of heat, artificial lighting or ventilation, they shall be included with the appropriate "Services" element and the cost shall be stated separately.

2. The cost of finishes or suspended ceilings to soffits immediately below roofs shall be shown separately.

Total area of ceiling finishes, (m2).

	£	Area m2	All-in unit rate £
Ceiling finishes			
3.3.1 Finishes to ceilings			
3.3.2 Suspended ceilings			

Preliminaries ..... % of remainder of contract sum.

Element and design criteria	Total cost of element £	Cost of element per m2 of gross floor area £	Element unit quantity	Element unit rate £	Specification
4.1 FITTINGS AND FURNISHINGS			–	–	4.1.1 Fittings, fixtures and furniture Fixed and loose fittings and furniture including shelving, cupboards, wardrobes, benches, seating, counters and the like. Blinds, blind boxes, curtain tracks and pelmets. Blackboards, pin-up boards, notice boards, signs, lettering, mirrors and the like. Ironmongery. 4.1.2 Soft furnishings Curtains, loose carpets or similar soft furnishing materials. 4.1.3 Works of art Works of art if not included in a finishes element or elsewhere. NOTE: Where items in this element have a significant effect on other elements a note should be included in the appropriate element. 4.1.4 Equipment Non-mechanical and non-electrical equipment related to the function or need of the building (e.g. gymnasia equipment).

Fittings and furnishings	Quantity	Cost £
4.1.1 Fittings, fixtures and furniture		
4.1.2 Soft furnishings		
4.1.3 Works of art		
4.1.4 Equipment		

Preliminaries ..... % of remainder of contract sum.

5.1 SANITARY APPLIANCES

Fittings to be noted as grouped or dispersed.

Sanitary appliances type and quality	Number	Cost of unit £	Total £
Baths, basins, sinks, etc. W.C's, slop sinks, urinals and the like. Toilet-roll holders, towel rails, etc. Traps, waste fittings, overflows and taps as appropriate.			
	–		
	–		

Preliminaries ..... % of remainder of contract sum.

5.2 SERVICES EQUIPMENT

Kitchen, laundry, hospital and dental equipment, and other specialist mechanical and electrical equipment related to the function of the building.

NOTE:

Local incinerators shall be included with "Refuse disposal" (5.3.2).

Services equipment type and quality	Number	Cost of unit £	Total £
	–		
	–		

Preliminaries ..... % of remainder of contract sum.

164

Element and design criteria	Total cost of element £	Cost of element per m² of gross floor area £	Element unit quantity	Element unit rate £	Specification
5.3 DISPOSAL INSTALLATIONS Number of sanitary appliances and special services equipment served should be stated.			–	–	**5.3.1 Internal drainage** Waste pipes to "Sanitary appliances" (5.1) and "Services equipment" (5.2). Soil, anti-syphonage and ventilation pipes. Rainwater downpipes. Floor channels and gratings and drains in ground within buildings up to external face of external walls. NOTE: Rainwater gutters are included in "Roof drainage" (2.3.3). **5.3.2 Refuse disposal** Refuse ducts, waste disposal (grinding) units, chutes and bins. Local incinerators and flues thereto. Paper shredders and incinerators.

Specification	Total £	Cost per m² of gross floor area £
Disposal installations		
5.3.1 Internal drainage		
5.3.2 Refuse disposal		

Preliminaries ...... % of remainder of contract sum.

5.4 WATER INSTALLATIONS

5.4.1 Mains supply

Incoming water main from external face of external wall at point of entry into building including valves, water meters, rising main to (but excluding) storage tanks and main taps. Insulation.

5.4.2 Cold water service

Storage tanks, pumps, pressure boosters, distribution pipework to sanitary appliances and to services equipment.
Valves and taps not included with "Sanitary appliances" (5.1) and/or "Services equipment" (5.2). Insulation.

NOTE:
Header tanks, cold water supplies, etc., for heating systems should be included in "Heat source" (5.5).

5.4.3 Hot water service

Hot water and/or mixed water services.
Storage cylinders, pumps, calorifiers, instantaneous water heaters, distribution pipework to sanitary appliances and services equipment.
Valves and taps not included with "Sanitary appliances" (5.1) and/or "Services equipment" (5.2). Insulation.

5.4.4 Steam and condensate

Steam distribution and condensate return pipework to and from services equipment within the building including all valves, fittings, etc. Insulation.

NOTE:
Steam and condensate pipework installed in connection with space heating or the like shall be included as appropriate with "Heat source" (5.5) or "Space heating and air treatment" (5.6).

Number of cold water draw-off points ....

Number of hot water draw-off points ....

Number of steam and condensate draw-off points ....

Preliminaries ..... % of remainder of contract sum.

Water installations	Total £	Cost per m² of gross floor area £
5.4.1 Mains supply		
5.4.2 Cold water service		
5.4.3 Hot water service		
5.4.4 Steam or condensate		

Element and design criteria	Total cost of element £	Cost of element per m² of gross floor area £	Element unit quantity	Element unit rate £	Specification
5.5 HEAT SOURCE Boiler rating in kilowatts .... kW Preliminaries ...... / of remainder of contract sum.			kW (kilowatts)		Boilers, mounting, firing equipment, pressurising equipment instrumentation and control, I.D. and F.D. fans, gantries, flues and chimneys, fuel conveyors, fuel oil and/or gas supplies. Cold and treated water supplies and tanks, fuel oil and/or gas supplies, storage tanks, etc., pipework (water or steam mains) pumps, valves and other equipment. Insulation. NOTES: 1. Chimneys and flues which are an integral part of the structure shall be included with the appropriate structural element. 2. Local heat source shall be included with "Local heating" (5.6.4). 3. Where more than one heat source is provided each shall be analysed separately.
5.6 SPACE HEATING AND AIR TREATMENT $$\dfrac{Tm^2 \ *}{Gross\ floor\ area} = \dfrac{m^2}{m^2} =$$ * Where Tm^2 is the total net area in square metres of the various compartments treated or served.			Cube of treated space as defined —— Tm^3		(i) Heating only by:- 5.6.1 Water and/or steam Heat emission units (radiators, pipe coils, etc.) valves and fittings, instrumentation and control and distribution pipework from "Heat source" (5.5). 5.6.2 Ducted warm air Ductwork, grilles, fans, filters, etc., instrumentation and control. 5.6.3 Electricity Cable heating systems, off-peak heating system, including storage radiators. NOTE: Electrically-operated heat emission units other than storage radiators should be included under "Local heating" (5.6.4). 5.6.4 Local heating Fireplaces (except flues), radiant heaters, small electrical or gas appliances, etc. 5.6.5 Other heating systems (ii) Air treatment:- NOTES: 1. System described as having: "Air treated locally" shall be deemed to include all systems where air treatment (heating or cooling) is performed either in or adjacent to the space to be treated. (contd.)...

5.6 SPACE HEATING AND AIR TREATMENT (contd.)

"Air treated centrally" shall be deemed to include all systems where air treatment (heating or cooling) is performed at a central point and ducted to the space being treated.

2. The combination of treatments used shall be stated, i.e.:-

Heating	Dehumidification or drying
Cooling	Filtration
Humidification	Pressurisation

   and whether inlet extract or recirculation.

3. High velocity system shall be identified as:-

Fan Coil	Induction units 2 Pipe
Dual duct	" " 3 "
Reheat	" " 4 "
Multi-zone	Any other system (state which).

5.6.6 Heating with ventilation (air treated locally)
Distribution pipework ducting, grilles, heat emission units including heating calorifiers except those which are part of "Heat source" (5.5) instrumentation and control.

5.6.7 Heating with ventilation (air treated centrally)
All work as detailed under (5.6.6) for system where air treated centrally.

5.6.8 Heating with cooling (air treated locally)
All work as detailed under (5.6.6) including chilled water systems and/or cold or treated water feeds. The whole of the costs of the cooling plant and distribution pipework to local cooling units shall be shown separately.

5.6.9 Heating with cooling (air treated centrally)
All work detailed under (5.6.8) for system where air treated centrally.

NOTE:
Where more than one system is used, design criteria specification notes and costs should be given for each.

Space heating and air treatment	Total £	Cost per m² of gross floor area £
5.6.1 Water and/or steam		
5.6.2 Ducted warm air		
5.6.3 Electricity		
5.6.4 Local heating		
5.6.5 Other heating systems		
5.6.6 Heating with ventilation (air treated locally)		
5.6.7 Heating with ventilation (air treated centrally)		
5.6.8 Heating with cooling (air treated locally)		
5.6.9 Heating with cooling (air treated centrally)		

Preliminaries ..... % of remainder of contract sum.

Element and design criteria	Total cost of element £	Cost of element per m² of gross floor area £	Element unit quantity	Element unit rate £	Specification
5.7 **VENTILATING SYSTEM** $\dfrac{Tm^2 *}{Gross\ floor\ area} = \dfrac{m^2}{m^2} =$ * Where Tm² is the total net area in square metres of the various compartments treated or served. Preliminaries ..... % of remainder of contract sum.			Cube of treated space as defined —— Tm³		Mechanical ventilating system not incorporating heating or cooling installations including dust and fume extraction and fresh air injection, unit extract fans, rotating ventilators and instrumentation and controls.
5.8 **ELECTRICAL INSTALLATIONS** Total electric load in kilowatts ....kW (tabulate illumination levels by principal functions) Total number of power outlets					5.8.1 **Electric source and mains** All work from external face of building up to and including local distribution boards including main switchgear, main and sub-main cables, control gear, power factor correction equipment, stand-by equipment, earthing, etc. NOTES: 1. Installations for electric heating ("built-in" systems) shall be included with "Space heating and air treatment (5.6.3). 2. The cost of stand-by equipment shall be stated separately. 5.8.2 **Electric power supplies** All wiring, cables, conduits, switches from local distribution boards, etc., to and including outlet points for the following:— {see sub-table below} NOTE: The cost of the power supply to these installations should, where possible, be shown separately. (Contd.)

Sub-table within Specification (5.8.2):

	Total £	Cost per m² of gross floor area £
Electric power supplies		
General purpose socket outlets		
Services equipment		
Disposal installations		
Water installations		
Heat source		
Space heating and air treatment		
Gas installation		
Lift and conveyor installations		
Protective installations		
Communication installations		
Special installations		

5.8 ELECTRICAL INSTALLATIONS (Contd.)

Total number of lighting points ......

Illumination in lux lx

5.8.3 Electric lighting

All wiring, cables, conduits, switches, etc., from local distribution boards and fittings to and including outlet points.

5.8.4 Electric lighting fittings

Lighting fittings including fixing. Where lighting fittings supplied direct by client, this should be stated.

Light fittings type and quality	Number	Cost £

Preliminaries ..... % of remainder of contract sum.

Electrical installations	Total £	Cost per m² of gross floor area £
5.8.1 Electric source and mains		
5.8.2 Electric power supplies		
5.8.3 Electric lighting		
5.8.4 Electric lighting fittings		

5.9 GAS INSTALLATIONS

Number of draw-off points ....

Town and natural gas services from meter or from point of entry where there is no individual meter: distribution pipework to appliances and equipment.

Number of draw-off points

Preliminaries ..... % of remainder of contract sum.

Element and design criteria	Total cost of element £	Cost of element per m² of gross floor area £	Element unit quantity	Element unit rate £	Specification
5.10 LIFT AND CONVEYOR INSTALLATIONS The number of rush period passengers for which the installation has been designed should be stated. Lifts The number, capacity speed, number of stops, number of doors and height served should be stated. Capacity of hoists to be given in kilogrammes. Escalators Rise and travel of escalators should be stated.			-	-	5.10.1 Lifts and hoists The complete installation including gantries, trolleys, blocks, hooks and ropes, downshop leads, pendant controls and electrical work from and including isolator. NOTES: 1. The cost of special structural work, e.g. lift walls, lift motor rooms, etc., shall be included in the appropriate structural elements. 2. Remaining electrical work shall be included with "Electric power supplies" (5.8.2). 3. The cost of each type of lift or hoist shall be stated separately. 5.10.2 Escalators As detailed under 5.10.1. 5.10.3 Conveyors As detailed under 5.10.1.

Lift and conveyor installations	Total £	Cost per m² of gross floor area £
5.10.1 Lifts and hoists		
5.10.2 Escalators		
5.10.3 Conveyors		

Preliminaries ..... % of remainder of contract sum.

5.11 PROTECTIVE INSTALLATIONS

Sprinklers - The number of outlets, control mechanism and area served by each control mechanism should be given.

$$\text{Gross floor area} = \frac{\text{Tm}^2 \text{ *}}{} = \text{m}^2 = \text{m}^2$$

* Where Tm^2 is the total net area in square metres of the various compartments treated or served.

5.11.1 Sprinkler installations

The complete sprinkler installation and CO_2 extinguishing system including tanks control mechanism, etc.

NOTE:
Electrical work shall be included with "Electric power supplies" (5.8.2).

5.11.2 Fire-fighting installations

Hosereels, hand extinguishers, asbestos blankets, water and sand buckets, foam inlets, dry risers (and wet risers where only serving fire-fighting equipment).

5.11.3 Lightning protection

The complete lightning protection installation from finials conductor tapes, to and including earthing.

NOTE:
The cost of lightning protection to boiler and vent stacks shall be stated separately.

	Total £	Cost per m² of gross floor area £
Protective installations		
5.11.1 Sprinkler installations		
5.11.2 Fire-fighting installations		
5.11.3 Lightning protection		

Preliminaries ..... % of remainder of contract sum.

Element and design criteria	Total cost of element £	Cost of element per m² of gross floor area £	Element unit quantity	Element unit rate £	Specification
5.12 COMMUNICATION INSTALLATIONS			–	–	The following installations shall be included:–
					<table><tr><td rowspan="2">Communication installations</td><td>Total £</td><td>Cost per m² of gross floor area £</td></tr><tr><td></td><td></td></tr><tr><td>Warning installations (fire and theft) Burglar and security alarms Fire alarms Visual and audio installations Door signals Timed signals Call signals Clocks Telephones Public address Radio Television Pneumatic message systems</td><td></td><td></td></tr></table>
Preliminaries ..... % of remainder of contract sum.					NOTES: 1. The cost of each installation shall be stated separately if possible along with an indication of the specification. 2. The cost of the work in connection with electrical supply shall be included with "Electric power supplies" (5.8.2).
5.13 SPECIAL INSTALLATIONS			–	–	All other mechanical and/or electrical installations (separately identifiable) which have not been included elsewhere, e.g. Chemical gases; Medical gases; Vacuum cleaning; Window cleaning equipment and cradles; Compressed air; Treated water; Refrigerated stores. NOTES: 1. The cost of each installation shall, where possible, be shown separately along with an indication of the specification. 2. Items deemed to be included under "Refrigerated stores" comprise all plant required to provide refrigerated conditions (i.e. cooling towers, compressors, instrumentation and controls, cold room thermal insulation and vapour sealing, cold room doors, etc.) for cold rooms, refrigerated stores and the like other than that required for "Space heating and air treatment" (5.6.8 and 5.6.9).
Preliminaries ..... % of remainder of contract sum.					

173

Builder's work in connection with mechanical and electrical services.

NOTES:

1. The cost of builder's work in connection with each of the services elements shall, where possible, be shown separately.

2. Where tank rooms, housings and the like are included in the gross floor area, their component parts shall be analysed in detail under the appropriate elements. Where this is not the case the cost of such items shall be included here.

Services elements	£	Cost of BWIC per m² of gross floor area £
5.1 Sanitary appliances		
5.2 Services equipment		
5.3 Disposal installations		
5.4 Water installations		
5.5 Heat source		
5.6 Space heating and air treatment		
5.7 Ventilating system		
5.8 Electrical installations		
5.9 Gas installations		
5.10 Lift and conveyor installations		
5.11 Protective installations		
5.12 Communication installations		
5.13 Special installations		
5.14 BUILDER'S WORK IN CONNECTION WITH SERVICES	—	—
Preliminaries ...... % of remainder of contract sum.		

Element and design criteria	Total cost of element £	Cost of element per m² of gross floor area £	Element unit quantity	Element unit rate £	Specification
5.15 BUILDER'S PROFIT AND ATTENDANCE ON SERVICES					Builder's profit and attendance in connection with mechanical and electrical services. NOTE: The cost of profit and attendance in connection with each of the services elements shall, where possible, be shown separately. |	£	Cost of BP&A per m2 of gross floor area £
Services elements		
5.1 Sanitary appliances		
5.2 Services equipment		
5.3 Disposal installations		
5.4 Water installations		
5.5 Heat source		
5.6 Space heating and air treatment		
5.7 Ventilating system		
5.8 Electrical installations		
5.9 Gas installations		
5.10 Lift and conveyor installations		
5.11 Protective installations		
5.12 Communications installations		
5.13 Special installations			
Preliminaries ...... % of remainder of contract sum.					
Sub-total excluding External works, Preliminaries and Contingencies	£				

175

Element and design criteria	Total cost of element £	Specification	Cost of sub-element £	Element unit quantity	Element unit rate £
6.1 SITE WORKS Cost per m² gross floor area £..........		6.1.1 Site preparation Clearance and demolitions Preparatory earth works to form new contours		m²	
		6.1.2 Surface treatment The cost of the following items shall be stated separately if possible:- Roads and associated footways Vehicle parks Paths and paved areas Playing fields Playgrounds Games courts Retaining walls Land drainage Landscape work		m²	
		6.1.3 Site enclosure and division Gates and entrance Fencing, walling and hedges		m	
		6.1.4 Fittings and furniture Notice boards, flag poles, seats, signs		number	
Preliminaries ..... % of remainder of contract sum.					
6.2 DRAINAGE Cost per m² gross floor area £..........		Surface water drainage Foul drainage Sewage treatment. NOTE: To include all drainage works (other than land drainage included with "Surface treatment" (6.1.2)) outside the building to and including disposal point, connection to sewer or to treatment plant.		—	—
Preliminaries ..... % of remainder of contract sum.					

Element and design criteria	Total cost of element £	Specification	Cost of sub-element £	Element unit quantity	Element unit rate £
6.3 EXTERNAL SERVICES Cost per m² gross floor area £..........		6.3.1 Water mains Main from existing supply up to external face of building. 6.3.2 Fire mains Main from existing supply up to external face of building; fire hydrants. 6.3.3 Heating mains Main from existing supply or heat source up to external face of building. 6.3.4 Gas mains Main from existing supply up to external face of building. 6.3.5 Electric mains Main from existing supply up to external face of building. 6.3.6 Site lighting Distribution, fittings and equipment. 6.3.7 Other mains and services Mains relating to other service installations (each shown separately).		–	–

		6.3.8 Builder's work in connection with external services
		Builder's work in connection with external mechanical and electrical services: e.g. pits, trenches, ducts, etc.
		    6.3.1
		    6.3.2
		    6.3.3
		    6.3.4
		    6.3.5
		    6.3.6
		    6.3.7
		
		NOTE:
		The cost of builder's work shall be stated separately for each of the sub-sections (6.3.1) to (6.3.7).
				–	–

		6.3.9 Builder's profit and attendance on external mechanical and electrical services
		    6.3.1
		    6.3.2
		    6.3.3
		    6.3.4
		    6.3.5
		    6.3.6
		    6.3.7
		
		NOTE:
		The cost of profit and attendances shall be stated separately for each of the sub-sections (6.3.1) to (6.3.7).
				–	–

Preliminaries ...... % of remainder of contract sum.					

		Gross floor area of ancillary buildings (m²)

6.4 MINOR BUILDING WORK

Cost per m² gross floor area £ ....

6.4.1 Ancillary buildings

Separate minor buildings such as sub-stations, bicycle stores, horticultural buildings and the like, inclusive of local engineering services.

| — |

Preliminaries ..... % of remainder of contract sum.

6.4.2 Alterations to existing buildings

Alterations and minor additions, shoring, repair and maintenance to existing buildings.

PRELIMINARIES

Cost per m² gross floor area £ ....

..... % of remainder of contract sum.

Priced items in Preliminaries Bill and Summary but excluding contractors' price adjustments. Individual costs of the main preliminary items should be given.

NOTES:

(i) Professional fees will not form part of the cost analysis.

(ii) Lump sum adjustments shall be spread pro-rata amongst all elements of the building and external works based on all work excluding Prime Cost and Provisional Sums.

TOTAL (less Contingencies)

Drawings: Drawings should always accompany an Amplified Cost Analysis.

STANDARD FORM OF COST ANALYSIS

<u>SECTION 5:   PERMISSION TO SUBMIT COST ANALYSES TO BCIS</u>

Where cost analyses are submitted by subscribers of the Building Cost Information Service, it is understood that permission has been obtained from the appropriate authority and the following letters have been drafted to facilitate this.

<u>Suggested form of letter to a Building Owner and the Contractor</u>

Dear Sir,

<u>Name of Project</u>

We are subscribers to the Royal Institution of Chartered Surveyors' Building Cost Information Service, and are collaborating in the production of statistics concerning costs of buildings.   The above is one of the projects in respect of which we would wish to report cost information.

Costs will be reported under element headings but individual bill rates will not be quoted.   Since the cost information will be in some detail it should be emphasised that, unless you wish otherwise, we do not propose to report any details concerning the names of the building owner, the architect or other professional consultants or of the contractor, nor the precise name and location of the project.   All that will be stated is the type of building, the general location and the date of tender.   Subject to the architect's and your own approval, sketch plans and elevations will be included to illustrate the design/shape of the block.   This information will be passed on only to quantity surveyor members of the Royal Institution of Chartered Surveyors who are subscribers to the Service. It is confidential to them and will not be broadcast further.   No change in this arrangement will be made without your prior knowledge and consent.

As the information contained in priced Bills of Quantities is confidential to the contracting parties, we do not feel that we could properly make use of it even in summarised form without the permission of yourselves and the contractor (or the building owner).

We should be grateful if you would kindly give your permission in this case.   If possible, it would be most helpful if you would consent to give blanket approval, so far as your own interest is concerned, to any future information of this kind being reported by us in respect of contracts with which we are jointly concerned without the need of further specific requests in each case.

We are similarly asking the permission of the contractor (building owner).

Yours faithfully,

<u>Suggested form of letter to the Architect</u>

Dear Sir,

<u>Name of Project</u>

We are subscribers to the Royal Institution of Chartered Surveyors' Building Cost Information Service and are collaborating in the production of statistics concerning tender costs of building.   The above is one of the projects in respect of which we would wish to submit a cost analysis.

It is felt that if sketch plans and elevations accompanied the analysis they would help the members of BCIS to interpret the costs with a better knowledge of the contract.   The drawings would convey the design and shape of the building far better than any wordy description could do.   The purpose of this letter is, therefore, to ask your permission to submit copies of sketch plans and elevations to be reproduced along with the analysis.

We should be grateful if you would kindly give your permission in this case.   If possible, it would be most helpful if you would consent to allow us to submit drawings in respect of other contracts with which we are jointly concerned without the need of further specific requests in each case.

Yours faithfully,

APPENDIX B

Nomograms

In Chapter 13 a calculator for relating income, expenditure and loan charges was described. This device is a form of *nomogram*. Graphical methods of this type are useful in calculating values or illustrating the range of choice that may be available in a standardized mathematical relationship.

The simplest form of nomograms are those used for addition and subtraction. Three are illustrated in Figures B1, B2 and B3. The first has been scaled for the same values as in the lower quadrant of the calculator referred to above, and could be used for the same purpose. A nomogram is in fact a form of graph with the axes parallel and the field reduced to a single line.

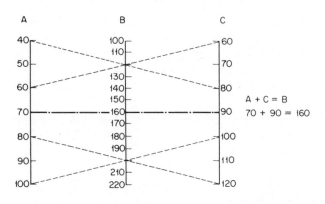

Figure B.1

Figure B1 has equal graduations on scales A and C; the central scale B gives the total. Any calculation is carried out by laying a straight edge across the three scales. Draw the outer scales on two trial calculations, using pairs of numbers that will have the same totals, and this will fix the position of the inner scale. In this arrangement the inner scale will have graduations at intervals half those on the outer scales; the values on this scale can be entered directly by measurement against a scale marker or by further trial calculations.

Figure B2 is plotted with unequal graduations on the outer scales. This results in the inner scale being displaced from the symmetrical central position. The exact position is determined as before by trial calculations. The number of steps in the graduation on the inner scale is given by the sum of the steps on the two outer scales.

Figure B3 is plotted with unequal graduations and, therefore, is asymmetrical. In this instance the outer scales are reversed in direction, which changes the relations in the

180

calculation, the outer scale C now indicating the total of scales A and B.

Figure B4 is a nomogram set out for multiplication and division. The outer scales are numbered in the reverse direction and the third central scale is drawn between the

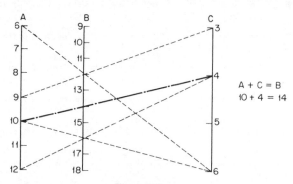

Figure B.2

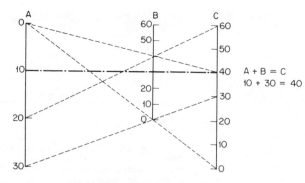

Figure B.3

zero points. Scale C indicates the product of the values on scales A and B_1, or scale A is the quotient of values of scale C divided by scale B_1. It can be seen that the central scale has also been graduated with scale B_2, so that scale A gives the product of scales B_2 and C. The values, which are underlined in the example, can be seen to be the reciprocals of those on the reverse side of the line.

Figure B5 is a similar nomogram, set out to relate cost per square metre on scale B, area per place on scale A, and cost per place on scale C. The procedure for setting out this figure is the same as before. The range of values that are expected are plotted on the outer scales, and the position of the line and its division into graduations is determined by trial examples.

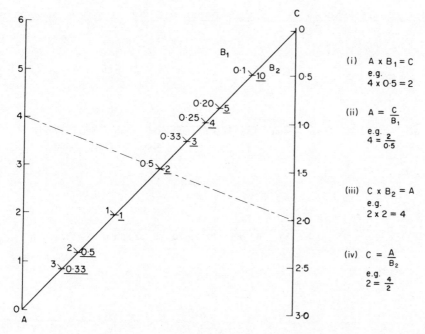

Figure B.4

Multiplication and division can also be carried out, using logarithms, by the processes of addition and subtraction.

Figure B6 is a nomogram using logarithmic scales and is similar in construction to Figure B1. The product of the two outer scales is given by a line cutting the inner scale. The graduations can be set out by using the divisions from a slide rule or by simply plotting values from logarithmic tables to suitable scales.

Nomograms can also be used to assist the solution of equations with more than three variables. Figure B7 shows an example which could be used to solve the function $y = p \cdot g \cdot r$. A straight edge is placed to correspond to the value of p and g on scales A and B. The product appears on scale C, and this is then related to the value of r measured on scale D. The final product equal to y is given on scale E. In this example the scales are logarithmic, and since it is essential that the total or products of the first pair of functions should appear in the third column C, it is

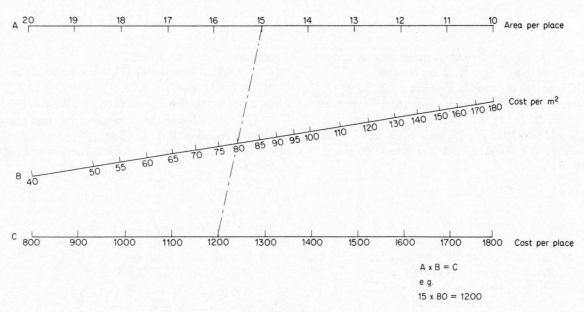

Figure B.5

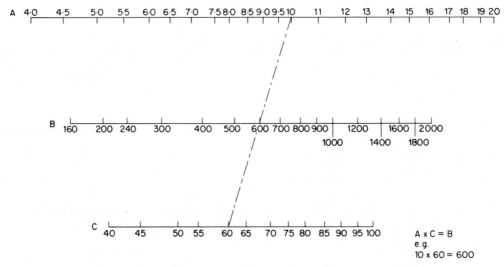

Figure B.6

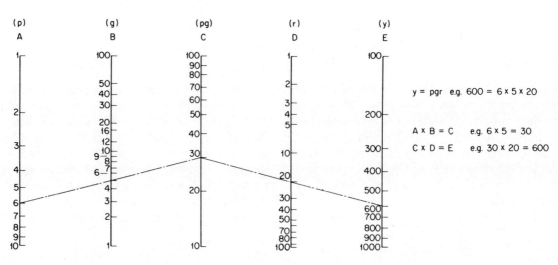

Figure B.7

necessary to set out the nomogram in the form described at Figure B3, which has the outer scales reversed.

If the equation had been in the form $y = 2 . p . g . r^2$, the first column, A, could have been numbered with the present scalar marks divided by two. Similarly the divisions on scale D could be related to a sequence of squares, i.e. the value marked as 4 would be marked as 2, and 100 would be marked as 10.

References

Adams, Douglas. *Nomography* (Hamden, Connecticut: Archar Books, 1946)

Allcock and Jones. *Nomograms* (London: Pitman, 1950)

Giet, A. *Abacs or Nomograms,* translated by Head and Phippen (London: Iliffe and Son, 1956)

Levens, A. S. *Nomography* (London: Chapman and Hall, 1948)

Optimizing Techniques

Linear Programming

Chapter 6, Cost Geometry, discussed the use of differentiation to determine design parameters from planning situations which could be expressed as quadratic equations. This appendix describes a method of finding an optimum in conditions that are controlled by linear equations.

An example might be a process, which has two outputs, articles A and B. The amounts of materials, labour, and plant used for each will differ as will the expected unit profit. Since the resources at any time will be finite the problem is to determine the number of articles of each type that should be produced to maximize the profit. In more general terms it is necessary for the procedure to indicate a decision that will maximize the objectives within the limitations of expressed constraints.

In this example if x_a represents the number of articles of type A to be produced and the profit on each is £2 and the profit on type B is £4, then the total profit will be given by the equation

$$2x_a + 4x_b = \text{total profit} = P_t.$$

This equation can be plotted on a graph with axes representing x_a and x_b for a particular value of the total profit. For example if the total profit expected was £1 the line

representing the equation would run from the co-ordinates $(x_a = 0, x_b = 250)$ to $(x_a = 500, x_b = 0)$. If this total profit was to be £900, the line would run from co-ordinates $(x_a = 0, x_b = 225)$ to $(x_a = 450, x_b = 0)$. Similar lines can be plotted for profits £800, £700 etc. giving a contour map of values increasing with the distance from the origin, as shown in Figure C.1.

Suppose that the constraints that limit the production capacity are as shown:

Resources	Inputs		
Total		Article A	Article B
Materials 5,600 units		7	16
Labour 2,880 hours		4·8	6
Machine 990 hours		1	3

Also that the profits will not be earned unless at least 100 units of both article A and B are produced. These constraints can be written as mathematical statements

$$7x_a + 16x_b \leqslant 5{,}600$$
$$4{\cdot}8x_a + 6x_b \leqslant 2{,}800$$
$$x_a + 3x_b \leqslant 990$$
$$x_a \geqslant 100$$
$$x_b \geqslant 100.$$

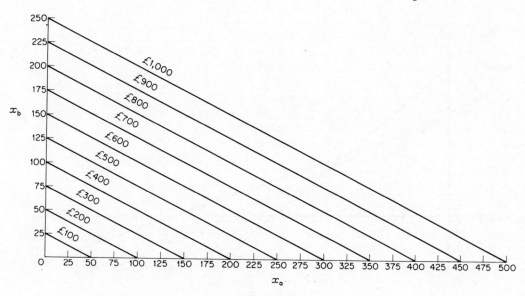

Figure C.1

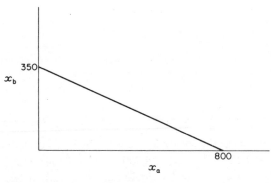

Figure C.2

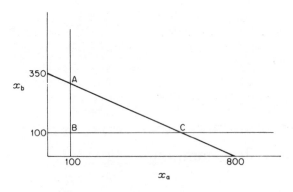

Figure C.3

These inequalities can also be plotted on the same axes as those in Figure C.1, but now the lines plotted indicate the junction between the zones that contain co-ordinates for articles A and B which satisfy the constraints and the zones where the pairs of numbers are not acceptable. For example consider the constraint for materials, plotted in Figure C.2.

Since the statement is $7x_a + 16x_b \leqslant 5,600$, if no articles of type A were produced, i.e. $x_a = 0$ the maximum number for type B would be 350, alternatively if no articles of type B were produced the maximum for type A would be 800. Therefore the line joining ($x_a = 0, x_b = 350$) and ($x_a = 800, x_b = 0$) is the boundary between a zone which is permitted and a zone that is excluded, i.e. any point between the origin and the line will have co-ordinates, or numbers for articles A and B that will be possible. The two minimum constraints applied to the profits, plotted on the same axis, are shown in Figure C.3, in this instance it is the rectangles between the lines and the axes which would

not meet the conditions.

For those constraints considered so far the only zone in which a point with co-ordinates satisfying the conditions would be the triangle ABC. Figure C.4 plots the five constraints and the profit contours within the permitted zone, the maximum profit is found at the junction of the restraints for materials and labour. The optimum numbers for the production of article A is 358 and for article B 193, giving a maximum profit of £1,488.

It is obvious that if it could have been predicted that the maximum profit occurred at the point where the lines representing the constraints for labour and materials crossed it would only be necessary to solve the problem by the method of simultaneous equations. However it is usually impossible to predict which pair of constraints will be critical, and furthermore it would be impossible to represent graphically a situation relating to three or more variables.

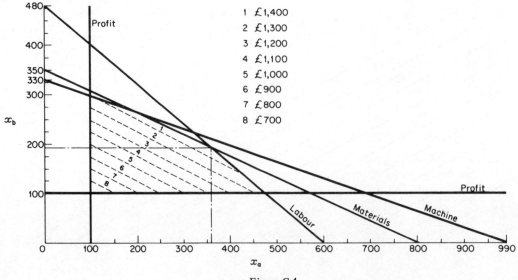

Figure C.4

184

A method of ordering the mathematical solution to problems of this type has been developed under the general title of linear programming. The numerical example which follows is based on two variables to reduce the amount of computation but also so that the result can be proved by graphical methods. Carrying out the calculation is assisted by using a 'tableau' which formalizes the algebraic process; and this method is also used for programming computers to solve problems of this type. At the end of this appendix the example is also solved by normal algebraic calculation (*see* Annexe C.1) which explains the basis of the Tableau method.

EXAMPLE 1

	House A	House B	Total
Bricks used per house	9M	12M	1,020M
Timber used per house	10 m³	10 m³	1,000 m³
Unit profit	£4,000	£5,000	
Site usage houses per hectare	25	12·5	

Site area 6 hectares with not less than 90 houses.

From this data where x_1 represents the number of houses of Type A and x_2 the number of Type B the following equations can be derived:

$$x_1 + x_2 \geqslant 90 \qquad \text{(Houses)}$$

$$\frac{x_1}{25} + \frac{x_2}{12\cdot5} \leqslant 6 \qquad \text{(Land usage)}$$

$$9x_1 + 12x_2 \leqslant 1,020 \qquad \text{(Bricks)}$$

$$10x_1 + 10x_2 \leqslant 1,000 \qquad \text{(Timber)}$$

$$4x_1 + 5x_2 = \text{Profit}$$

These equations can be turned into equalities, that is the signs for not greater than or equal and not less than or equal can be eliminated, by introducing a device known as the 'slack variable'. In the equations below these are represented by the functions x_3, x_4, x_5, and x_6. The essential property of a slack variable is that it can only be a positive number or equal to zero.

$$x_3 - x_1 - x_2 = -90$$
$$x_1 + 2x_2 + x_4 = 150$$
$$9x_1 + 12x_2 + x_5 = 1,020$$
$$x_1 + x_2 + x_6 = 100$$
$$\text{Profit} - 4x_1 - 5x_2 = 0$$

The first step in finding which combination of houses A and B gives the highest profit is to draw up a tableau. The various functions are set out across the top row, and the constants and the coefficients of the functions, are inserted

in the columns under the appropriate functions as shown in Tableau 1.1.

Tableau 1.1

Constants	x_1	x_2	x_3	x_4	x_5	x_6
−90	−1	−1	+1	0	0	0
150	1	(2)	0	1	0	0
1,020	9	12	0	0	1	0
100	1	1	0	0	0	1
0	−4	−5	0	0	0	0

The next stage is to draw up a new tableau which takes the first step towards maximizing the profit objective. Inspection of Tableau 1.1 shows that a change in the values of the co-efficient of x_2 will move the profit by 5 units whilst changes in x_1 will make a difference of only 4 units, the first procedure is therefore to identify a 'pivot' in the column of coefficients under x_2. The pivot is found by dividing the constants by the positive coefficients in each row, that is 150 is divided by 2, 1,020 is divided by 12 and 100 is divided by 1, giving 75, 85 and 100. The coefficient that gives the lowest quotient is marked at the pivot, in this instance the number is 2 in the second row.

Having marked the pivot number the second step is to calculate the new tableau by following three rules. The column of coefficients under x_2, the pivot column, are written as zero, apart from the pivot which is inserted with the value one. All the numbers in the same row as the pivot are divided by the pivot and the quotients entered in the new tableau.

All other figures are transposed by subtracting from the value in the original tableau the product of the number in the same row but in the pivot column and the number in the same column as the figure but in the pivot row.

Thus having identified the value 2 as the pivot, marked by the brackets in Tableau 1.1, the steps towards the second tableau are as follows:

The first step:

Tableau 1.2(a)

Constants	x_1	x_2	x_3	x_4	x_5	x_6
		0				
		1				
		0				
		0				
		0				

185

The second step:

Tableau 1.2(b)

Constants	x_1	x_2	x_3	x_4	x_5	x_6
		0				
75	$\frac{1}{2}$	1	0	$\frac{1}{2}$	0	0
		0				
		0				
		0				

The third step:

The figures -90, and 0 under the constant column and $+1$ under x_6 are changed by following the rules described above.

It is perhaps easier to consider this rule as describing a rectangle with the number to be modified at one end of a diagonal and the pivot at the other. If the other diagonal is then imagined, it is the product of the two numbers at the end of this diagonal, divided by the pivot which is subtracted from the figure being considered. In the partial Tableau 1.1(a) below the relevant diagonals for the constants -90 and 0, and the 1 under x_6 are marked with arrows and letters.

Tableau 1.1(a)

Constants	x_1	x_2	x_3	x_4	x_5	x_6

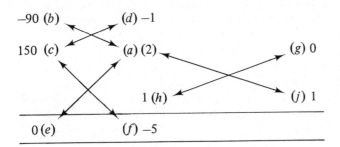

The application of the rule is therefore:

b is changed by the equation $b - \dfrac{d \times c}{a}$

e is changed by the equation $e - \dfrac{f \times c}{a}$

j is changed by the equation $j - \dfrac{h \times g}{a}$

or in numbers.

$$-90 - \frac{-1 \times 150}{2} = -15$$

$$0 - \frac{-5 \times 150}{2} = 375$$

$$1 - \frac{1 \times 0}{2} = 1$$

Tableau 1.2(c)

Constants	x_1	x_2	x_3	x_4	x_5	x_6
-15	$-\frac{1}{2}$	0	1	$\frac{1}{2}$	0	0
75	$\frac{1}{2}$	1	0	$\frac{1}{2}$	0	0
120	(3)	0	0	-6	1	0
25	$\frac{1}{2}$	0	0	$-\frac{1}{2}$	0	1
375	$-1\frac{1}{2}$	0	0	$+2\frac{1}{2}$	0	0

The third tableau is drawn up by identifying the pivot under x_1. The lowest quotient is given by dividing by the coefficient 3, and thus this number becomes the pivot.

Tableau 1.3

Constants	x_1	x_2	x_3	x_4	x_5	x_6
5	0	0	1	$-\frac{1}{2}$	1/6	0
55	0	1	0	$1\frac{1}{2}$	$-1/6$	0
40	1	0	0	-2	$\frac{1}{3}$	0
5	0	0	0	$(\frac{1}{2})$	$-1/6$	1
435	0	0	0	$-\frac{1}{2}$	$\frac{1}{2}$	0

Since the negative value under x_4 will produce an increase in the total profit a pivot must be identified in this column.

Tableau 1.4

Constant	x_1	x_2	x_3	x_4	x_5	x_6
10	0	0	1	0	0	1
40	0	1	0	0	$\frac{1}{3}$	-3
60	1	0	0	0	$-\frac{1}{3}$	4
10	0	0	0	1	$-\frac{1}{3}$	2
440	0	0	0	0	$\frac{1}{3}$	1

At this point values appear in the last row only under the function x_5 and x_6, but if a pivot is determined in either of these columns it will be found that the value of the total profit, which appears under the constant column in the last row, will be diminished rather than increased.

The results are read as follows, column x coefficient (1), value in constant column for the same row (60), therefore x_1 equals 60, x_2 equals 40, and the total profit £440 (x 1,000). It can also be noted that in the objective equation x_5 equals $\frac{1}{3}$ and x_6 equals 1, the meaning of these figures attached to the slack variables is that they indicate the extra profit that could be achieved if the constant represented by that particular variable were eased by one unit. In this example x_5 represents 1,000 bricks and

the unit of profit in £1,000. Therefore, if 1,000 more bricks were available the profit would increase by £333·30. Similarly x_6 represents 10 m³ of timber, if 10 m³ more timber were found £1,000 extra profit results. Thus it will be found if the tableau is re-worked with 101 (x 10) units of timber, the result will be $x_1 = 64$, $x_2 = 37$, profit £441 (x 1,000).

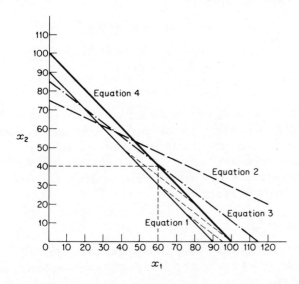

Figure C.5

Figure C.5 plots the equations of the constraints on a graph. This demonstrates that the point of maximum profit occurs where the lines representing Eqs. C.4 and C.3 cross, and projecting the lines on to the axis gives $x_1 = 60$ and $x_2 = 40$.

It will be understood that these methods can be applied to discover minimum costs, or whatever criteria is appropriate, with equal facility. The objective being written as Cost $+ N_1 x_1 + N_2 x_2 = 0$ and the tableaux operated to minimize this factor. There are also alternative methods of using tableaux for solving linear equations. Annexe 2 solves the above problem using the 'Simplex' method.

Example 2

	House A	House B	House C	Total
Bricks used per house	9 M	10 M	12 M	1,630 M
Timber used per house	8 m³	10 m³	12 m³	1,600 m³
Unit profit	£6,000	£8,000	£10,000	
Site usage houses per hectare	25	20	12·5	

Site area 8·8 hectares with not less than 150 houses and not less than 10 houses of each type.

From this data it is possible to write out the equations as in Example 1, it would also be possible to introduce three additional equations to deal with the requirement that there should be a minimum number of each house type, however, in this instance it is easier to recalculate and reduce the constraints with respect to the thirty houses i.e.

Bricks used $= 10 \times 9 + 10 \times 10 + 10 \times 12 = 310$ M

Timber used $= 10 \times 8 + 10 \times 10 + 10 \times 12 = 300$ m³

Land used $= \dfrac{10}{25} + \dfrac{10}{20} + \dfrac{10}{12·5} = 1·7$ hectares

The basic equations with slack variables therefore become:

$$-120 = x_4 - x_1 - x_2 - x_3 \qquad \text{(Houses)}$$
$$710 = 4x_1 + 5x_2 + 8x_3 + x_5 \qquad \text{(Site)}$$
$$1,320 = 9x_1 + 10x_2 + 12x_3 + x_6 \qquad \text{(Bricks)}$$
$$1,300 = 8x_1 + 10x_2 + 12x_3 + x_7 \qquad \text{(Timber)}$$
$$0 = -6x_1 - 8x_2 - 10x_3 + \text{Profit}$$

Tableau 2.1

Constants	x_1	x_2	x_3	x_4	x_5	x_6	x_7
−120	−1	−1	−1	1	0	0	0
710	4	5	(8)	0	1	0	0
1,320	9	10	12	0	0	1	0
1,300	8	10	12	0	0	0	1
0	−6	−8	−10	0	0	0	0

Tableau 2.2

	x_1	x_2	x_3	x_4	x_5	x_6	x_7
−31·25	−0·5	−0·375	0	1	0·125	0	0
88·75	0·5	0·625	1	0	0·125	0	0
255	3	2·5	0	0	−1·5	1	0
235	2	(2·5)	0	0	−1·5	0	1
887·5	−1	−1·75	0	0	1·25	0	0

Tableau 2.3

Constants	x_1	x_2	x_3	x_4	x_5	x_6	x_7
4	−0·2	0	0	1	−0·1	0	0·15
30	0	0	1	0	0·5	0	−0·25
20	1	0	0	0	0	1	−1
94	0·8	1	0	0	−0·6	0	0·4
1,052	0·4	0	0	0	0·2	0	0·7

In this example the interpretation of the last tableau is that the maximum profit is achieved by building 94 houses of type B and 30 of type C.

187

The ten houses of each type can be added to the results of this calculation and the usage of materials, etc. calculated to show which were the determining constraints. In this instance it proves to be the amount of timber and the size of the site.

Bricks used $10 \times 9 + 104 \times 10 + 40 \times 12 = 1{,}610$ M

Timber used $10 \times 8 + 104 \times 10 + 40 \times 12 = 1{,}600$ m^3

Site usage $\dfrac{10}{25} + \dfrac{104}{20} + \dfrac{40}{12 \cdot 5} = 8 \cdot 8$ hectares

Profit $10 \times 6 + 104 \times 8 + 40 \times 10 = £1{,}292$ (x 1,000)

Annexe C.1

Example 1 (Algebraic Method)

Equations with slack variables suitably transposed.

$$x_3 = x_1 + x_2 - 90 \qquad \text{(Eq. C.1)}$$
$$x_4 = -x_1 - 2x_2 + 150 \qquad \text{(Eq. C.2)}$$
$$x_5 = -9x_1 - 12x_2 + 1{,}020 \qquad \text{(Eq. C.3)}$$
$$x_6 = -x_1 - x_2 + 100 \qquad \text{(Eq. C.4)}$$
$$P = 4x_1 + 5x_2 \qquad \text{(Eq. C.5)}$$

Since the slack variables can only have positive values each equation can be examined to see if the profit can be increased. Thus in Eq. C.2 if x_1 were zero the maximum value for x_2 whilst keeping x_4 positive or zero would be 75. In Eq. C.3, the maximum value for x_2 keeping x_5 positive would be 85 and from C.4 the maximum would be 100. Therefore for these equations the maximum value for x_2 is 75 determined by C.2. It will be noted that this process is identical to that for identifying the pivot in Tableau 1.1.

The next step is to substitute the value of x_2 in Eq. C.2 in the four other equations.

i.e. from C.2 $x_2 = -\frac{1}{2}x_1 - \frac{1}{2}x_4 + 75$ \qquad (Eq. C.6)

and by substitution,

$$x_3 = \tfrac{1}{2}x_1 - \tfrac{1}{2}x_4 - 15 \qquad \text{(Eq. C.7)}$$
$$x_5 = -3x_1 + 6x_4 + 120 \qquad \text{(Eq. C.8)}$$
$$x_6 = -\tfrac{1}{2}x_1 + \tfrac{1}{2}x_4 + 25 \qquad \text{(Eq. C.9)}$$
$$P = \tfrac{3}{2}x_1 - \tfrac{5}{2}x_4 + 375 \qquad \text{(Eq. C.10)}$$

From Eq. C.7 if x_4 were zero there is no upper limit to the value of x_1 to keep x_3 positive, but from C.8 the maximum to keep x_5 positive would be 40, and from C.9 to keep x_6 positive the value of x_1 would be 50. Therefore it is Eq. C.8 which is the limiting constraint.

Thus from C.8 $x_1 = 2x_4 - \frac{1}{3}x_5 + 40$ \qquad (Eq. C.11)

and by substitution,

$$x_2 = -1\tfrac{1}{2}x_4 + \tfrac{1}{6}x_5 + 55 \qquad \text{(Eq. C12)}$$
$$x_3 = \tfrac{1}{2}x_4 - \tfrac{1}{6}x_5 + 5 \qquad \text{(Eq. C.13)}$$

$$x_6 = -\tfrac{1}{2}x_4 + \tfrac{1}{6}x_5 + 5 \qquad \text{(Eq. C.14)}$$
$$P = \tfrac{1}{2}x_4 - \tfrac{1}{2}x_5 + 435 \qquad \text{(Eq. C.15)}$$

From these equations if x_5 were zero the maximum value for x_4, keeping x_6 positive would be 10, (from Eq. C.14).

Thus from C.14 $x_4 = \frac{1}{3}x_5 - 2x_6 + 10$

and by substitution,

$$x_1 = \tfrac{1}{3}x_5 - 4x_6 + 60$$
$$x_2 = -\tfrac{1}{3}x_5 + 3x_6 + 40$$
$$x_3 = -x_6 + 10$$
$$P = -\tfrac{1}{3}x_5 - x_6 + 440$$

If either x_6 or x_5 were increased P would decrease therefore $P = 440$ is the maximum profit possible where $x_1 = 60$ and $x_2 = 40$. If the development of these equations is compared to Tableaux 1.1 to 1.4 it will be seen that the simple rules of the iterative method avoids a not uncomplicated algebraic process.

Annexe C.2

To solve Example 1 using the Simplex method, the first tableau is set out as below. The slack variables written at the side and the variables which are to be maximized along the top.

Tableau Anx 2.1

	x_1	x_2	Constant
x_3	−1	−1	−90
x_4	1	2	150
x_5	9	12	1,020
x_6	(1)	1	100
P	−4	−5	0

As in the earlier example the constants are divided by the positive values in the column and the minimum quotients indicates the pivot. However, at this point the operating rules change.

The value of the pivot is inverted i.e. where the numerical value is 3 it would be rewritten as $\frac{1}{3}$, the values row by row in the same column as the pivot are re-inserted in the next tableau with their signs changed and divided by the pivot. Values in the same row as the pivot are divided by the pivot. All other values are dealt with as before

i.e. Original value less values in the same row but in the pivot column multiplied by the value in the same column but in the pivot row, divided by the pivot.

In addition the label at the top of the pivot is exchanged for the label in the pivot row. The process continues as before until it is impossible to increase the objective.

Tableau Anx 2.2	x_6	x_2	Constant
x_3	1	0	10
x_4	−1	1	50
x_5	−9	(3)	120
x_1	1	1	100
P	4	−1	400

Tableau Anx 2.3	x_6	x_5	Constant
x_3	1	0	10
x_4	2	$-\frac{1}{3}$	10
x_2	−3	$\frac{1}{3}$	40
x_1	4	$-\frac{1}{3}$	60
P	1	$\frac{1}{3}$	440

In this example the value of the pivot in the first tableau is 1, thus the process of inversion is not apparent and only the signs in the pivot column change. The use of the reciprocal is demonstrated in tableaux annexe 2.2 and 2.3 for the pivot value 3. It will be seen that the last tableau is equivalent to the last stage of the last example (Tableau 1.4).

Expenditure Forecasting

This paper is reproduced with the permission of K. W. Hudson F.R.I.C.S., Chief Quantity Surveyor, Department of Health and Social Security. It is a slightly shortened version of a paper published in the Chartered Surveyor B and QS Quarterly dated Spring 1978. The authors wish to acknowledge their indebtedness to Mr Hudson.

From a statistical study of details of a large number of actual schemes submitted by the Regional Hospital Boards (Regional Health Authorities), guidance was produced for the likely contract duration of schemes in different cost categories. An analysis of the expenditure patterns of schemes was also performed. The cumulative monthly values of work executed, before the deduction of any retention monies or addition of fluctuations, were expressed as a percentage of the contract sum and plotted against percentage of contract period. In each cost category a line of best fit was drawn, and the resulting S-curve graphs of rate of expenditure were issued as guidance (Figure D.1).

A study of schemes costing £5 m and over showed that,

regardless of the actual size of the scheme, the rate of expenditure for the first two years was practically the same in every case (Figure D.2). The value of work executed in the first twelve months was £0·9 m, and in the second twelve months it was £2·1 m (i.e. £3 m in the first twenty-four months of the contract). The study also showed that the pattern of expenditure of large schemes followed S-curves of a type similar to those found for smaller schemes.

It will be appreciated that as the curves are lines of best fit, no one job will necessarily fit the curve exactly. However, when all jobs in a cost category are taken cumulatively, the forecast produces a close approximation to the actual value of work executed for schemes in that category.

In addition to the several small schemes in progress in any particular region, there could also be one or more large schemes with a cost of £5 m or over. If a large scheme were to run more quickly or more slowly than expected, it could cause the programme forecast to be inaccurate. A flexible forecasting technique was needed for these large schemes, which would enable a revised forecast to be made as soon as it became apparent that the scheme was not progressing as expected.

Cumulative expenditure curve for schemes costing approximately £ 4 M

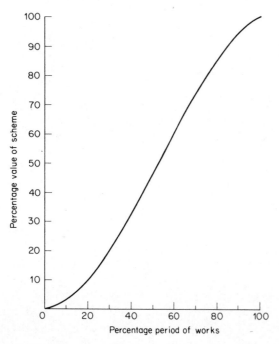

Figure D.1 Cumulative expenditure curve for schemes of approximately £4 m

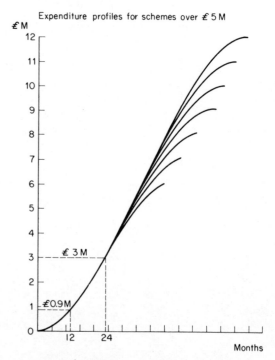

Figure D.2 Expenditure profiles for schemes over £5 m

The next step was to find a mathematical model for the expenditure profiles.

The Forecasting Formula

The equation of the S-curves was found to be an extremely close approximation to:

$$y = S \left[x + Cx^2 - Cx - \frac{1}{K}(6x^3 - 9x^2 + 3x) \right]$$

where

y = cumulative monthly value of work executed before deduction of retention monies or addition of fluctuations.

$$x = \frac{\text{month (m) in which expenditure } y \text{ occurs}}{\text{contract period } (P)}$$

(i.e. proportion of contract completed)

S = contract sum
C and K = parameters.

This formula can be used in two different ways:

(a) knowing C, K, contract sum and contract period, the cumulative value of work executed after any number of months can be calculated;
(b) knowing C, K, contract sum and cumulative expenditure in any month, the likely works duration can be calculated.

The C and K parameters for the guidance curves which had been issued for cost categories up to £4 m were found by taking any two points on a curve and reading off the x and y co-ordinates of these points. Each pair of x and y values was substituted into the forecasting formula to give two simultaneous equations, which were then solved for C and K. The parameters so obtained are referred to as 'standard' parameters. For schemes of £5 m and over, simultaneous equations were obtained by using a cumulative expenditure value of £0·9 m in twelve months and £3·0 m in 24 months. Standard C and K parameters were calculated in this way for schemes costing up to £12 m (Table D.1). The standard parameters form the basis of all the forecasts which are made. It is fortunate that this research was undertaken in the late 1960s because at that time schemes having similar contract sums had similar contract periods, and all large schemes had practically the same rate of expenditure in the first two years. This made the task of producing guidance and calculating standard C and K parameters relatively simple. At the present time the situation is far more variable. Contract periods for schemes of similar sizes differ considerably, and the rate of expenditure for the first two years in large schemes is no longer constant. In spite of this, however, the standard C and K parameters are as effective today as they were in the past.

Table D.1
Standard C and K parameters

Cost Category (£)	Standard Parameters C	K
10,000 to 30,000	− 0·409	7·018
30,000 to 75,000	− 0·360	5·000
75,000 to 120,000	− 0·240	4·932
120,000 to 300,000	− 0·200	4·058
300,000 to 1,200,000	− 0·074	3·200
2·0 M	0·010	4·000
3·0	0·110	3·980
4·0	0·159	3·780
5·0	0·056	3·323
6·0	0·192	3·458
6·5	0·154	3·401
7·0	0·172	3·557
7·5	0·131	3·445
8·0	0·142	3·538
8·5	0·099	3·404
9·0	0·104	3·456
9·5	0·061	3·317
10·0	0·063	3·344
10·5	0·019	3·207
11·0	0·018	3·218
11·5	− 0·025	3·089
12·0	− 0·028	3·090

Forecasting Expenditure for Individual Schemes

The forecasting formula provides the flexible technique which was required for large schemes because by changing C and K it is possible to simulate any expenditure rate. Increasing C gives a slower build-up and shorter run-down period, while decreasing C gives a faster build-up and longer run-down period.

Changing C has very little effect on the rate of expenditure over the central portion of the graph (Figure D.3). Increasing K produces a slower rate of expenditure over the central portion of the graph, with a faster build-up and shorter run-down period. Decreasing K gives a faster rate of expenditure over the central portion of the graph, with a slower build-up and longer run-down period (Figure D.4).

When a new scheme begins, the only way to forecast the likely pattern of expenditure is to use the standard C and K parameters for the cost category in which the scheme lies. The graph obtained from the standard parameters, contract sum and contract period is called the standard graph for the scheme.

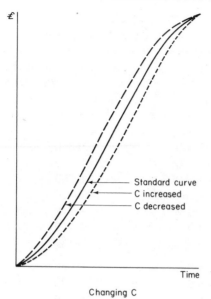

Figure D.3   Changing *C*

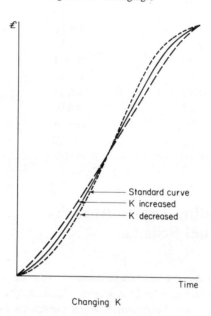

Figure D.4   Changing *K*

When the scheme has been in progress for a few months, it is possible to determine the *C* and *K* parameters of that particular scheme, as distinct from the standard parameters of the cost category in which the scheme falls. This is done by substituting two actual values of cumulative monthly expenditure into the forecasting formula, together with the months in which the expenditures occurred, and solving the pair of simultaneous equations obtained.

The two most recent observations of monthly expenditure are used, but first they are smoothed in conjunction with the previous three or five observations by means of a polynomial regression. This is done because the flow of expenditure on a scheme does not follow a regular smooth curve (although it is not so erratic as was first thought) and

192

although only two observations are necessary to determine *C* and *K*, the parameters will clearly be more realistic if they are based on a trend line which encompasses several observations of expenditure (Figure D.5).

If a scheme deviates from the original standard forecast, then *C* and *K* parameters for the scheme can be calculated and a new forecast made on the basis of observed expenditure to date. The new forecast can also make allowance for any revisions of the authorized sum or works duration. The figure substituted for *S* in the forecasting formula is initially the tender amount, but as the scheme progresses the latest revised authorized sum is used and, towards the end of the scheme, the estimated final account. Similarly, the number of months substituted for *P* is initially the original contract period, but as the scheme progresses the latest estimated works duration is used.

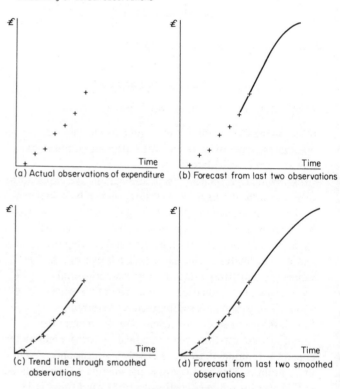

Figure D.5   Smoothing of actual observations

Forecasting of Likely Works Duration

The contract period originally stated for a scheme is seldom correct to the month: very few schemes reach completion sooner than expected, the majority anything from a few months to several months later than expected.

As long as the actual expenditure of a scheme follows the standard curve, the original contract period may be taken as being the best estimate of actual duration available.

Table D.2

Preparation of standard forecast Contract sum? 1230644* Contract period? 27.* C? 0·010* K? 4·000* Month at which forecast is to begin? 1.* Interval required? 1.* Cumulative exp. month 14660. 1. 36388 2. 64621. 3. 98797. 4. 138351. 5. 182723. 6. 231348. 7. 283665. 8. 339111. 9. 397122. 10.	457137. 11. 518592. 12. 580925. 13. 643574. 14. 705974. 15. 767565. 16. 827782. 17. 886064. 18. 941847. 19. 994569. 20. 1043667. 21. 1088579. 22. 1128741. 23. 1163592. 24. 1192567. 25. 1215106. 26. 1230644. 27. For graph press continue month at which plot to begin? 0.* *Figures entered manually	**Preparation of revised forecast** Enter contract sum C K Observation Month of Observation 1259085.* 0·010* 4·000* 656869.* 15.* Contract period 29. Enter seven actual readings press continue after each 3252200.* 376647.* 412807.* 462010.* 523310.* 602107.* 656869.* Smoothed readings 325296·212 376069·727 414250·182 460085·758 524753·182 601529·727 656965·212	S = ? 1259085.* P = ? 29.* IST Obs. = ? 601529·727* Month of Obs. = ? 14·000* 2nd Obs. = ? 656965·212* Month of Obs. = ? 15·000* C = 0·001 K = 5·412 Contract sum? 1259085.* Contract period? 29.* C? 0·001* K? 5·412* Interval required? 1.*	Cumulative exp. month 712213. 16. 766968. 17. 820868. 18. 873568. 19. 924727. 20. 973999. 21. 1021043. 22. 1065514. 23. 1107069. 24. 1145364. 25. 1180057. 26. 1210804. 27. 1237261. 28. 1259085. 29. For graph, press continue month at which plot to begin? 15.* *Figures entered manually.

When the actual expenditure begins to be consistently above or below the standard curve, it is necessary to find a revised estimate.

The forecasting model was given earlier as:

$$y = S\left[x + Cx^2 - Cx - \frac{1}{K}(6x^3 - 9x^2 + 3x)\right]$$

where x = month (m) in which expenditure y occurs, divided by the contract period (P). Substituting $x = m/p$ the formula can be transformed to give a cubic equation in P, the contract period:

$$\frac{Ky}{S}P^3 + (CK - K + 3)m.P^2 - (CK + 9)m^2.P + 6m^2 = 0$$

It is possible, by substituting the standard C and K parameters, the contract sum (S) and the latest expenditure £y which occurred in month m, to solve this cubic equation and obtain a new estimate of the likely works duration of the scheme.

Table D.2 shows the input/output using the D.H.S.S. forecasting programmes for a scheme of £1,230,644 in 27 months. A revised forecast was prepared after the scheme had been in progress for 15 months, at which time it had obviously fallen behind the standard curve and the authorized sum had been increased to £1,259,085. Figure D.6 shows graphically the results obtained.

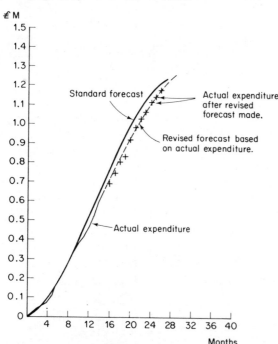

Figure D.6 Results of forecasting procedure

Problems which can Occur

Difficulties are to be expected when trying to apply a simple mathematical equation to a real life situation, particularly one as complex as erection of a building.

One of the main problems is that the method is essentially predictive, and in no way explanatory. If observed readings are used to obtain a forecast curve and, for some reason, the underlying relationship between expenditure and time has changed, then the forecast will be incorrect.

A possible problem, although it has never yet actually occurred, is that the cubic equation used to forecast likely works duration may have roots which are clearly unrealistic from the practical point of view. If this did happen, it would be necessary to apply professional judgement to the estimation of the likely works duration.

Two other situations have occasionally occurred in which professional judgement has had to be applied to the estimation of likely works duration. In the first of these, the forecast expenditure exceeds the contract sum and then decreases again (Figure D.7). Completion is most likely to occur at some point in time between the two months in which the forecast expenditure equals the contract sum. In the second case, the forecast expenditure shows no run down at the end of the contract (Figure D.8). Experience has shown that all jobs have a run down period, and completion will probably occur at a later date than that given by the forecast works duration.

Occasionally a forecast may show a negative expenditure flow during the first few months of a scheme (Figure D.9). This does not occur when using standard C and K parameters, but may happen when making a forecast based on

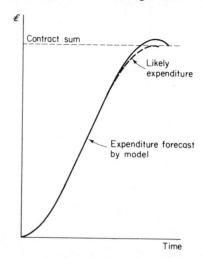

Figure D.7 Estimation of likely works duration

actual expenditure to date. When making such a forecast, however, it is only expenditure in future months which is of interest, and the forecast for months already past is therefore disregarded.

Recently, actual expenditure during the early months of a contract has frequently been greater than forecast expenditure. This is possibly due to contractors overloading the early trades in order to improve their cash flow situation.

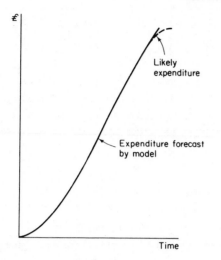

Figure D.8.

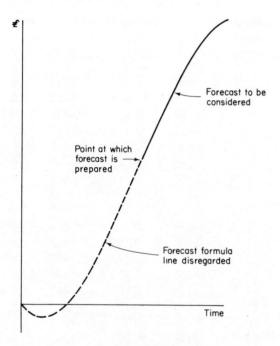

Figure D.9

D.O.E. for example, is using the model successfully for a whole variety of P.S.A. schemes such as telephone exchanges, post offices, Crown buildings, residential accommodation, etc. The D.O.E. was only able to do this, however, after standard C and K parameters had been calculated for P.S.A. schemes.

It should be possible for standard parameters to be calculated for any type of building e.g. schools, offices, prisons, housing estates, factories, etc. Cost categories would have to be determined for the particular type of building under consideration and data from as many completed schemes as possible analysed. It is unlikely that there will be, at the present time, constant rates of expenditure such as were found for large hospital schemes. Probably the best method of approach would be to plot percentage expenditure against percentage time in each cost category and then calculate C and K parameters for the lines of best fit.

The application of this system to provide a control mechanism for a building programme where perhaps more than a hundred schemes may be in progress requires some adjustment to the procedures described above. The basic need is to provide an estimate of the total expenditure which will fall within the financial years taking into account the fact that some contracts will be starting and finishing at random times during the year whilst others will be in progress throughout. Therefore additional programmes must be devised to carry out the mathematical analysis implied by the problems of timing. However, this appendix also refers to certain mathematical difficulties in the calculation of the curves, particularly the fact that there may be a maximum value to the curve preceding the expected completion date.

From research carried out by Frank Speechley, Regional Quantity Surveyor, and Mr. Graham Woods, a statistician with the North West Thames Regional Health Authority, it appears that the forecasting can be carried out with an acceptable degree of accuracy by omitting the process of averaging certificates and recalculating the parameters to the curve at monthly intervals for each scheme. As would be expected the factor which has most influence on the expenditure curve is the period of contract, thus a working programme can be built up by taking a realistic, and perhaps somewhat pessimistic, estimate of the likely contract period and basing all predictions on a series of standard curves. The contracts could be re-examined at suitable periods, perhaps six monthly, to determine whether the contract duration has changed. If the delays are significant new parameters can be calculated to give revised expenditure curves. Otherwise constant parameters could be held for each project throughout the period where it is producing certified expenditure. The impact of expenditure related to final accounts or contractors claims can be estimated and allocated to the appropriate years as the need arises.

Within six to eight months from the start of the contract however, the expenditure flow has usually returned to the forecast level.

At the end of a contract the actual expenditure curve continues for many months to run almost parallel to the x axis. This 'tail', which represents a very small amount of money, cannot be reproduced by the forecasting model. The model however, is effective up to practical completion and the 'tail' is really a management problem.

Buildings Other than Hospitals

Although the expenditure forecasting model was developed for hospital buildings it is not limited in its application. The

195

APPENDIX E

Discount Tables

The derivation of the following Tables E.1 to E.5 was given in Chapter 8, to which reference may be made.

Table E.1

Amount of £1: amount to which £1 invested now will accumulate in the years shown

Period: Number of years	*Rate of Compound Interest* 4%	5%	6%	7%
1	1·040	1·050	1·060	1·070
2	1·082	1·102	1·124	1·145
3	1·125	1·158	1·191	1·225
4	1·170	1·216	1·262	1·311
5	1·217	1·276	1·338	1·403
6	1·265	1·340	1·419	1·501
7	1·316	1·407	1·504	1·606
8	1·369	1·477	1·594	1·718
9	1·423	1·551	1·689	1·838
10	1·480	1·629	1·791	1·967
11	1·539	1·710	1·898	2·105
12	1·601	1·796	2·012	2·252
13	1·665	1·886	2·133	2·410
14	1·732	1·980	2·261	2·579
15	1·801	2·079	2·397	2·759
20	2·191	2·653	3·207	3·870
25	2·666	3·386	4·292	5·427
30	3·243	4·322	5·743	7·612
35	3·946	5·516	7·686	10·677
40	4·801	7·040	10·286	14·974
45	5·841	8·985	13·765	21·002
50	7·107	11·467	18·420	29·457
55	8·646	14·636	24·650	41·315
60	10·520	18·679	32·988	57·946
65	12·799	23·840	44·145	81·273
70	15·572	30·426	59·076	113·989
75	18·945	38·833	79·057	159·876
80	23·050	49·561	105·796	224·234
85	28·044	63·254	141·579	314·50
90	34·119	80·730	189·465	441·103
95	41·511	103·035	253·546	618·670
100	50·505	131·501	339·302	867·716

Table E.2

Present value of £1 payable at the end of the period of years shown.

Period: Number of years	*Rate of Compound Interest* 4%	5%	6%	7%
1	0·962	0·952	0·943	0·935
2	0·925	0·907	0·890	0·873
3	0·889	0·864	0·840	0·816
4	0·855	0·823	0·792	0·763
5	0·822	0·784	0·747	0·713
6	0·790	0·746	0·705	0·666
7	0·760	0·711	0·665	0·623
8	0·731	0·677	0·627	0·582
9	0·703	0·645	0·592	0·544
10	0·676	0·614	0·558	0·508
11	0·650	0·585	0·527	0·475
12	0·625	0·557	0·497	0·444
13	0·601	0·530	0·469	0·415
14	0·577	0·505	0·442	0·388
15	0·555	0·481	0·417	0·362
20	0·456	0·377	0·312	0·258
25	0·375	0·295	0·233	0·184
30	0·308	0·231	0·174	0·131
35	0·253	0·181	0·130	0·094
40	0·208	0·142	0·097	0·067
45	0·171	0·111	0·073	0·048
50	0·141	0·087	0·054	0·034
55	0·116	0·068	0·041	0·024
60	0·095	0·054	0·030	0·017
65	0·078	0·042	0·023	0·012
70	0·064	0·033	0·017	0·009
75	0·053	0·026	0·013	0·006
80	0·043	0·020	0·009	0·004
85	0·036	0·016	0·007	0·003
90	0·029	0·012	0·005	0·002
95	0·024	0·010	0·004	0·002
100	0·020	0·008	0·003	0·001

Table E.3
Present value of £1 payable at the end of each year shown (Years Purchase)

Period: Number of years	Rate of Compound Interest			
	4%	5%	6%	7%
1	0·962	0·952	0·943	0·935
2	1·886	1·859	1·833	1·808
3	2·775	2·723	2·673	2·624
4	3·630	3·546	3·465	3·387
5	4·452	4·329	4·212	4·100
6	5·242	5·076	4·917	4·767
7	6·002	5·786	5·582	5·389
8	6·733	6·463	6·210	5·971
9	7·435	7·108	6·802	6·515
10	8·111	7·722	7·360	7·024
11	8·760	8·306	7·887	7·499
12	9·385	8·863	8·384	7·943
13	9·986	9·394	8·853	8·358
14	10·563	9·899	9·295	8·745
15	11·118	10·380	9·712	9·108
20	13·590	12·462	11·470	10·594
25	15·622	14·094	12·783	11·654
30	17·292	15·372	13·765	12·409
35	18·665	16·374	14·498	12·948
40	19·793	17·159	15·046	13·332
45	20·720	17·774	15·456	13·606
50	21·482	18·256	15·762	13·801
55	22·109	18·633	15·991	13·940
60	22·623	18·929	16·161	14·039
65	23·047	19·161	16·289	14·110
70	23·395	19·343	16·385	14·160
75	23·680	19·485	16·456	14·196
80	23·915	19·596	16·509	14·222
85	24·109	19·684	16·549	14·240
90	24·267	19·752	16·579	14·253
95	24·398	19·806	16·601	14·263
100	24·505	19·848	16·618	14·269

Table E.4
Annual Sinking Fund to replace £1 at the end of the period of years shown

Period: Number of years	Rate of Compound Interest			
	3	4	5	6
1	1·000	1·000	1·000	1·000
2	0·493	0·490	0·488	0·485
3	0·324	0·320	0·317	0·314
4	0·239	0·235	0·232	0·229
5	0·188	0·185	0·181	0·177
6	0·155	0·151	0·147	0·143
7	0·131	0·127	0·123	0·119
8	0·112	0·109	0·105	0·101
9	0·098	0·095	0·091	0·087
10	0·087	0·083	0·080	0·076
11	0·078	0·074	0·070	0·067
12	0·070	0·067	0·063	0·059
13	0·064	0·060	0·056	0·053
14	0·059	0·055	0·051	0·048
15	0·054	0·050	0·046	0·043
20	0·037	0·034	0·030	0·027
25	0·027	0·024	0·021	0·018
30	0·021	0·018	0·015	0·012
35	0·017	0·014	0·011	0·009
40	0·013	0·011	0·008	0·006
45	0·011	0·008	0·006	0·005
50	0·009	0·007	0·005	0·003
55	0·007	0·005	0·004	0·002
60	0·006	0·004	0·003	0·001
65	0·005	0·003	0·002	0·001
70	0·004	0·003	0·002	0·001
75	0·004	0·002	0·001	0·001
80	0·003	0·002	0·001	
85	0·003	0·001	0·001	
90	0·002	0·001	0·001	
95	0·002	0·001		
100	0·002	0·001		

Table E.5
Amount payable annually over the period of years shown
which is equivalent to £1 payable at the beginning of the
period (Mortgage instalments)

Period: Number of years	Rate of Compound Interest			
	4%	5%	6%	7%
1	1·040	1·050	1·060	1·070
2	0·530	0·538	0·545	0·553
3	0·360	0·367	0·374	0·381
4	0·275	0·282	0·289	0·295
5	0·225	0·231	0·237	0·244
6	0·191	0·197	0·203	0·210
7	0·167	0·173	0·179	0·186
8	0·149	0·155	0·161	0·167
9	0·134	0·141	0·147	0·153
10	0·123	0·130	0·136	0·142
11	0·114	0·120	0·127	0·133
12	0·107	0·113	0·119	0·126
13	0·100	0·106	0·113	0·120
14	0·095	0·101	0·108	0·114
15	0·090	0·096	0·103	0·110
20	0·074	0·080	0·087	0·094
25	0·064	0·071	0·078	0·086
30	0·058	0·065	0·073	0·081
35	0·054	0·061	0·069	0·077
40	0·051	0·058	0·066	0·075
45	0·048	0·056	0·065	0·074
50	0·047	0·055	0·063	0·072
55	0·045	0·054	0·062	0·072
60	0·044	0·053	0·062	0·071
65	0·043	0·052	0·061	0·071
70	0·043	0·052	0·061	0·071
75	0·042	0·051	0·061	0·070
80	0·042	0·051	0·061	0·070
85	0·041	0·051	0·060	0·070
90	0·041	0·051	0·060	0·070
95	0·041	0·050	0·060	0·070
100	0·041	0·050	0·060	0·070

t-Tables

The derivation and use of *t* is given in Chapter 7.

Table F.1
Percentage Points of the *t* − distribution

v	$P = 50\%$	25%	10%	5%	2·5%	1%	0·5%	0·1%
1	1·00	2·41	6·31	12·7	25·5	63·7	127	637
2	0·82	1·60	2·92	4·30	6·21	9·92	14·1	31·6
3	0·77	1·42	2·35	3·18	4·18	5·84	7·45	12·9
4	0·74	1·34	2·13	2·78	3·50	4·60	5·60	8·61
5	0·73	1·30	2·01	2·57	3·16	4·03	4·77	6·86
6	0·72	1·27	1·94	2·45	2·97	3·71	4·32	5·96
7	0·71	1·25	1·89	2·36	2·84	3·50	4·03	5·40
8	0·71	1·24	1·86	2·31	2·75	3·36	3·83	5·04
9	0·70	1·23	1·83	2·26	2·68	3·25	3·69	4·78
10	0·70	1·22	1·81	2·23	2·63	3·17	3·58	4·59
11	0·70	1·21	1·80	2·20	2·59	3·11	3·50	4·44
12	0·70	1·21	1·78	2·18	2·56	3·05	3·43	4·32
13	0·69	1·20	1·77	2·16	2·53	3·01	3·37	4·22
14	0·69	1·20	1·76	2·14	2·51	2·98	3·33	4·14
15	0·69	1·20	1·75	2·13	2·49	2·95	3·29	4·07
16	0·69	1·19	1·75	2·12	2·47	2·92	3·25	4·01
17	0·69	1·19	1·74	2·11	2·46	2·90	3·22	3·96
18	0·69	1·19	1·73	2·10	2·44	2·88	3·20	3·92
19	0·69	1·19	1·73	2·09	2·43	2·86	3·17	3·88
20	0·69	1·18	1·72	2·09	2·42	2·85	3·15	3·85
21	0·69	1·18	1·72	2·08	2·41	2·83	3·14	3·82
22	0·69	1·18	1·72	2·07	2·41	2·82	3·12	3·79
23	0·69	1·18	1·71	2·07	2·40	2·81	3·10	3·77
24	0·69	1·18	1·71	2·06	2·39	2·80	3·09	3·74
25	0·68	1·18	1·71	2·06	2·38	2·79	3·08	3·72
26	0·68	1·18	1·71	2·06	2·38	2·78	3·07	3·71
27	0·68	1·18	1·70	2·05	2·37	2·77	3·06	3·69
28	0·68	1·17	1·70	2·05	2·37	2·76	3·05	3·67
29	0·68	1·17	1·70	2·05	2·36	2·76	3·04	3·66
30	0·68	1·17	1·70	2·04	2·36	2·75	3·03	3·65
40	0·68	1·17	1·68	2·02	2·33	2·70	2·97	3·55
120	0·68	1·16	1·67	2·00	2·30	2·66	2·91	3·46
∞	0·67	1·15	1·64	1·96	2·24	2·58	2·81	3·29

Bibliography

Building Design Evaluation: Costs in Use, by P. A. Stone (Spon).

Building Economics and Cost Planning, by C. D. Browning (Batsfords).

Cost Planning of Buildings, by D. J. Ferry (Crosby Lockwood).

Economics of Planned Development, by N. Litchfield (Estates Gazette).

Estimating and Cost Control, by J. Nisbet (Batsfords).

Planning Law and Procedure, by A. E. Telling (Butterworths).

The attention of the reader is also drawn to the many excellent Government publications on various aspects of building, available from H.M. Stationery Office, and particularly to the following:

Cost Control in Building Design: A Programmed Text, by the Department of the Environment.

Building Bulletin No 4: Cost Study, by the Department of Education and Science.

Flats and Houses 1958, by the Department of the Environment.

Homes for Today and Tomorrow, by the Department of the Environment.

Index